Early Education Program Administration Toolkit

*Intentionally building capacity
in individuals and early childhood organizations*

ALTHEA PENN

Early Education Program Administration Toolkit:
Intentionally building capacity in individuals and early childhood organizations

Library of Congress Cataloging in publication data
Penn, Althea
Early Education Program Administration Toolkit: Intentionally building capacity in individuals and early childhood organizations/Althea Penn – 1st ed.
p.cm.
Includes biographical references.
School management and organization – United States.
School Supervision –Unites States.

Attention corporations, universities, colleges, and professional organizations: Quantity discounts are available on bulk purchases of this book for educational, gift purposes, or as premiums for increasing magazine subscriptions or renewals. Special books or book excerpts can be created to fit specific needs. For further information, please contact Althea Penn, Penn Consulting (Training and Publishing) at apenn@pennconsuting.org.

DEDICATION

This toolkit is dedicated to my daughters, Alethia and Alynthia. They represent the hardworking early educators and program administrators that work diligently to cultivate potential in the next generation. May you be empowered by this toolkit of administrative forms and reference materials.

If one advances confidently in the direction of his dreams, and endeavors to live the life which he has imagined, he will meet with a success unexpected in common hours.
–Henry David Thoreau

Plans fail for lack of counsel, but with many advisers they succeed.
–King Solomon of Israel Proverbs 15:22

Connect with me:
Twitter: http://twitter.com/pennconsulting
Facebook: http://www.facebook.com/althea.penn
Website: www.pennconsulting.org
Email: apenn@pennconsulting.org

Introduction

Webster's Dictionary defines a tool as a "…device that aids in accomplishing a task or something necessary (or an instrument or apparatus) used in performing an operation or necessary in the practice of a vocation or profession." Early education program administrators are charged with recruiting, supervising, serving students and staff, and enlisting community support. Whether you are beginning a new program or school year this entails assembling volumes of records. There are numerous forms to be adopted and this toolkit will make your job easier. It provides every tool you need to plan and administer a program that promotes optimal development in each stakeholder. The forms comply with current federal and state rules and regulations, in addition to the National Health and Safety Standards of the American Academy of Pediatrics and the National Board of Health. Using the toolkit will help protect your rights, save time, and money. Why re-invent the wheel when the work has already been done for you? Best wishes for a successful school year.

Table of Contents

Section 1 Student Records 2
Biting Fact Sheet 3
Biting Report Form 5
Diabetes Health Care Emergency Action Plan............................. 6
Enrollment Form 8
Emergency Medical Authorization 10
Release And Waiver Of Liability For Administering An Asthma Inhaler............................. 10
Family Agreement.. 11
Physical Exam Form 13
Food Allergy Action Plan.. 14
Infant/Toddler Feeding And Care Plan 18
Developmental Checklist 20
Parent And Family Manual 21
Parent Manual (Faith Based)... 50
Nutritious Snack List... 63
Recalled Over The Counter Medications List 68
Medical Illness Log 75
Medical Injury Log.. 76
Montessori Program Handbook Materials 77
Early Childhood Checklist 82
Early Childhood Narrative Assessment 84
Infant/Toddler Daily Report.. 85
Sample Experiential Learning Program Overview 88
Excerpt From Disorder Fact Sheet Resource Booklet: 89
Differentiated Learning Plan 93
Daily Observation Form... 99
Attendance Record 100
Section 2 Staff Records 102
Application For Employment... 103
Personal Philosophy Essay Questions... 109
Personnel Manual.. 110
Daily Schedules And Lesson Plans 122
Daily Activity Report 123
Employee's Documentation Checklist 159
Staff Training Record 160
Documentation Of Orientation Training 161
Child Care Staff Health Assessment 162
Instructional Staff Duties And Responsibilities 164
Teacher Candidate Interview Questions...................................... 167
Interview Rating Scale 169
Instructional Performance Evaluation 170
Classroom Observation 172
Instructional Performance Evaluation... 174

Notification Of Unsatisfactory Performance 177
Pastoral/Church Leader Reference Form 178
Statement Of Faith...179
Payroll Schedule 180
Time Off – Overtime Request Form 181
Weekly Time Card/Attendance Record 182
Hiring Practice Checklist..186
Terminating An Employee Checklist 189
Americans With Disabilities Act (ADA) 190
Section 3 Management 191
Writing A Business Plan 192
Direct Deposit Authorization Form...197
Delinquent Tuition Letter 198
Grant Readiness Checklist/Assessment...199
Invoice 201
Emergency Drill Reporting Form..202
Section 4 Instructional Resources 207
Excerpt From Disorder Fact Sheet Resource Booklet: 210
Differentiated Learning Plan 213
Childcare Health And Safety Checklist..216
Weekly Lesson Plan 218

ACKNOWLEDGMENTS

I would be remiss if I did not mention the support team that has enabled me to provide this resource. First, I must acknowledge God, by whose grace I am strengthened and empowered to share the tools and gifts which He has so bountifully showered upon my life and ministry to others. Secondly, my husband and greatest supporter, Mike. He tirelessly supports my every creative endeavor with bountiful encouragement. I must also mention the faculty and staff of The Shepherd's Training Academy, the Association of Christian Schools International, the American Academy of Pediatrics, and the Association for Supervision and Curriculum Development. These organizations provide a plethora of educational tools that make excellent teaching, healthy child development, and maximized student achievement a reality in every classroom. Lastly, my grandchildren (Michael and Kendall) who are my inspiration. May their generation return to the ancient paths and blueprints of the good life. It is my heart's desire that educational leaders will use these resources to promote healthy development in the little ones of the flock. They are the "next big thing."

1 Student Records

Biting Fact Sheet

Biting is a a typical phase of early childhood development, however, it can be a challenging behavior of **toddlers and two year olds**. Because it is often unsettling and potentially dangerous, it is important for parents to address biting when it occurs.

When a child bites another child, intervene immediately between the child who bit and the bitten child. Stay calm; don't overreact, yell or give a lengthy explanation.

Use your voice and expression to show that biting is not acceptable. Look into the child's eyes and say calmly but firmly, "I do not like it when you bite people." For a child with more limited language, just say "No biting people." Point out how the biter's behavior affected the other person. "You hurt him and he's crying." Encourage the child who was bitten to tell the biter "You hurt me." Encourage the child who bit to help the other child by getting the ice pack, etc.

Offer the bitten child comfort and first aid. Wash bro- ken skin with warm water and soap. Observe universal blood borne pathogen precautions if there is bleeding. Apply an ice pack or cool cloth to help prevent swelling. If the bitten child is a guest, tell the parents what happened. Suggest the bitten child be seen by a health care provider if the skin is broken or there are any signs of infection (redness or swelling).

Preventing biting
Reinforce desired behavior. Notice and acknowledge when you like what your child is doing, especially for showing empathy or social behavior, such as patting a crying child, offering to take turns with a toy or hugging gently. Do not label, humiliate or isolate a child who bites.

Discourage play which involves "pretend" biting, or seems too rough and out of control.

Help the child make connections with others.

Why do children bite and what can we do? Children bite for many different reasons, so in order to respond effectively it's best to try and find out why they are biting.

If your child experiments by biting immediately say "no" in a firm voice, and give him a variety of toys to touch, smell and taste and encourage sensory-motor exploration.

If your child has teething discomfort, provide cold teething toys or safe, chewy foods.

If your child is becoming independent, provide opportunities to make age-appropriate choices and have some control (the bread or the cracker, the yellow or the blue ball), and notice and give positive attention as new self-help skills and independence develop.

If your child is using muscles in new ways, provide a variety of play materials (hard/soft, rough/smooth, heavy/light) and plan for plenty of active play indoors and outdoors.

If your child is learning to play with other children, try to guide behavior if it seems rough (take the child's hand and say, "Touch Jorge gently—he likes that") and reinforce pro-social behavior (such as taking turns with toys or patting a crying child).

If your child is frustrated in expressing his/her needs and wants, state what she is trying to communicate ("you feel mad when Ari takes your truck" or "you want me to pay attention to you").

If your child is threatened by new or changing situations such as a parent returning to work, a new baby, or parents separating, provide special nurturing and be as warm and reassuring as possible, and help him or her talk about feelings even when he or she says thing like "I hate my new baby."
• Consult with a professional if your child seems to be acting out due to unusual stress.
• If the child continues biting over several weeks or does not seem to care about the consequences, seek professional help. It is unusual for a preschool age (3-5 year old) child to continue to bite and he/she need to be evaluated for developmental concerns.
Adapted from California Child Health Article by Cheryl Oku, Infant/Toddler Specialist

BITING REPORT FORM

Behavioral Documentation Procedures: Fill out this form to be filed in the office. Fill out incident reports for each child involved. These incident reports will be read and signed by parent and staff member. One copy will be placed in each child's file and one copy will be given to parent or guardian of children involved. Remember to observe confidentiality when filling out the forms. Refrain from using the biter's name on the recipient' form and vice versa.

Date:_____ Time of bite:_____

Name of Biter:_____

Name of Recipient:_____

Describe area of bite (part of body, was skin broken, etc.):

Description of Area and Incident: (who was in the room including children, level of activity, what activity was going on, if transition, who saw, what happened immediately before and after the biting, each child's reaction etc.)

Staff response to Biter and recipient, including any first aid measures:

Identify any stress factors on the child who did the biting from the childcare setting:

Identify any stress factors on the child who did the biting from the family setting:

Identify any stress factors on staff:

Ideas on what caused biting behavior:

Prevention Plan:

Diabetes Health Care Emergency Action Plan

Student Information		
Name:	DOB:	Grade:
Address:		
Father/Guardian:	Phone (home):	Phone (work):
Mother/Guardian:	Phone (home):	Phone (work):
Other Emergency Contacts		
Name:	Relationship:	Phone:
Name:	Relationship:	Phone:
Physician:		Phone:
Hospital:	Transport: [ ] Parent [ ] Ambulance [ ] Other	

Emergency items to be left at school:
[ ] Glucose tablets   [ ] Blood glucose meter
[ ] Snacks   [ ] Insulin
[ ] Syringes   [ ] _____
[ ] _____   [ ] _____

In the event of an insulin reaction, the procedure routinely followed at school is to give some form of sugar such as 1/2 carton of milk followed with crackers and peanut butter, 1/2 cup fruit juice or 1/2 cup non diet soda. If the student is unconscious, "911" is called. I approve the above health care action plan as written. Yes ___ No ____

Please make the following changes to the health care action plan:

_____

_____

_____

List other additional information or significant special health concerns of this student:

_____

_____

_____

I give permission for emergency blood glucose testing by the school nurse using equipment I have provided. I understand that when the school nurse is not available for emergency blood glucose testing, the parent/guardian will be notified or "911" will be called. Yes _____ No _____
Additional directions regarding blood glucose testing:

_____

_____

_____

Written and prepared by

Nurse _____ Date _____

Physcian _____ Date _____

Reviewed and signed by

Parent/guardian _____ Date _____

The diabetes care plan should be revised according to the child's specific needs every ninety days.

[Insert logo here]

(Your school's name) Academy
[Insert your address, telephone number, website, email]

ENROLLMENT FORM

_____
Entrance Date (mm/dd/yyyy)   Withdrawal Date (mm/dd/yyyy)   Birth date (mm/dd/yyyy)

_____
Child's Name (last, first, middle initial)

_____
Child's Nickname   Gender   Age

_____
Home Address (Street Address, City, State and Zip Code)

(_____)_____
Home Telephone Number   Child's Primary Language

_____
School attending (school age children only)

(_____)_____   (_____)_____
Mother's Cell Telephone Number   Father's Cell Telephone Number

_____   (_____)_____
Father's Name/Home Address/Telephone Number, if different from child's

_____   (_____)_____
Place of Employment/Address of Employment/Business Number with extension

_____   (_____)_____
Mother's Name/Home Address/Telephone Number, if different from child's

_____   (_____)_____
Place of Employment/Address of Employment/Business Number with extension

Regular Care Arrangements: Lives with [ ] Both Parents [ ] Mother [ ] Father [ ] Other:_____
Are there any custody arrangements for your child? _____ If yes, please describe:

_____
(A court order with supporting documentation describing custody arrangements and restrictions must be provided.)

_____
Child's Legal Guardian(s) [ ] Both Parents [ ] Mother [ ] Father [ ] Other

Transportation arrangement to and from school: _____

Legal guardians' formal education: _____
                                    Highest grade completed and institution

Child care or education experience(s) of parent/guardian: _____

8

Pick up/Drop off Authorizations: My child may be released to the person(s) signing this agreement or to the following:

Name	Address (include complete street address, city, state and zip code)	Telephone	Rel. to child

Emergency Contacts: Persons to contact in case of an emergency when parents cannot be reached. These people are authorized to make medical decisions concerning my child.

Name	Address (include complete street address, city, state and zip code)	Telephone

_____   (___)_____
Pediatrician or child's primary health care source name   Telephone number

_____   (___)_____
Dentist name   Telephone number

Our school does not exclude children with special needs if we can provide a safe environment. The following information is requested to help us plan services for your child.

Does your child have any allergies or food restrictions?_____ If yes, please describe and attach care plan:

_____

Does your child have any diagnosed special needs, medical or mental conditions? _____ If yes, please describe:

_____

Are your child's activities restricted by any special needs, developmental disabilities, medical or other conditions? _____ If yes, please describe: _____

The following special accommodation(s) may be required to most effectively meet my child's needs while at this school.   (circle one) NONE YES

_____

My child is currently on medication(s) prescribed for long-term continuous use and/or has the following pre-existing illness, allergies, or health concerns unmentioned above: (circle one) NONE YES

_____

Medical Insurance Information
Insurance Carrier _____ Insured's Name _____

Primary Care Physician Name _____ Telephone (___)_____

ID or Policy # _____ Member Service Number (___)_____

Special needs of parents (e.g. inability to climb stairs, difficulty lifting child, hearing, vision, etc.):

EMERGENCY MEDICAL AUTHORIZATION

Should my child suffer an injury or illness while in the care of [Insert your name] and the facility is unable to contact me/us immediately, it shall be authorized to secure such medical attention and care for the child as may be necessary. I/We agree to keep the facility informed of changes in telephone numbers, etc. where I/We can be reached. The facility agrees to keep me informed of any incidents requiring professional medical attention involving my child. Permission is granted to take my child to the nearest appropriate medical facility, and the facility and its medical staff have my authorization to provide treatment that a physician deems necessary for the well being of my child. I agree to accept the financial responsibility for all medical and transportation expenses incurred.

In consideration of the registration of my child, I release [Insert your name] and their related companies, directors, officers, employees and agents, from any claims, losses, damages or costs (including attorneys' fees) caused by or arising from my child's registration, use of the facility, or participation in the programs and activities conducted by the program other than to the extent caused by the negligent or willful misconduct of the program and their related companies, directors, officers, employees and agents.

Release and Waiver of Liability for Administering an Asthma Inhaler

Release between [Insert your school's name] and (parent(s)/guardian(s) name) who are the Parent(s)/Guardian(s) of (child's name). (parent(s)/guardian(s) name) have requested [Insert your name] provide emergency treatment for their child at [Insert your name] Program and take certain actions described in the child's "Asthma Care Plan" (Authorization), which is attached to this Release and is hereby incorporated by reference.

The parties agree that (parent(s)/guardian(s) name)releases [Insert your school's name] and its officers, employees or agents from all liability which may arise as a result of [Insert your school's name] administering asthma treatment or following the directions in the Authorization (including any additional physician's instructions or clarifications) as long as such employees or agents exercise reasonable care in taking such actions. (parent(s)/guardian(s) name) also releases [Insert your school's name] and its officers, employees or agents from all liability arising out of the use of any materials and/or equipment supplied by the parent(s)/guardian(s) in connection with the asthma treatment as long as such employees or agents exercise reasonable care in the use of such materials or equipment.

This Release shall be governed by the laws of the State of _____, where [school name] is located.

Parent Signature(s) _____ Date _____

FAMILY AGREEMENT

PLEASE CHECK ALL THAT APPLY:

___ The school agrees to obtain written authorization from me before my child participates in routine transportation, field trips, special activities away from the facility, and water-related activities occurring in water that is more than two (2) feet deep.

___ TRANSPORTATION: I hereby ___ give ___ do not give − consent for my child to be transported and supervised by the operation's employees. ___ for emergency care

___ FIELD TRIPS: I hereby ___ give ___ do not give − my consent for my child to participate in Field Trips:

___ WATER ACTIVITIES: I hereby ___ give ___ do not give − my consent for my child to participate in Water Activities: ___ sprinkler play ___ splashing/wading pools ___ swimming pools water ___ table play

___ VIDEO/PHOTOGRAPHY: I give permission for my child to be photographed and videotaped for use by or on behalf of the facility for educational, training, curriculum, marketing, observation, security, and similar purposes. ___ Yes ___ No

___ DAYS/HOURS: [Insert your name] agrees to provide educational services for my child on: (circle all that apply) Monday Tuesday Wednesday Thursday Friday from _____a.m. to _____p.m..

___ MEALS: The program will provide meals (lunch, morning and afterschool snack) which are in compliance with United States Department of Agriculture guidelines. I agree to provide substitute meals which meet USDA guidelines in the event my child has medical reasons for a substitution and a physician's statement.

___ MEDICATION AUTHORIZATION: Before any medication is dispensed to my child, I will provide a written authorization, which includes: date, name of child, name of medication, prescription number, if any; dosage; date and time of day medication is to be given. Medicine will be in the original container with my child's name marked on it.

___ AUTHORIZATION TO DISPENSE EXTERNAL PREPARATIONS: I/we authorize [Insert your school's name] employees permission to apply one or more of the following topical ointments/preparations to my child in accordance with the directions on the label of the container.

_____ Baby Wipes

_____ Band-aids

_____ Neosporin or similar ointment

_____ Bactine or similar first aid spray

_____ Sunscreen

_____ Insect Repellent

_____ Non-Prescription ointment (such as A & D, Desitin, Vaseline)

_____ Baby Powder

Other (please specify) _____

___ SAFETY: My child will not be allowed to enter or leave the facility without being escorted by the parent(s), person authorized by parent(s), or facility personnel.

___ RECORDS: I acknowledge it is my responsibility to keep my child's records current to reflect any significant changes as they occur, e.g. telephone numbers, work location, emergency contacts, child's physician, child's health status, and immunization records, etc.

___ INCIDENT REPORTS: The school agrees to keep me informed of any incidents, including illnesses, injuries, adverse reactions to medications, exposure to communicable disease, which include my child.

___ CONFERENCES/PROGRESS REPORTS: I am advised that the school will notify me of my child's progress, issues relating to his/her care and any individual special needs.

___ PARENT INVOLVEMENT: [Insert your name] encourages parents to volunteer and attend all functions. I will receive monthly communication regarding these events and opportunities.

___ VOLUNTEER: I volunteer to work _____ hours a week/month with the school.

___ ATTENDANCE: Child's arrival time _____ Child's departure time_____

___ ILLNESS: Notify the staff when my child or any family member has a contagious disease.

___ CARE PLANS/HEALTH ASSESSMENTS: I agree to obtain special care plan(s) and health assessment(s) for my child according to the schedule recommended by the American Academy of Pediatrics or required by state rules and regulations.

___ NO EMPLOYMENT: I will not solicit, employ or enter into any contract with any employee of [Insert your name] to perform child care or similar services under any circumstances without the express consent of [Insert your name]. If I employ or contract with any employee of [Insert your name] or person who within one year of the date of such employing or contracting was employed or under contract with [Insert your name], I will pay the School a placement fee of $5,000.

___ PARENT HANDBOOK: I have received, reviewed and understand the Parent Handbook and related information concerning the school and the educational services provided by [Insert your name]. I will use the program in accordance with the terms of the Parent Handbook and the policies and procedures made available at the facility. Use of the facility and the services may be denied in the event I do not comply with the terms of this Agreement, or when determined by the administration to be in the best interests of my child or the children enrolled in the afterschool program. The availability of these services are subject to change at any time.

___ REGISTRATION AND PAYMENTS: Registration must be fully completed prior to my child attending the afterschool program. Where applicable, all registration fees and/or tuition fees must be paid in connection with the registration of my child and use of the program.

___ TERMINATION OF ENROLLMENT: If the parent/legal guardian terminates the child's enrollment, we will suggest an approach to provide a comfortable transition for your child. Refund of payments for services will be limited to policies outlined in the handbook. In the event of noncompliance with the conditions described in the admission agreement and policies that the parent/legal guardian reviewed, accepted, and signed, we will meet with the parent/legal guardian to make a plan for corrective action that specifies the expected action and the period after which termination will occur for continued noncompliance. Program staff members will offer support to the family to achieve compliance and follow the school's grievance procedure. If the corrective action plan is not successful, unless the grievance procedure results in an alternative approach, termination of services will occur. Parent/legal guardian is responsible for fees as outlined in the termination policy (usually equal to one week's tuition).

RECEIPT OF WRITTEN OPERATIONAL POLICIES:
I acknowledge receipt of the facility's operational policies including those for discipline and guidance.

Signature (Parent/Guardian) _____

Date _____

Signature (Parent/Guardian) _____

Date _____

PHYSICAL EXAM FORM

To be completed by parent:

Child's Name: _____

Address: _____ City: _____ Zip: _____

Phone: _____ DOB: _____ Race: _____ Sex: _____

Family Physician: _____ Address: _____ Last Visit:_____

Family Dentist: _____ Address: _____ Last Visit:_____

Allergies: _____

To be completed by the physician:

Immunization Status At Visit ( ) Complete ( ) Incomplete Please attach immunization certificate

Indicate dates) completed:

Developmental Screening/Testing: _____

Vision Testing: _____

Hearing Testing: _____

Speech Test: _____

Vital Data: T _____ P _____ R _____ BP _____

HT_____ inches or cms. _____% wt _____lbs. or kg. _____%

Stature:_____

Head Circumference: _____ % _____ up to 3 years old

Chest Circumference: _____ % _____ up to 1 year old

Laboratory

Hematocrit _____% Or Hemoglobin _____ Mg/100ml

Urinalysis Ph _____ Blood _____ Protein _____ Keytones _____ Glucose _____

Urobilinogen _____ Nitrite _____ Specific Gravity _____ If Clear Of Concentrated_____

Sickle Cell   Date:_____ Results: _____

Blood Lead   Date: _____ Results: _____

Well Baby Tanner Rating: _____

Circle below and provide care plan or additional comments:

Skin & Nails	Normal	Abnormal	Comments-please see _____
Head & Hair	Normal	Abnormal	Comments-please see _____
Eyes	Normal	Abnormal	Comments-please see _____
Ears	Normal	Abnormal	Comments-please see _____
Nose	Normal	Abnormal	Comments-please see _____
Mouth & Throat	Normal	Abnormal	Comments-please see _____
Teeth & Gums	Normal	Abnormal	Comments-please see _____
Neck	Normal	Abnormal	Comments-please see _____
Chest & Lungs	Normal	Abnormal	Comments-please see _____
Heart	Normal	Abnormal	Comments-please see _____
Abdomen	Normal	Abnormal	Comments-please see _____
Femorals	Normal	Abnormal	Comments-please see _____
Genitalia	Normal	Abnormal	Comments-please see _____
Extremities	Normal	Abnormal	Comments-please see _____
Gait	Normal	Abnormal	Comments-please see _____
Neurological	Normal	Abnormal	Comments-please see _____

Recommended accommodations: _____

_____

I certify that this child is free from communicable disease as of this examination.

DOCTOR'S SIGNATURE: _____ DATE:_____

Food Allergy Action Plan

I/we provide consent for my/our child's health care professional to release information and to communicate with my/our child's teacher/child care provider to discuss information relating to this care plan.

Parent/legal guardian signature _____ Date _____

Student's Name:_____**D.O.B:**_____

ALLERGIC TO:_____

STEP 1: TREATMENT

<u>Symptoms:</u> Asthmatic: Yes* No *Higher risk for severe reaction	<u>Give Checked</u> <u>Medication**:</u> **(To be determined by physician authorizing treatment)
If a food allergen has been ingested, but *no symptoms*:	Epinephrine Antihistamine
Mouth Itching, tingling, or swelling of lips, tongue, mouth	Epinephrine Antihistamine
Skin Hives, itchy rash, swelling of the face or extremities	Epinephrine Antihistamine
Gut Nausea, abdominal cramps, vomiting, diarrhea	Epinephrine Antihistamine
Throat† Tightening of throat, hoarseness, hacking cough	Epinephrine Antihistamine
Lung† Shortness of breath, repetitive coughing, wheezing	Epinephrine Antihistamine
Heart† Weak or thready pulse, low blood pressure, fainting, pale, blueness	Epinephrine Antihistamine
Other† _____	Epinephrine Antihistamine
If reaction is progressing (several of the above areas affected), give:	Epinephrine Antihistamine

†Potentially life-threatening. The severity of symptoms can quickly change.

DOSAGE

Epinephrine: inject intramuscularly (circle one) EpiPen® EpiPen® Jr. Twinject® 0.3 mg Twinject® 0.15 mg _____

Antihistamine (must be completed for over the counter and prescription medications):
give_____medication/dose/route _____
Other: give_____
medication/dose/route _____
IMPORTANT: Asthma inhalers and/or antihistamines cannot be depended on to replace epinephrine in anaphylaxis.

Needed Accommodations (Please describe accommodation and why it is necessary. Attach additional pages if needed to provide complete information.)

14

Needed Accommodations (Please describe accommodation and why it is necessary. Attach additional pages if needed to provide complete information.):

Special equipment or medical supplies:

Training needed for staff:

STEP 2: EMERGENCY CALLS

1. Call 911. State that an allergic reaction has been treated, and additional epinephrine may be needed.

2. Dr. _____ Phone Number: _____

3. Parent_____ Phone Number(s) _____

4. Emergency contacts:

Name/Relationship Phone Number(s)

a. _____ 1.)_____ 2.) _____

b. _____ 1.)_____ 2.) _____

EVEN IF PARENT/GUARDIAN CANNOT BE REACHED, DO NOT HESITATE TO MEDICATE OR TAKE CHILD TO MEDICAL FACILITY!

Parent/Guardian's Signature_____

Date_____

Doctor's Signature_____

Date_____

Adapted from the Food allergy and Anaphylaxis Network *Food allergy care plan* www.foodallergy.org

HEALTH CARE PLAN FOR ASTHMA MANAGEMENT

Student: _____ DOB: _____ Sex: _____

Parent/Guardian #1: _____

Home phone: _____ Cell: _____ Work number: _____

Parent/Guardian #2: _____

Home phone: _____ Cell: _____ Work number: _____

Emergency Contact: _____
                   Name   Relationship   Phone

Health Care Provider: _____ Phone: _____

■■■

Does the student have allergies? □ No   □ Yes

What triggers an asthma episode (check all that apply)
    □ Exercise   □ Animals   □ Pollen   □ Mold   □ Dust/chalk dust

    □ Respiratory infections   □ Change in temperature   □ Strong odors/fumes

    □ Food _____   □ Other _____

Early symptoms of an asthma episode (check all that apply)
    □ runny nose   □ coughing   □ itchy throat

    □ sneezing   □ wheezing   □ tightness in chest

    □ irritable   □ short of breath   □ other _____

Does the student have any activity restrictions? □ No   □ Yes, (health care provider note needed)

Has the student been hospitalized for an asthma episode? □ No   □ Yes, when: _____

Does the student recognize early symptoms of his/her asthma episodes? □ No   □ Yes   □ Some

Will a peak flow meter be used during school hours? □ No   □ Yes, (authorization needed)

    Green Zone – doing well; can participate in usual activities: 80% or more personal best _____

    Yellow Zone -- asthma control unstable; having symptoms: 50-79% of best peak flow _____

    RED ZONE – Medical Alert; assistance needed, call parents and 911: less than 50% _____

Please list asthma medication(s): □ None   □ As needed   □ Daily

Name of medication(s)	When/ how many times per day	Oral / Inhaler / Nebulizer

Will asthma medication be needed during school hours? □ No   □ Yes, (authorization needed)
Please provide written authorization for all forms. Medication authorization forms must be signed every ten days. Care plans must be updated quarterly or as prescriptions or conditions change. Emergency Plan:

Steps to take during an asthma episode:
1. Check peak flow, if authorized by health care provider.
2. Give medication(s), as authorized by health care provider.
3. If student condition does not improve within 15-20 minutes, notify parent.
4. Seek emergency medical care if the student has any of the following:
✓ Coughs constantly, breathes more than 50 bpm at rest
✓ No improvement 15-20 minutes after initial treatment with medication and a relative cannot be reached.
✓ Difficulty breathing with: chest and neck pulled in, stooped body posture, struggling or gasping for air
✓ Trouble walking or talking
✓ Stops playing and cannot start activity again
✓ Lips or fingernails are blue or gray
Other recommendations or accommodations:

The information on this form will be shared with staff who have a need to know.

Parent/Guardian Signature:_____ Date:_____

Physician Signature: _____ Date: _____

(Your school's name) Early Learning Center
Infant/Toddler Feeding and Care Plan

In an attempt to smoothly facilitate your child's transition into our class, please fill out the following form. This information is confidential.

Child's Name _____ Date _____

Birthdate_____

Does the child take a bottle?   Yes [ ]   No [ ]
Is the bottle warmed?   Yes [ ]   No [ ]
Does the child hold own bottle?   Yes [ ]   No [ ]
Can the child feed self?   Yes [ ]   No [ ]
Does the child eat:
    Strained Foods   [ ]   Whole Milk   [ ]
    Baby Foods   [ ]   Table Food   [ ]
    Formula   [ ]   Other   [ ]
What type formula used? _____
Amount of formula to be given? _____
Updated amounts of formula? _____ Date _____
                                  _____ Date _____
                                  _____ Date _____
Does the child take a pacifier? Yes [ ]   No [ ]
When? _____
Food likes _____ Food dislikes _____
Allergies- including any premixed formula
_____

Child's Schedule
Breakfast _____
       Approximate Time   Types and approximate amount of food

Lunch   _____
       Approximate Time   Types and approximate amount of food

Dinner   _____
       Approximate Time   Types and approximate amount of food

Morning Nap _____ Afternoon Nap _____
          Approximate Time   Approximate Time

Instructions for the introduction of solid foods _____
_____

As needed, please list updated instructions regarding adding new foods or other dietary changes.
_____

Has your child had any feeding problems? (Please describe in detail) _____

Is your child: __ breast fed __ bottle fed __ weaned
Supplemental infant information:

Describe your child's present napping pattern _____

_____

Does your child usually cry when going to sleep? __ No __ Yes
Does your child cry when waking? __ No __ Yes
Do you have any special ways of helping your child go to sleep?

_____

_____

Elimination patters (toileting/diapering): _____

Things that comfort your child: _____ scare child: _____

Cultural habits/issues that may affect your child's behavior: _____

_____

Who will care for your child when he/she is sick: _____
Does your child have any special needs (serious illness, medications, treatments, allergies, food intolerance, conditions, behaviors, etc.? Please describe and have your pediatrician submit a care plan and update it every 90 days.

_____

_____

_____

Has your child had any surgical procedures? __ No __ Yes Describe:

_____

What special training, if any, must the staff have to provide care? _____

Please indicate which of the following diseases your child has previously experienced:

__ Whooping Cough   __ Pneumonia   __ Mumps

__ Chicken Pox   __ Measles (10 day)   __ Allergies

__ Eczema   __ High Temperature (Over 103)   __ Neurological

__ Roseola (24 Hr. Measles)   __ Rubella (3 day-German Measles) __ Recurrent Ear Infections

__ Other _____
Please take a moment to tell us anything else that would help us to provide the best care for your child.

_____

_____

Developmental Checklist

Developmental milestones are things most children can do by a certain age. They are basic goals for development. Check the milestones your child has reached. Take this with you and talk with your child's doctor if you are concerned.

0 to 2 months

___ Able to raise head off floor or bed and turn to both sides when lying on tummy
___ Holds head up, briefly bobbing, when in sitting position
___ Moves arms and legs vigorously
___ Pays attention to someone's face in his or her direct line of vision
___ Watches and follows moving object or person with eyes
___ Quiets or startles in response to noise or voice
___ Vocalizes - gurgles, coos, and smiles

3 to 5 months

___ Lifts head and chest up easily with arm support while lying on stomach
___ Holds head up steadily when supported in sitting position
___ Watches hands; holds and begins reaching for objects
___ Looks at, mouths, and begins to shake objects when put into hands
___ Often holds head and hands in midline
___ Squeals and laughs - vocalizes and smiles at familiar persons more than strangers
___ Recognizes breast or bottle

6 to 8 months

___ Rolls over in both directions - tummy to back and back to tummy
___ Begins sitting without support and in high chair
___ Begins creeping on tummy - pushes up to hands or knees or all fours
___ Bangs and shakes toys - transfers toy from hand to hand
___ Looks to floor when something falls
___ Begins burbling (dada, baba)
___ Turns toward sounds in all directions
___ Cries when left alone; prefers to be with
___ Takes pureed and/or semi-solid foods from spoon
___ Uses whole hand to pick up small objects or pieces of food

9 to 11 months

___ Sits steadily and changes position without falling
___ Begins creeping on hands and knees
___ Begins pulling to stand and walking around furniture
___ May stand alone. Walks with both hands held
___ Uses thumb and first finger to pick up small objects, being pointing or poking
___ Uncovers hidden toy
___ Responds to own name
___ Responds appropriately or imitates familiar verbal request, such as "wave bye-bye," "play peek-a-boo," or "play pat-a-cake"
___ Bites and chews cracker. eats mashed table food, finger feeds, drinks from cup with help

Parent/Guardian Signature _____ Date _____

[Insert your logo]

[Enter Your School Name]
Parent and Family Manual
20____-20____
Revised

"It is far easier to shape a child than to repair an adult." -Dr. Tony Evans

…I am not built to sit still, keep my hands to myself, take turns, be patient, stand in line, or keep quiet. I need motion, I need novelty, I need adventure, and I need to engage in the world with my whole body. Let me play! (Trust me I am learning) -Anonymous

Table of Contents

General Information
Letter from the Director
Mission Statement
Philosophy
Program Overview

The ABC's of [Your school's name]: [insert page numbers after adding distinctive policies and biographical sketches of administrative staff]

A	Administration and Staff	
	Admissions Procedures: Registration, Fees, and Tuition	
	Attendance: Arrival and Dismissal Procedures	
B	Birthdays	
C	Child Abuse and Neglect	
	Communication: Home-School Connection	
	Cultural Sensitivity Policy	
D	Discipline Policy	
	Dress	
E	Emergencies	
F	Family Expectations	
G	Generous Donations	
H	Health and Safety	
I	Information About Toddler Care	
J	Join Us!	
K	Kaleidoscope of Activities	
L	Language and Culture	
M	Medication, Illness, and Injury Policies	
N	Nap and Rest Time	
	Nutrition: Food Policies	
O	Open Door Policy	
P	Personal Belongings	
	Pre-School Program	
	School-Age Program	
Q	Quality Assurance	
R	Resources and Services	
S	Student-Teacher Ratios	
T	Termination of Childcare Services	
U	Unusual Issues	
V	Voluntary Pre-Kindergarten	
W	Water and Sand Play Policy	
X	(E)Xceptional Students- Individuality	
Y	Yearbook	
Z	Zero Tolerance	

GENERAL INFORMATION

Ages Served: 12 months – 5 years
Emergency Closings
CLOSED per [YOUR SCHOOL'S County DOE] actions
Calendar Year: July 1st- June 30th
Vacation Days (no payments due):
August 6th , 2011- August17th, 2012
December 21st , 2011 - January 4th , 2012

Days of Operation: Monday – Friday

Hours of Operation: Before Care 7 a.m. – 8 a.m. School hours 8 a.m. – 4 p.m.
After Care 4 p.m. – 6 p.m.

Late Pick Up Fees: $5.00 for first five minutes, $1 per minute afterward
Registration Fee: Annual fee- $150.00 nonrefundable
Weekly payment:
Infants $X/wk.
Toddlers $X/wk
Preschool $X/wk.
Before care $X/wk.
Afterschool care $X/wk.

Weekly rates apply year-round including teacher planning days, legal holidays and any student absences.

Note: The school participates in various programs which offer subsidies. The subsidies may vary depending upon eligibility and attendance. Credits for these programs will be reflected on the families' invoices.
Payment Schedule: Due each Friday for the upcoming week
Daily Meals: Breakfast, lunch, and afternoon snack
Toys: Leave at home, please
Clothing: Please provide a change of clothing, closed toe shoes are required
All items must be labeled
Enrollment Termination: Non-payment; excessive late payments; Non-compliance with conduct policy as stated; Needs unable to be met by school; Physical/verbal abuse by parent
Field Trips: Must be paid in advance
Parent Conferences: Twice yearly: December and May; others may be scheduled

Dear Parents,

Welcome to ([YOUR SCHOOL'S NAME]). We are extremely fortunate to have a state of the art program. This year, we have become a Science, Technology, Engineering, and Mathematics (STEM)-focused child development program. Being a STEM program means that we use learning opportunities to have students observe, classify, compare and contrast, and problem solve. For example, when children state that they came to school in a cloud, the teacher will take the opportunity to teach about fog. Bugs, rain, our beautiful garden, butterflies, blocks, etc. all become "teachable moments" for learning about the universe around us and its principles.

Our lead teachers are certified professionals with a wealth of experience in intentionally cultivating a child's potential. We are very proud of the dedication of the staff to the early childhood development profession and their pursuit of excellence in teaching and learning. We are excited about the opportunities we have available for your child.

We are glad that you have chosen [YOUR SCHOOL'S NAME] for your child's education. We appreciate your commitment and confidence in our ability to educate and care for your children. We have an open door policy and are happy to have you stop in, observe your child's classroom, and participate in our program.

This handbook of important information is for you to read and to refer to during your child's early years of learning. Once you have read the information, please complete, sign, and return the Handbook Agreement Form on page ____ to the office for our records. By signing, you acknowledge that you have read the policies and procedures. Note: The Parent Handbook may be amended by [YOUR SCHOOL'S NAME] and its agents as the needs of the school change.

For additional information, please feel free to contact me at 770-XXX-XXXX or [email address]. May your family's relationship with us be positive and rewarding!

Sincerely,

[Your name and signature]
Director

"The truly gifted educators are those who care for their students and show them the "awesomeness" of the world around them—and then go the extra mile to help them find their unique and purposeful place in it."
-Anonymous

[YOUR SCHOOL'S NAME]

Mission Statement
The mission of [Your school's name] is to provide quality care and education for the children of [name] community.

Vision Statement
Our goal is to provide accessible, affordable, high-quality early education by keeping the learner's needs at the center of decision-making and working in partnership with families and our dynamic, multicultural community.

Philosophy
We believe in the value of human diversity and the fair treatment of all people. Our primary goal is to provide a nurturing environment that supports all children as they become creative, independent, responsible, fully-functioning, self-directed individuals who have a strong sense of self and accomplishment. Secondly, as adults, we must strive to continue learning and growing in our relationships with others to role model a peaceful environment and surround the children with understanding and warmth.

Program Overview
Our developmentally appropriate program is child-centered and based on best practices research in Early Childhood Education. Our belief is that the best way for children to learn is through play, and our classrooms reflect this belief by providing a planned environment that is designed to stimulate children's interest. Our individualized educational approach meets each child's different and unique needs and interests.

The program focuses on the child's cognitive, social-emotional, psychomotor, language and communication, and creative development. Learning centers encourage children to choose freely from a wide range of play and learning experiences, and help them recognize, understand, and express their own emotions as well as to sympathize with the emotions of others.

We use the *[blank] Curriculum* for all age groups. Children learn best through hands-on experiences with people, materials, events, and ideas; this principle, validated by research, is the basis of *[blank]* approach to teaching and learning. On-going observation of children is documented and shared with parents through classroom bulletin board displays, reports, newsletters, and parent conferences. Our program enables children to reach their fullest potential.

Objectives
The daily schedule provides children with opportunities to make meaningful choices and actively learn in their environment. Children's time is spent in learning centers, group activities such as creative movement, music, storytelling, and dramatization. Field trips are also part of the pre-school children's experiences. Days are planned so children will:

- ☺ feel safe, nurtured, loved, and respected
- ☺ have a wide variety of age appropriate materials and toys
- ☺ participate in stimulating, interactive activities, and hands-on experiences
- ☺ join in activities willingly without feeling pressured
- ☺ have predictable routines that include active and quiet times
- ☺ make choices
- ☺ solve problems and think critically
- ☺ are allowed to make mistakes and can laugh about it

☺ have parents as partners
☺ know that their unique abilities and cultural backgrounds are honored
☺ are in small class size with low teacher ratios
☺ receive individual attention and affection
☺ develop satisfying relationships with other children and adults
☺ develop self-discipline
☺ experience successes in order to develop a positive self-image
☺ learn to respect the personal and property rights of others
☺ develop intellectual, physically, creatively, socially, and emotionally

[YOUR SCHOOL'S NAME]Child Development Center
[YOUR SCHOOL'S ADDRESS]

Infant Daily Schedule (6 to 12 months)

Schedules for infants are used as a guide for the day. Infant classroom schedules are responsive to individual children's needs. Infants who eat table foods follow a schedule, while younger infants eat at appropriate intervals based on their indicators to staff that they are hungry. Infants eating table food follow the program's snack and meal schedule, while younger infants eat at appropriate intervals based on their indicators to staff that they are hungry. Developmental activities including sensory, large motor (both indoors and outdoors), and small motor activities happen throughout the day as children are interested. Routines, such as diapering, eating, and napping, occur throughout the day to meet each child's unique schedule.

6:00-7:00   Staff members greet children and parents and assists with storage of personal belongings. Children are provided opportunities for free choice play in learning centers (reading, listening, dramatic play, art, manipulative play, music).

7:00-8:30   Potty breaks and diaper changes as needed.

8:30-9:30   Breakfast snack for older babies, diaper changing, feeding

9:30-10:30   Circle time -(Prayer and Interactive Bible story) developmental activities and experiences (sensory, small motor, music, and language), diaper changing, naps as needed

10:30-11:15   Large motor/outdoor play time

11:15-11:35   Check and change diapers as needed

11:35-12:15   Lunch for older infants, diaper changing, feeding, floor play

12:15-2:30   Story time and naps, as needed

2:30-3:30   Snack for older infants, diaper changing, feeding

3:30-4:00   Large motor/outdoor play time

4:00-4:30   Check and change diapers as needed

4:30-5:30   Music and movement- developmental activities and experiences

5:30-6:00   Story time

6:00-6:15   Check and change diapers, prepare for supper

6:15-7:00   Supper and departure

[YOUR SCHOOL'S NAME]Child Development Center
[YOUR SCHOOL'S ADDRESS]

Toddler Daily Schedule (13 months to 35 months)

6:00-7:00	Staff members greet children and parents and assists with storage of personal belongings. Children are provided opportunities for free choice play in learning centers (reading, listening, dramatic play, art, manipulative play, music). Potty breaks and diaper changes as needed.
7:00-7:30	Circle time: songs, stories and finger plays. Children develop calendar skills (months/days, seasons and weather). Gross motor skills development through active indoor activities.
7:30-8:00	Prepare for morning snack. Wash hands and faces. Potty break and diaper change.
8:00-8:30	Morning snack-children are encouraged to develop self-feeding skills.
8:30-8:45	Cleanup and wash hands.
8:45-9:15	Circle Time-Devotions (Prayer and Interactive Bible story with the teacher, the children will be a part of the action in the story.)
9:15-9:30	Potty breaks and diaper changes as needed. Wash hands and faces.
9:30-10:15	Early literacy activities: Pre-reading and math lessons. Children learn to recognize the alphabet and numbers (count) 0-10. Art project time - Arts and Craft.
10:15-10:30	Potty breaks and diaper changes as needed.
10:30-11:30	Outdoor play-weather permitting. Explore the outdoors. Children will learn about trees, leaves, grass etc. Gross motor activities: running, jumping, climbing and riding.
11:30-12:00	Potty breaks and diaper changes as needed.
12:00-12:30	Lunch time-occasionally served family style. Cleanup and wash hands.
12:30-12:45	Potty breaks and diaper changes as needed.
12:45-1:15	Music and Movement. Interactive learning songs. Children are introduced to various types of music and songs for play.
1:15-1:30	Story time with teacher and prepare for nap. Potty breaks and diaper changes as needed.
1:30-3:00	Rest period or nap time.
3:00-3:30	Potty breaks and diaper changes as needed. Prepare for snack.
3:30-4:00	Afternoon Snack - Cleanup and wash hands.
4:00-5:00	Outdoor play weather permitting. Play outside on the playground. Potty breaks and diaper changes as needed.
5:00-6:00	Free choice play in learning centers. Teachers interact with the children as they play and are introduced to musical toys and books, alphabet books and blocks, and number concepts. Caregivers facilitate fine and gross motor skills development through play with finger paint, markers, paint and brushes, puzzles, blocks, play gyms, vinyl mats, push and pull toys, and riding equipment.
6:00-6:15	Potty breaks and diaper changes as needed. Prepare for supper.
6:15-7:00	Supper and dismissal

[YOUR SCHOOL'S NAME]Child Development Center
[YOUR SCHOOL'S ADDRESS]

Three and Four Year Old Class Daily Schedule

6:00-7:00	Staff members greet children and parents and assists with storage of personal belongings. Children are provided opportunities for free choice play in learning centers (reading, listening, dramatic play, art, manipulative play, music). Potty break-children are taught proper hand washing technique during each break.
7:00-7:45	Circle time: songs, stories and finger plays. Children develop calendar skills (months/days, seasons and weather). Gross motor skills development through active indoor activities.
7:45-8:15	Wash hands and faces. Potty break.
8:15-9:00	Circle Time and Interactive Bible story with the teacher, the children will be a part of the action in the story. Calendar skills.
9:00-9:15	Cleanup and wash hands.
9:15-9:45	Morning Snack-children are encouraged to develop self-feeding skills.
9:45-10:00	Potty break. Wash hands and faces.
10:00-10:45	Early literacy activities: Pre-reading and math lessons. Children learn to recognize the alphabet and numbers (count) 0-10. Art project time - Arts and Craft.
10:45-11:00	Potty break
11:00-12:00	Outdoor play-weather permitting. Explore the outdoors. Children will learn about trees, leaves, grass etc. Gross motor activities: running, jumping, climbing and riding.
12:00-12:15	Potty break
12:15-12:45	Lunch time-occasionally served family style. Cleanup and wash hands.
12:45-1:00	Potty break
1:00-1:15	Interactive learning songs. Children are introduced to various types of music and songs for play.
1:15-1:30	Story time with teacher and prepare for nap. Potty break
1:30-3:00	Rest period or nap time.
3:00-3:30	Potty break. Prepare for snack.
3:30-4:00	Afternoon Snack time. Cleanup and wash hands.
4:00-5:00	Outdoor play weather permitting. Play outside on the playground. Potty break
5:00-6:00	Free choice play in learning centers. Teachers interact with the children as they play and are introduced to musical toys and books, alphabet books and blocks, and number concepts. Caregivers facilitate fine and gross motor skills development through play with finger paint, markers, paint and brushes, puzzles, blocks, play gyms, vinyl mats, push and pull toys, and riding equipment.
6:00-6:15	Potty break - Prepare for supper.
6:15-7:00	Supper and dismissal

[YOUR SCHOOL'S NAME] School or Child Development Center
[YOUR SCHOOL'S ADDRESS]

Extended Care Daily Schedule
5-12 years

6:00-7:00   Children are greeted warmly and assisted in storing personal belongings. Opportunities to rest quietly or play in free choice learning centers.
7:00-7:15   Restroom Break
7:15-7:45   Morning Snack and cleanup
7:45-8:00   Gather belongings and load school buses for school attendance.

3:00-3:15   Store personal belongings and restroom break
3:15-3:45   Afterschool snack and cleanup
3:45-4:00   Restroom break
4:00-5:00   Outdoor play (weather permitting)
5:00-5:15   Restroom break
5:15-6:00   Homework Tutorial, guest speakers, group rap sessions, computer lab time and/or free choice play. Reading and Storytelling time, Listening centers.
6:00-6:15   Restroom Break. Prepare for supper.
6:15-7:00   Supper and dismissal

Holiday/Teacher Workday Care 5-12 years of age

6:00-7:00	Children are greeted warmly and assisted in storing personal belongings. Opportunities to rest quietly or play in free choice learning areas.
7:00-7:15	Restroom Break
7:15-8:15	Circle time: Bible Story, Prayer, and Songs, Review rules through story telling, role play, etc., calendar skills and weather
8:15-9:30	Language Arts-Integrated art and language activities (spelling, poetry, reading)
9:30-9:45	Restroom Break
9:45-10:15	Morning snack
10:15-11:15	Outdoor play (weather permitting)
11:15-11:30	Restroom break
11:30-12:00	Math Fun-Integrated numbers, music and computer
12:00-12:15	Restroom break
12:15-12:45	Lunch
12:45-1:00	Restroom break
1:00-1:30	Foreign Language exploration
1:30-3:00	Rest period. Children nap or listen to soft music, play quietly with puzzles or read.
3:00-3:15	Store personal belongings and restroom break
3:15-3:45	Afternoon snack and cleanup
3:45-4:00	Restroom break
4:00-5:00	Outdoor play
5:00-5:15	Restroom break
5:00-6:00	Homework Tutorial, guest speakers, group rap sessions, computer lab time and/or free choice play in learning centers. Reading and Storytelling time, Listening centers.
6:00-6:15	Restroom Break. Prepare for supper.
6:15-7:00	Supper and dismissal

Administration and Staff
[YOUR SCHOOL'S NAME] has a Director, an Assistant Director, and Staff who work collaboratively to provide the services aforementioned.

Director
[Insert five sentence biographical sketch]

Assistant to the Director
[Insert five sentence biographical sketch]

Staff
Our administrative team and board of directors hire well-qualified staff to work with the children. Each classroom has a full-time staff member who holds, at a minimum, a Child Development Associate Credential or a Bachelor of Science degree in Early Childhood as well as experience in early childhood centers. All full-time and part-time staff satisfy the Georgia Department of Early Care and Learning: Bright from the Start 10-hour training requirement. Each staff member has passed the required criminal background check. All staff complete a minimum of twelve hours of in-service training each year in addition to our monthly staff training sessions. [YOUR SCHOOL'S NAME] facilitates continuous professional development opportunities for the staff.

Additional qualified assistants support our regular staff and come to us through the local colleges and technical schools. Students may visit the classrooms to complete their course-required observations. These students observe and may interact with the children, but are not caregivers counted towards the student-teacher ratios. If there is a change in staff, we will always inform you about the change in personnel and ask for your support during the transition period.

Admission Procedures: Registration, Tuition, and Fees
Admission Procedures
The [School's name] admits children ages 12 months (walking) to 5 years of age. [YOUR SCHOOL'S NAME] and all its agencies do not discriminate based on race, gender, religion, or ethnic background. Parents/guardians need to complete a registration form that includes information on: family background, emergency contacts, health issues, statement of fees, attendance policies, behavior management, and provide parental releases for photography, videotaping, and field trip participation. All registration forms must be kept current; if you move, change emails, change telephone or cell phone numbers, please contact the office at once. Our school year runs from August to June with closings based on the calendar for [name] County Public School's calendar.

In order to be considered for enrollment the following forms must be submitted:

- Enrollment Form
- Emergency Medical Authorization Form
- Birth Certificate
- Medication Authorization Form (if applicable)
- Field Trip Permission Forms
- Immunization Form
- Family Agreement
- Authorization to Dispense External Preparations Form
- Food Allergy Action Plan (if applicable)
- Special Care Plan for Asthma (if applicable)
- Special Care Plan for Diabetes (if applicable)

We will make all of the necessary forms available to you and help you with any questions. Please thoroughly review the handbook and forms before signing the family agreement. A parent / guardian planning to withdraw their child from [YOUR SCHOOL'S NAME], must notify the director in writing and provide ten days notice.

Registration Fee

A school year registration fee of $150.00 is required for <u>each child</u> at the time of registration and/or enrollment renewal. This is <u>non-refundable fee</u> and is not part of the tuition fees.

Tuition Fees

Tuition fees are set by [YOUR SCHOOL'S NAME], and we constantly strive to assure modest rates. Taken into account are low student-teacher ratios that ensure high quality learning; as suggested by NAEYC.

Tuition Rates

The tuition rates are as follows and apply to the hours of operation of 8:00 a.m. – 4:00 p.m.:
Infants
Toddler
Preschool
Aftercare
Before Care

In addition, on-site before and after care is available from 7:00 a.m. – 8:00 a.m.; and from 4:00 p.m. – 6:00 p.m. This additional service of care is charged weekly at the rate of $X.00 per hour/per week.

Payment of weekly rates apply year-round including teacher planning days, legal holidays and any student absences (including illness).

Sibling Discount

Families with two children enrolled in the center will receive a discount. In such cases, the first child's tuition will follow the regular rates; additional children will have their tuition discounted by $10 per week.

Payment Schedule

Tuition payment is due before service is rendered. Payment is due each Friday prior to the starting week. <u>Late payments will incur a penalty fee of $x.00, per day, to be applied to all accounts where tuition is not paid on/ before the due date.</u>

1. Weekly: The payment is due on Monday of each week or on the first day of attending school. If the payment is not received a $x.00 late fee will be added to the account.
2. Monthly: The payment is due the first business day of each month or the first day of attending school. If the payment is not received a $x.00 late fee will be added to the account.
3. It must be understood that in order to hold a child's slot payment must be made regardless to attendance. **Tuition is based upon a contract not attendance.

Non-Sufficient Check

You may pay by cash, check (made payable to "[YOUR SCHOOL'S NAME]") at the office or by credit or debit card online. If a check is returned, we will notify you and will require payment in cash plus $30.00 to cover the service charge. After the second returned check, we will accept electronic payment. Tuition discounts are offered to parents that agree to monthly ACH withdrawals.

Accounts that become in the arrears by 2 weeks are subject to suspension from the program and are subject to termination after 30 days. Accounts that have been terminated for non-payment are subject to a new registration fee. Children that have been suspended or terminated for non-payment will not be allowed to return to the center until FULL payment and ALL late fees have been paid and the account brought up to date.

No account may go into deficit. THERE ARE ABSOLUTELY NO EXCEPTIONS TO THIS POLICY.

Tuition payments may be made directly at the preschool by credit/debit card, check or money order only. NO CASH PAYMENTS ARE ACCEPTED at the preschool. Tuition payments must be placed in the payment drop-box. Receipts are distributed on a monthly basis, but may be issued earlier upon request. Year-end statements for income tax purposes can be provided by [YOUR SCHOOL'S NAME].

Any adjustments necessary due to *extended* closure of school due to natural disasters will be dealt with as necessary.

Parents receiving subsidies are required to pay the difference between their tuition rate and the subsidy. For example, if your tuition rate is $X per week and your subsidy pays for $X per week, you are responsible for the $X difference per week. No tuition credit will be given for absences (even due to illness) or vacations.

Late Pick Up and Fees

In case of late pickup, the parent must call the school at (770) xxx-xxxx, NO LATER THAN 5:30 P.M. The phone call allows the Director and/or classroom teacher to reassure your child that she/he has not been abandoned. A late fee of $5.00 for the first five minutes and $1.00 for each minute after 6 pm will be assessed. Chronic lateness may result in your child being dropped from the program. This policy will be strictly enforced.

If your child has not been picked up within one hour of closing time, the proper authorities will be called which may include: [name] County Police and/or the Department of Children and Families.

Attendance: Arrival and Dismissal Procedures

Arrival Procedures

All children must be brought to their classrooms escorted by their parents and signed in on a daily basis. Arrival is the time for parents, children, and staff to start the day off by greeting one another, sharing information and settling in. Family members, parents, guardians, or relatives must be listed on the emergency contact forms to be considered pre-approved for drop-off and pick-up. Children should arrive by 8:30 a.m. in order to take advantage of the entire morning program. In order to facilitate the transition at arrival, please encourage your child to: say good morning, sign-in, and wash his /her hands, leave toys and/or inappropriate books in your car.

Parking

Parents may park in the designated parking spaces. Please **do not block the emergency pass** through lane or park in front of the building.

Dismissal Procedures

All children must be signed out on a daily basis. Departure from the center is a time for reconnecting, sharing information, and gathering items to go home. Please call ahead if you are going to be late (see

"Late Pick Up and Fees" section). Only those people listed on your emergency contact form may pick up your child. Written permission for an exception will be permitted if the *parent* sends a handwritten note or fax to (770) xxx-xxxx. You must also call to inform us that the fax was sent. Please let these people know that ***we will ask them for a photo I.D.***. Please check your emergency contact form to make sure it is complete and updated. Remember that the person picking up your child must be at least 18 years of age in order to sign him/her out.

Transportation Verification:
Daily: Your child must be signed in upon arrival and signed out at dismissal every day by the adult who receives drop off and/or facilitates pick up. The time and full signature, NO INITIALS ALLOWED, must be written on the attendance sheet. Georgia Child Passenger Restraint Law requires children under 4'9" tall and eight years old to ride in a child safety seat. The driver is held responsible for compliance with the law. Violators of Georgia Child Passenger Restraint Law will be liable to the penalty and fees. They may also be reported to the Department of Child and Family Services for negligence. **Please do not leave any child in the car while you run in to the class to sign your [YOUR SCHOOL'S NAME] child in**. Besides being against the law, it is also dangerous. Our children are very curious and have been watching you drive for a while and may want to try it out if they are left on their own even for a short time. **In our [YOUR SCHOOL'S NAME] vehicles, all passengers will be buckled in.** Transportation to and from our program is the responsibility of the parent. Field trip transportation is arranged by our staff and will be provided to and from the after school site by chartered bus. The vehicle will have a licensed driver. The staff will maintain a roster of children to be transported and check attendance before loading the vehicle, upon arrival, upon unloading, entry and exit of field trip locations. We will maintain a record of all transportation (e.g. location, times, directions, etc.), a copy of your child's emergency medical information (special care plans, medication, authorizations, etc.), and an annual vehicle inspection form on the vehicle. All staff members have evidence of First Aid and CPR training.

Attendance/Absences:
Regular attendance is a requirement of tuition subsidy programs. It is important that your child attends every day in order to receive the maximum benefit of this program so that your child is prepared to succeed in school.

Please note: It is a State requirement that parents/guardians comply with the center's attendance policy as well as any of its other policies and procedures. The state Pre-K program allows a center to dismiss a child who does not follow these rules.

Birthdays
Birthdays are special times to celebrate. Please speak with your child's teacher regarding birthday celebration guidelines specific to his / her classroom. If you do not celebrate birthdays, please inform the Director and your child's teacher. **Also, outside foods are not allowed. This includes goodie bags filled with food items during the holidays and birthdays. All allergies and food omissions must have a statement from a doctor and a copy of the form will be placed in the child's file and in the kitchen.**

The following are alternative ways to celebrate special occasions.
Non-Food Ideas
- A puzzle/book/educational toy to be used in the classroom
- Cultural toys/outfits for the classroom
- Stickers
- Toothbrushes
- Notebooks, pencils, crayons, markers, and/or erasers

Non-Food, No-Cost Activities
- Plant/teach art and/or craft activities
- Share one or two cultural activities
- Volunteer for a day

Please be considerate of all children's feelings when a birthday is to be celebrated outside of school. If the entire class is not invited, distribution of the invitations is up to the family. The teachers will happily distribute invitations if the entire class is invited.

Child Abuse and Neglect
Staff members are required by law to report any <u>suspected</u> cases of child abuse or neglect. Please see the brochure from the Department of Children and Families for more information.

Communication: Home-School Connection
A strong home-school connection ensures that the child will benefit greatly from their school experiences. We support families by providing information and support that connects the home and school so that your child can develop his/her fullest potential. There are many ways a parent may become involved at our school.

Parent-Teacher Communication
- ☺ Bulletin boards in front of each classroom
- ☺ Activity documentation within the classrooms
- ☺ Parent-Teacher conferences*
- ☺ Newsletters
- ☺ Informal arrival and dismissal sharing

*Parent conferences are scheduled twice per year; in November and in April. Please see your child's teacher to schedule specific dates and times. For more ways to connect home and school, please see the section under "Join Us!"

Cultural Sensitivity Policy
[YOUR SCHOOL'S NAME] is committed to diversity and cultural sensitivity. We do not discriminate based on race, gender, religion, or ethnic origin. Many cultural events are incorporated in our program, such as the celebration of birthdays and holidays. Families who do not participate in these celebrations at home and wish their children to be excused from such celebrations need only to speak to the Director of the program. We will honor the wishes of each family with sensitivity and diligence.

Culture and family traditions are a part of our regular learning experiences. Families are invited to share their culture and traditions, especially foods and recipes that are enjoyed at home and at family celebrations. We will adopt these ideas into our curriculum and routines.

We admit students without regard to race, culture, ethnicity, sex, national origin, ancestry, special health needs, developmental or behavioral concerns, or disabilities. The curriculum reflects respect for different cultures, without stereotyping of any culture. Program staff members try to communicate in the language best understood by the family. If that language is not spoken English or the family does not understand written English, the program will find a trusted adult who uses the family's language to translate for the family or provide translated materials. In addition, the program will suggest ways for family members to communicate with program staff when the program does not have a translator available. For example, the program may help the family to identify a bilingual person in the family's community who can write out the family's communication in English and translate notes that the program writes in English for the family. Staff members will provide opportunities for the child to learn English.

Discipline Policy
We believe that children learn by doing. Conscious discipline (using natural consequences), redirection, time away, and positive guidance regarding appropriate behavior, are our methods of teaching children self-control and self-discipline. At [YOUR SCHOOL'S NAME], discipline does not take the form of a punishment. Children encounter situations in their everyday environment that require them to problem-solve. We provide a safe environment in which your child can have a safe outlet to handle these situations in a positive and productive way. We arrange quarterly visits by an early childhood mental health consultant or intervention specialist to observe teacher/caregiver interactions with our students and advise staff members about approaches to manage challenging behaviors. This program explicitly prohibits corporal punishment, psychological abuse, humiliation, abusive language, physical restraints, restriction of access to large-motor physical activities, and withdrawal or forcing of food and other basic needs. Before they are hired, all teachers/caregivers sign an agreement to implement the facility's discipline policies that includes the consequence for staff members who do not follow the discipline policies. If a child's behavior is unresponsive to the usually effective discipline measures described previously, the program will seek help from a qualified early childhood mental health consultant or as a last result, terminate enrollment.

Dress
Children are expected to be dressed in comfortable clothing appropriate for active play according to the weather. Children work in the garden and many other "messy" activities as part of our hands-on curriculum, they **will** get dirty. Please do not send them in clothes reserved for special occasions. In addition, all children need an extra set of labeled clothing left at school. Please place this set of clothing in a plastic bag labeled with the child's name on the outside. **Please dress your child in safe, close-toed shoes such as tennis shoes or sneakers for safety.**

Lost clothing is a problem most of us cannot afford. Help us and help yourself by clearly marking your child's name on jackets, sweaters and changes of clothing.

Small hair ornaments are not recommended for infants and toddlers, as they can fall out and pose as a choking hazard. In cases where children are old enough to wear beads in their hair, please make sure that the beads are secure and will not fall out.

Emergencies
Closing
In case of an emergency closing during the school day, the director shall notify parents by email or telephone. Parents are asked to pick-up their children within one hour of being notified. The school follows the county DOE schedules and directives, therefore, if [X county DOE] announces over the radio, TV, or [YOUR SCHOOL'S NAME] website that it will close due to weather emergency or other conditions, the will also close. We urge each family to have a plan for emergency closing during school hours. Please make sure that our office has your current emergency contact information.

Fire Drills
The director conducts fire drills once a month at different times during the day to make sure that we are prepared in case of a fire. The Director will immediately notify you by email or telephone in the event of any emergency. Please see procedures posted on the parent bulletin board.

Lockdowns

In case of a lockdown, our first responsibility is the safety of the children. We will not release children to anyone without proper identification. Please register family or friends with [YOUR SCHOOL'S NAME]'s emergency system so that you are informed of procedures.

Family Expectations
It is inappropriate for any child, family member or guardian, to be physically violent, verbally abusive, or engage in disruptive behavior toward another child, parent/ guardian, relative of an enrolled child, or personnel. This policy includes sexual harassment. For the protection of the children and personnel, such conduct will not be tolerated and any person engaged in such behavior will be immediately removed from the premises by either an administrator or local law enforcement. Inappropriate or disruptive behavior, by child, parent, guardian, or relative of an enrolled child may be the basis for termination of the child's enrollment. Please note that employees are prohibited from "babysitting" after hours. Employees who do so are subject to employment termination.

Generous Donations- Thank you!
Donations are gladly accepted. If you would like to make a donation, please see the classroom teacher or Director and a "wish list" of recommended items will be provided to you. All large donations should be given to the Director. She will assign the donations to the appropriate classrooms.

In addition, we can always use: "gently" used toys, books, buttons, greeting cards, purses, ribbons, calendars, tiles, dramatic play props, spools, phones, jewelry, dress-up costumes, collage materials, and paper/ plastic recyclables.

Many employers offer matching gifts for your generous contributions. We are also affiliated with several "give back" programs whereby the school earns up to 5% of your purchases at Office Depot and Kroger stores.

Health and Safety Policy
Health Care Documents: Immunizations / Physicals
Our school only accepts children into our program with a current physical examination and an up-to-date immunization certificate. Documentation of performance and findings of a checkup that includes all preventive health services, including oral health services, that the child needs according to current recommendations of the American Academy of Pediatrics. Documentation must be signed and dated by the child's physician, licensed pediatric or family nurse practitioner, or family practice physician. The information on the submitted form must be updated, initialed, and dated at each subsequent age-appropriate health assessment, or a new form must be completed, signed, and dated. Information generated by a health care professional's electronic medical record system is acceptable as long as it provides the required information. (No child is allowed to attend if the physical or immunizations forms are outdated. **It is the responsibility of the parent to ensure that their child's health records are current and accurate.** Parents may submit a notarized statement if an exemption for religious reasons is requested. If upon review of a child's health record it is determined that a nationally recommended preventive health service (e.g., vision, hearing, dental examination, immunization) has not been performed enrollment will be suspended until the physical exam is conducted or the immunization record and/or care plan is updated.

Accidents
All accidents, no matter how small, are reported by the teachers or Director to the parent on the appropriate form by the end of the school day. The parent will immediately be called by the Director in the event of any serious accidents/ injuries and for all accidents/ injuries above the neck. Parents will be asked to sign the form, return it, and the form will be kept on file. In case of severe emergency, we will call "911" and then the parent(s).

Parents /guardians are responsible for and expected to share any accidents and injuries that occur off the pre-school premises so that when the child comes to school with bruises or injuries we are knowledgeable about the situation.

Biting

Biting is a typical phase of development for children between the ages of 15-36 months and is one way to express feelings and relieve tension. When a child is bitten, we respond by following normal accident procedures. Our teachers work with the child to help him/ her understand that biting is not acceptable behavior. However, in cases of repeated occurrences, the Pre-School Director will work with the family to develop a behavior modification plan.

Reasons for and strategies for addressing biting:

- **Teething:** When teeth are coming through, applying pressure to the gums is comforting, and infants will use anything available to bite. Obviously, if this is a likely cause, then a teething ring or objects to bite will lessen the infant's need to bite other people.
- **Excitement and over-stimulation:** When some very young children are very excited, even happily so, they may behave in an out-of-control fashion.
- **Impulsiveness and lack of self-control:** Infants sometimes bite because there is something there to bite. This biting is not intentional in any way, but just a way of exploring the world.
- **Curiosity:** Young infants and toddlers learn about emotion (shock, fear, amusement, and the like) through exploring. Often they act out in order to observe responses. This behavior is repeated if the reaction is entertaining. Caregivers use redirection to avert this type of behavior.
- **Frustration:** Too many challenges, too many demands, too many wants, too little space, and too many obstacles may lead a child to bite, especially before they have the capability to express frustration through using their words.

Our staff members are trained to do the following to try to minimize the biting behavior:

- Let the child know in words and manner that biting is unacceptable. Adults' most stern manner and words should be reserved for acts such as biting.
- Provide caring attention to bother the biter and the victim.
- Examine the context in which the biting occurred and look for patterns. Was it crowded? Too few toys? Too little to do? Too much waiting? Is the biting child getting the attention and care he/she deserves at all times? Did someone or something provoke the child?
- Change the environment, routines, or activities if necessary.
- Work with the biting child on resolving teething pressure, interpersonal conflict, or frustration in a more appropriate manner, including using words if the child is capable.
- Observe a child who is a short-term chronic biter to get an idea about when he or she is likely to bite. Some children, for example, may bite not when they are angry or frustrated, but when they are very excited.
- Identify children likely to be bitten and make special efforts to reduce their chance of becoming victims.
- Don't casually attribute willfulness or maliciousness. Infants explore anything that interests them with the mouth, and that includes other bodies. They have more sensors in the mouth than their fingertips.
- If biting continues, continue to observe the group closely. Apply additional resources as necessary to shadow the child.

What can parents do?

Removing significant stressors on the child at home, such as a too demanding a schedule or difficult transitions, which will make it easier for a child to handle times of stress that do arise. If the child bites other children in your presence, take the same steps suggested above for teachers, immediately after the biting occurs and look for ways to adapt the environment to prevent biting in the future. If the child is biting at the child care center, there is very little you can do other than keep in close communication with the child's teachers. Fortunately, biting is a developmental stage that passes.

What if your child is bitten?

There's not much worse than seeing a bite mark on your child, and worse, infant and toddler bites are often on the face. All of our parental primal instincts as our child's protector come into play. It is natural to be upset. But try and keep in mind that it is a consequence of the group situation and not really the fault of the child, the family, or the program. Your child might as easily have been the biter. Keep communication lines open with the teacher.

Information about Infant and Toddler Care
Primary Care
Each child will be assigned a primary caregiver who is responsible for the child's well-being in the classroom and charting the child's progress; for communicating information and concerns to parents; and for that child's well-being in the classroom. Work schedules of all staff will be posted and arrangements for conferences should be made with the lead teacher.

Curriculum
Developmental goals are based upon the Early Learning and Development Standards across the Essential Domains of School Readiness. The domains are as follows:

Social and Emotional Development. The standards for Social and Emotional development involve behaviors that reflect children's emotional growth and their growing ability to successfully navigate their social worlds through interactions with teachers and peers. These standards include a focus on children's developing abilities to regulate attention, emotions, and behavior, and to establish positive relationships with familiar adults and with peers. Research indicates that early skills of social competence and self-regulation are foundational to children's long-term academic and social success (National Research Council, 2008). Curriculum topics or strands in the social and emotional domain are *Self* and *Relationships*.

Physical Well-Being and Motor Development Physical Well-Being and Motor Development standards address motor skills and health practices that are essential for children's overall development. These skills include the ability to use large and small muscles to produce movements, to touch, grasp and manipulate objects, and to engage in physical activity. These standards also describe the development of health practices that become part of children's daily routines and healthy habits such as nutrition and self-help. These skills and behaviors play an important role in children's physical well-being and set children on a path leading toward a healthy lifestyle. Healthy children are more likely to attend school, to be physically active, and to learn more effectively (Bluemenshine and others, 2008). The two strands in this domain are *Motor Development and Physical Well-Being*.

Approaches Toward Learning. Approaches Toward Learning centers on the foundational behaviors, dispositions, and attitudes that children bring to social interactions and learning experiences. It includes children's initiative and curiosity, and their motivation to participate in new and varied experiences and challenges. These behaviors are fundamental to children's ability to take advantage of learning opportunities, and to set, plan, and achieve goals for themselves. This domain also includes children's level of attention, engagement, and persistence as they do a variety of tasks. These factors are consistent predictors of academic success (Duncan et al., 2007). Finally, children's creativity, innovative thinking and flexibility of thought allow them to think about or use materials in unconventional ways, and to express thoughts, ideas and feelings in a variety of media. The standards in the domain Approaches Toward Learning are organized in the following strands: *Initiative*; *Engagement and Persistence*; and *Creativity*.

Language and Literacy. The standards for language and literacy reflect knowledge and skills fundamental to children's learning of language, reading and writing. Young children's language competencies pertain to their growing abilities to communicate effectively with adults and peers, to express themselves through language, and to use growing vocabularies and increasingly sophisticated language structures. Early literacy skills include children's developing concepts of print, comprehension of age-appropriate text, phonological awareness, and letter recognition. Research has identified early skills of language and literacy as important predictors for children's school readiness, and their later capacity to learn academic knowledge (National Early Literacy Panel, 2008). The Language and Literacy domain consists of the following strands: *Listening and Speaking, Reading and Writing.*

Cognition and General Knowledge. This domain includes those cognitive processes that enable all other learning to take place, as well as children's knowledge of the social and physical world. This domain is organized into the strand, *Cognitive Skills* and those concepts and skills in **sub-domains**, *Mathematics, Social Studies* and *Science*.

Cognitive Skills. This strand refers to the underlying cognitive mechanisms, skills and processes that support learning and reasoning across domains, including the development of memory, symbolic thought, reasoning and problem-solving.

Children in the infant and toddler classrooms follow a daily schedule which is posted. Teachers plan developmentally appropriate experiences daily, focusing on the individual and differentiated needs of the children, and work with the children individually as well as in small and large groups. We place great emphasis on routines and self-help skills.

Toilet Training
We are more than happy to encourage potty training as long as the child is ready (usually between the ages of two and three years old). The process needs to begin at home for approximately two weeks with success before it can be successfully implemented at the center. Toilet learning occurs when the child shows readiness for using the toilet and the family is ready to support the child's involvement in doing so. Readiness indicators include desire to perform self-body care, ability to remain dry for at least 2 hours at a time, communication skills to understand and express concepts related to toileting, ability to get onto and sit with minimal assistance on a toilet adapted for the child's size or appropriately sized, and awareness of the sensations associated with releasing urine and stool. Parents will be responsible for supplying pull-ups and wipes. **Children will be allowed to come to the center in cotton training pants/underwear after the child has been accident free for two consecutive weeks, in pull-ups. Communication between the parent and the caregiver is imperative during the transition from diapers to toilet.**

Diapers
Parents are required to provide an ample supply of diapers and wipes. The preschool does not store any

EXTRA diapering items. It is also the parent's responsibility to check periodically to determine the need to replenish these items. Each child has his/her own clear labeled diaper bin, either in infant/young toddler or older toddler/preschool room, depending on the age of children. Diapers are checked frequently and changed every 2 hours, or more often if required. Diapers containing feces are changed immediately. The diaper changing table is cleaned and disinfected immediately between each diaper change and hand washing of child care provider and child is performed after every diaper change.

This facility allows use of disposable absorbent diapers that prevent spills of feces or urine. Exceptions require documentation by the child's health care professional of the medical reason for using cloth diapers. If cloth diapers are used, they must meet the following criteria: the diaper has an absorbent inner lining completely contained within an outer covering made of waterproof material that prevents the escape of feces and urine, or the cloth diaper is adherent to a waterproof cover. No soiled clothing has its contents dumped or is rinsed at the child care facility. Disposable diapers are placed in a hands-free, plastic-lined, lidded container. Soiled cloth items are completely contained in a non-permeable, sealed plastic bag before being moved from the location where the child is being changed. Soiled cloth diapers may be stored in a labeled container with a tight-fitting lid provided by an accredited commercial diaper service. Otherwise they are placed in a sealed plastic bag for removal from the facility by an individual child's family. At no time are dishes, bottles, lunch boxes, or any other articles involved with food or beverages placed within a diapering or toileting area; nor are any surfaces outside the diapering or toileting area ever in contact with any object that could be contaminated by soiled diapers or soiled underclothing.

Food/Meals
Current research shows that children need a variety of nutrient-dense foods that include protein, carbohydrates, oils, vitamins, and minerals, with an amount of calories that prevents hunger, fosters healthy growth, and prevents obesity. Children learn to self-feed and develop lifelong healthful habits by being introduced to developmentally appropriate solids and observing eating modeled by others. We serve the following meals: morning and afternoon snack and lunch according to the United States Department of Agriculture's food program guidelines. Please complete and submit the infant and/or toddler feeding plan as applicable. At one year of age, children are introduced to new foods and follow our regular lab menu, including whole milk, unless medical restrictions are noted by a physician. Meals are provided with portion size as outlined by the childcare licensing agency and USDA. Mothers who are breast-feeding are encouraged to come during meal times. Please speak to the Director for more information.

Join Us!
PTA
Our parents are very involved, and we are all partners when it comes to your children! They help organize fund-raisers, field trips, amazing initiatives, and meet on a regular basis. They will communicate dates and times for you to become involved. Please join!

Parent Orientation/ Open House
The staff will hold a Parent Orientation/Open House at the beginning of the school year. This is an opportunity to learn about the policies of the school, meet your child's teacher, and visit the classroom for a "model" day.

Parent Visits
Parent visits to the center during the school hours are welcome and encouraged. There are also many opportunities during the year for parent help in projects and as chaperones on field trips. Parents may plan classroom visits with the teachers or you may visit any time you wish (see "Open Door Policy").

Parent-Child Resource Library
We encourage each child to take a book home each evening to read at home with the family. Help your child select an age-appropriate book, check the book out, and take the time to read at home and discuss. Please return the book within two weeks so that others can also enjoy it. If you have any books that you would like to donate to the library, please leave them with the Director. We appreciate your contributions!

Kaleidoscope of Activities
Enrichment
Our school is so fortunate to be able to take advantage of the many local cultural programs offered. We occasionally offer enrichment classes for students during the year. The classes are held once a week and include areas such as creative movement, sports, art, dance, robotics, cooking, and piano. These classes are in addition to our regular pre-school programming and, as such, an additional fee is charged for participation. Classes are limited in size and age groups.

Field Trips
Our program of activities includes visits to special places within the community. We take special precautions to insure safety. We will notify you in advance of planned field trips and will require your written permission for your child to attend. Field trips are treated as enrichment programs and the cost for the entrance fees and transportation costs are above and beyond the tuition fees and must be paid prior to the child attending the field trip.

Parent chaperones are always welcome. Chaperones must be 21 years or older and are utilized on a first-come-first- serve basis. At times, parent chaperones that participate in field trips will be asked to pay for their own admission, and may be asked to drive their own vehicle to the place of visit. Only children who are enrolled at the time of the field trip are eligible to participate.

(Optional policy) Travel away from the facility is limited to walking excursions or those for which parents/legal guardians can drive their own children or the children are transported in a vehicle provided or arranged by the program/facility that is equipped with age-appropriate seat restraints for the children who are traveling in them. Each child wears identification with the child's name and the name and contact information of the child care program in a fashion that does not allow it to be easily read from a distance by a stranger. Staff members carry medical authorization, photographs, and emergency contact information for each child. A parent/legal guardian must sign an informed consent for the specific trip for the child to go on that trip.

Teachers/caregivers keep toddlers and preschool-aged children together through use of a travel rope (a knotted rope stretched between 2 teachers/caregivers to which children hold on while they walk), by having an adult hold each child's hand, or by another means that keeps the children physically connected to an adult at all times. A designated adult supervises the children at the front of each group, and another adult supervises children at the back of each group.

Language and Culture
Language and Culture
The families come from diverse backgrounds and speak different languages. At the Pre-School we will be sensitive to these linguistic and cultural needs. We encourage children developing their home language skills and the acquisition of a second language.

Medication and Illness Policies
Medication

Written consent is required for all medication (e.g. over the counter, prescriptions, creams, injections, and the like). All prescriptions must be in original containers labeled with the child's name. Your child will be watched closely once medication is given, to see if any noticeable adverse reactions are happening. Should any adverse reactions be noticed, you will be notified immediately to come and pick up your child. All non-prescription medications must be in the original containers bearing the original label, child's name and age, expiration date and directions for dosages. Please drop off and pick up any medication with the director. The medication will be given according to the times on the prescription. [School name] will not administer medication to a child longer than ten days, unless there is written authorization from your physician. Authorizations to Dispense Medication must be updated every ten days. In addition, we will administer emergency care to any child who has asthma or allergies and needs to be treated with an inhaler or antihistamine in accordance with the instructions provided by the child's doctor. We will review our policies annually in order to assure that it meets the requirements of the Americans With Disabilities Act of 1990, 42 U.S.C. §§ 12181-89 and its implementing regulation, 28 C.F.R. pt. 36.

Illness and Injury Policy
Please do not send your child to school ill. We operate under [Name of state] Childcare Licensing regulations that do not allow actively sick children to be in the classroom. The staff is trained in First Aid/ CPR and recognizes the signs of communicable disease and other illness.
If the child needs to be sent home because of illness, the Director will call the parent and the child must be picked up within the hour. The school has only limited facilities to make your ill child comfortable and we must guard the health of others in the pre-school. When the parent cannot be reached, the person listed as an emergency contact by the parent will be called. The child will be released to that person. Re-admittance to the program is allowed after 24 hours of normal temperature (below 99 degrees), and/or no other signs of illness for 24 hours, or by a doctor's signed statement.

A written statement of good health from a doctor will be required to return to the school when:
1. A child has contagious symptoms (e.g. vomiting, diarrhea, fever, rash or others listed on the National Board of Health's Communicable Disease chart).
2. A child has a diagnosed communicable disease (strep, head lice, pink eye, impetigo, etc.). We do not require a statement when a child has had chicken pox, but we will do a visual check to make sure all the pox are dried.
3. A child has undergone surgery or has been hospitalized.

Children returning with signs of illness or disease will be refused admittance. If a child is well enough to come to school, it is expected that s/he will participate in all activities.

In the event of a medical emergency the director will immediately call 9-1-1 and notify parents. Staff members will initiate life-saving techniques as appropriate. We will remove other children from the area and the director will call the parent(s) as applicable. Your child will be transported by emergency medical services to [Name, address, and telephone of nearest medical facility]. After the crisis, the staff will complete an incident report and turn it into the director. The director will inform Bright from the Start within 24 hours of incident.

Notification of Communicable Diseases
Parents are responsible for notifying the Director of the center IMMEDIATELY upon learning that their child has a communicable disease. Parents of every child enrolled will be notified of communicable diseases that occur in within 24 hours. The Health Department will be notified within 48 hours of any suspected outbreak of noticeable communicable disease.

Too Cold, Too Hot

Children play outdoors except when weather or air quality poses a significant health risk, defined as a wind chill factor at or below -15°F and a heat index at or above 90°F or poor air quality (e.g., an ozone alert) per the National Weather Service. Scheduled outdoor play activities and times may be shortened when conditions approach these limits. Precipitation (rain or snow) does not preclude outdoor play unless a child's inner clothing becomes wet. A special needs care plan or doctor's statement is required to make an accommodation for special needs. We also believe in the need for fresh air and outdoor play. When it is too cold (below -15°F) or too hot above 98°F) outdoors, we take a brisk walk outside, play in shaded areas, or provide alternate indoor activities.

Sunscreen and Sun Injury

Outdoor areas provide protection from the sun with shade and protection from wind with vegetation or wind-reducing fencing. Children use sunscreen and dress for the weather and sun exposure. Parents are urged to apply sunscreen on their children before they come to school. If a child does receive a sun injury, we will follow the Illness Policy. If sunscreen or insect repellant are sent to school, parents must complete and Authorization to Dispense External Preparations form before the staff can apply it. As appropriate for the weather, families must provide outdoor clothing that keeps their child dry and comfortable such as a raincoat, warm coat, boots, snow pants, mittens, and hats for cold weather or days when precipitation is expected. For sunny days, children must have lightweight clothing that is sun protective, including long-sleeved shirts and hats.

Tooth Brushing

Each classroom will have a daily supervised tooth brushing activity that models and teaches good dental hygiene and prevents cross-contamination between children, toothbrushes, and toothpaste. To ensure proper hygiene each child will be given her/his own labeled toothbrush and toothpaste which will be stored in a holder or individually marked Ziploc bags and kept out of the reach of children when not in use. Toothbrushes will be changed every three months. Classroom staff will insure that toothbrushes are rinsed and stored properly after use.

Nap and Rest Time

The daily program includes a quiet rest time as part of the children's daily schedule. Some children may need sleep; others only rest. We try to accommodate each child's rest needs. We want your child to feel comfortable during rest time. The school provides a crib or cot sheet for rest time. Infants younger than 12 months are placed on their backs for every sleep time unless the child's health care professional completes a signed-and-dated statement that the child requires a different sleep position. Infants always sleep in a crib on a firm surface. The crib must meet current standards of the US Consumer Product Safety Commission (CPSC) and ASTM for infant sleep equipment. Infants who fall asleep outside a crib are put in their cribs on their backs to continue sleeping. Except for a fitted sheet to cover the mattress and a pacifier, no other items are in an occupied crib with an infant, and nothing is attached to the crib or within reach of the child. Wedges, infant positioners, and blankets may not be used unless prescribed by the child's health care professional with a written note.

Nutrition: Food Policies

The center serves breakfast, lunch, and an afternoon snack. Daily menus provide a healthy and well-balanced diet. Portions and balances are in accordance with the USDA and CCFP (Child Care Food Program) requirements. Children from 1 to 2 years are served whole milk. Substitutions can only be made with a doctor's note.

1. Substitutions will be made for food that your physician confirms *in writing* are harmful to your

child (allergies, cholesterol, etc.).
2. Religious requirements will be honored, as we are able.
3. Other meal substitutions must be healthy and/ or in line with our food program menu. **NO fast foods of any kind will be allowed in the center at any time.**

Breakfast is served beginning at 8:00 a.m. and ending at 8:30 a.m. for the pre-school side; for the toddler side, breakfast begins at 8:30 am and ends at 9:00 a.m.; this time may vary for the younger groups. However, for school age students, breakfast will be served between 8:00 a.m. and 8:15 a.m. Mealtimes are on a set schedule in accordance with CCFP guidelines.
Special diets, including nutrient concentrates and supplements, may be served only upon written instruction from the child's physician. No exceptions or substitutions will be made for children who simply do not care for an item. Each child will receive every item on the menu to encourage, teach, and model the consumption of a balanced meal. Food is never used to punish or to bribe, nor will a child be forced to eat every item presented.

Eating together is a social learning experience. Children and teachers eat together; teachers eat the same meal in order to demonstrate and role model appropriate eating behavior and manners, proper conversation techniques, and trying new and different foods in a family-style dining experience.

Open Door Policy
Parents are always welcome and encouraged to visit our classrooms at any time. Open-door policy visits are an opportunity for parents to participate and observe their child's behavior. However, if you wish to discuss your child's progress, please make arrangements with your child's teacher to schedule a parent-teacher conference.

Personal Belongings
Each child has a cubby with his/her name on it. This is a special place for each child's jackets, extra clothes, blankets, and most treasured art projects. Please check your child's cubby each day and take home items such as important communication from teachers or administrators, clothes for laundering, and art work for display at home.

Toys from home create many problems in educational settings. For the safety of the children, the following are prohibited: electronic devices, jewelry, guns, swords, gum, candy, action figures, and money. ***Please leave personal belongings at home or in the car.*** Jewelry such as necklaces and hoop earrings can pose a threat to the safety of the children. We suggest that these items are saved for special occasions. Please do not allow your child to bring these items unless special permission has been given (e.g. show and tell, exhibits, and so forth). All banned items will be confiscated and returned to the parent. Our program **takes no responsibility for valuable items brought or worn to school.**

Pre-School Program
We implement the *[X] Curriculum* in the pre-school classrooms. The *[X] Curriculum* is based on the principles of active learning and key experiences. Our pre-school children are given opportunities to challenge themselves and advance their learning through art, science, music, literacy, blocks, sand and water, math, logic, language, and physical activities. We provide "hands-on" meaningful experiences that enrich the learning process. Children develop critical thinking skills by direct manipulation of the environment that surrounds them. As adults, we facilitate learning to enable the children to continue moving towards learning success. The children and teachers partner in the learning process. The teacher records and documents daily observations and conduct assessments in order to plan for your child's interests and needs. In addition, we incorporate the Georgia Early Learning and Development Standards (GELDS) of learning in order to align ourselves with Common Core and Georgia Department of

Education (GDOE) Performance Standards. Our curriculum meets the state requirements of early learning standards. This year we are very excited to add a focus on Science, Technology, Engineering and Mathematics (STEM) into our curriculum. Ask your teachers (and your child!) about STEM, and learn about how they are engaged in meaningful, hands-on, experiential, inquiry-based activities that teach them about the world!

School-Age Program
We provide supervised before- and after-school and vacation time care and enrichment programs for school-aged children. The curriculum includes academics, physical activity, healthful nutrition, recreation, completion of schoolwork, social relationships, and use of community resources, all of which are coordinated with school and home life. The goal of this program is to equip students to excel academically, especially in science, technology, engineering, the arts, and math. Activities include free choice learning experiences, at least 60 minutes of indoor and outdoor physical activity, time and settings for schoolwork and recreation alone or in a group, field trips to community facilities, relationships with understanding and comforting adults, and rest. Regular communications occur at least weekly among the children's schoolteachers, parents/legal guardians, and child care program staff members.

Quality Assurance
To assure the implementation of best practice in Early Childhood Education, we use the Infant/Toddler and Early Childhood Environment Rating Scales (ITERS and ECERS) to evaluate the space and furnishings, personal care routines, listening and talking, activities, interactions, program structure, and parent and staff interaction.

Resources and Services
Bright from the Start: Georgia Department of Early Care and Learning
2 Martin Luther King Jr. Drive SE, 754 East Tower Atlanta, Georgia 30334
404-656-5957 1-888-442-7735
Georgia Department of Family and Children Services
Please contact the local DFCS office in your county or the local police department.
After hours (between 5 p.m. and 8:30 a.m.) call 1-855-GACHILD
Georgia Poison Control Center
Toll Free: 1.800.222.1222 Local: 1.404.616.9000

Student- Teacher Ratios
Student-teacher ratios meet group size quality indicators as recommended by Georgia Department of Early Care and Learning: Bright from the Start:

Infants less than one (1) year old or children under eighteen (18) months who are not walking	1:6
One (1) year olds who are walking	1:8
Two (2) year olds	1:10
Three (3) year olds	1:15
Four (4) year olds	1:18
Five (5) year olds	1:20
Six (6) years and older	1:25

Disenrollment or Termination of Services
Our school reserves the right to revoke the enrollment of a child (ren) for any of the following reasons:
- Non-payment or excessive late payment of tuition fees
- Violation of the rules and regulations of the pre-school as outlined in this Parent Handbook and

Agreement
- Physical and/or verbal abuse of staff or children by parent, child, guardian, or family member

Transitions

Transitioning from one classroom to another can be both an exciting and stressful time for young children as well as their families. We take measures to ensure that each child's transition is an enjoyable experience by taking into consideration his or her chronological age, overall development, and teacher recommendations. Please see your child's teacher for transition guidelines specific to your child's age group and individual needs. Typically students are promoted each fall unless there is a need to remain with a group for the child's best interests (e.g. until potty trained or verbal).

Unusual Issues

The Director and teachers are always on alert for unusual issues. These include: strangers on the property, unidentified packages, marks or bruises on children, etc. We report each of these to the proper authorities so that they can be addressed appropriately. **Facility entrances are observed by a staff member and maintained locked from the outside but easily opened from the inside by school-aged children or adults. An alarm is activated when a door is opened from the inside other than the monitored entrance/exit door so that no one can leave the building unnoticed. The security system includes an alarm if anyone gains entrance without being recognized by the administration. The administration and support staff** are the only ones authorized to operate the security system and monitor entrances to the building and the doors from the reception area into child care areas. Please do not prop doors or provide access to unauthorized individuals. Pets are not allowed on the property.

Water and Sand Play Policy

All rooms are equipped with covered sand and water tables on wheels. This allows the tables to be used indoors or out. Tables are kept in the classrooms. Teachers provide close supervision to maintain good hygiene practices. Fresh water is used for each session of water play for a group of children and drained when the activity is complete. When swimming, wading, or other gross motor play activities in water are part of the program, each infant or toddler has 1:1 supervision with a teacher/caregiver having a hand on the infant or toddler at all times during the activity. For preschool-aged children, the required child:staff ratio during water activities for preschoolers is 4:1, and for school-aged children, 6:1. Clean sand is used and replaced frequently. Sand is securely covered when not in use.

(E)Xceptional Students- Individuality

Each child is a unique individual who will be loved and treasured for who they are by the teachers and other personnel. We recognize that each child has talent, intelligence, and is capable of learning. We strive to create the best learning environment and provide for the needs of each child. Toward this goal, our curriculum varies from child to child as it is structured to meet his/her individual and differentiated needs. Your child may report that s/he is doing something different than his/her classmates. This may be true based on what each child needs in order to progress satisfactorily. We support inclusion of children with special needs and will make every effort to meet the needs of families with children with special needs.

Yearbook

Each teacher will compile numerous photographs of your child and his interactions with his/her peers and teachers during activities and field trips throughout the year. All of these educational experiences can be placed in a CD full of memories!

Zero Tolerance

We have a zero tolerance for: mistreatment of children in any form; alcohol, drug, and smoking of any kind on the premises; weapons, guns, or dangerous supplies brought to the school. All chemicals are locked in secure cabinets or stored out of reach of the children.

FAITH BASED PRESCHOOL
Parent Manual

…you *are* a chosen generation, a royal priesthood, a holy nation, His own special people,
that you may proclaim the praises of Him who called you…
1 Peter 2:9a

Preparing future leaders to impact the world for Jesus Christ…

Phone: 678.XXX.XXXXFax: 678.XXX.XXXX
YOURSCHOOL@yahoo.com   www.YOURSCHOOL.com
Mailing address:
P. O. Box XXXXX
Atlanta, GA 30359

Why Christian education? Researchers strongly suggest that a child's moral development is almost complete by age nine. Because your child's education environment and source shapes them in several ways:

• Academically
• Socially
• Morally and Spiritually

"The function of education, therefore, is to teach one to think intensively and to think critically. But education which stops with efficiency may prove the greatest menace to society. The most dangerous criminal may be the man gifted with reason, but with no morals." -Dr. Martin Luther King, Jr.

FAITH BASED PRESCHOOL

Table of Contents

1. INTRODUCTION	Page
Greetings	4
Mission and Philosophy of Education	5
Methodology	6
Statement of Faith	7
Student Outcomes	9
2. POLICIES AND PROCEDURES	
Admission Policies	11
Waiting List	11
School Tour	11
Registration	12
Sessions	12
Hours of Operation	11
Registration Fee	12
Tuition Payments	12
Late Charge	12
Returned Check Fee	12
Late-Pick-Up Policy	12
Calendars	13
Absences/Holidays	13
Snacks and Lunches	14
Vacation Credit	13
Withdrawal From School	16
3. STAFF AND CURRICULUM	
Staff	16
Overall Curriculum	16
Chapel Bible Stories	17
Discipline	17
Daily Schedule	17
4. PARENT-SCHOOL COMMUNICATIONS	
Parent Observations/Conferences	18
Change of Address/Phone	18
Number/Emergency Pick-up	18
Newsletters	18
Information Boards	18
Parent Meetings	18
Volunteer Opportunities	18
5. HEALTH	
Medication	19
Immunization Check List	20
6. OPERATIONAL POLICIES	
Attendance	20
Arrival and Departure	21
Clothing	22

Share Items/Toys	22
Lost and Found	22
Naps	22
Birthdays	22
Accidents/Injury Requiring Medical Care	22
Emergency Preparedness	23
School Pictures	23
Testing	23
School Visits	24
School Events	24
Peer Group/Family Member Visits	24
Supplies	25

FAITH BASED PRESCHOOL

Greetings in the precious name of our Lord and Savior, Jesus Christ:

Welcome to FAITH BASED PRESCHOOL! We provide a comprehensive kindergarten program which engages and develops the whole child. Daily teaching and learning objectives focus on your child's development in the following areas: Social, Emotional, Physical, Cognitive and Spiritual. We believe parents are a child's first and most important teacher; thus, we encourage your involvement in our program and value your insight into your child's unique learning style. Our desire is to help your child discover God's purpose and plan for his life while encouraging the development of their gifts and talents. Each day will be filled with stimulating and innovative activities which encourage each child to reach his/her full potential. Our daily schedule includes a balance of teacher guided and child initiated enrichment activities.

Our small class size provides the opportunity to connect with your child individually and provide a sound academic foundation. We hope that your child will consider our program a second home…a place where they are valued and nurtured unconditionally…a place where laughter and play are important to their development…a place where their individuality is appreciated and responded to. You will find we are very knowledgeable with regards to current research in child development. Please make the most of every opportunity to observe, listen to and learn from this community of learners. We believe teaching is a calling and are committed to facilitating the learning of children, parents and one another. We are delighted to embrace this role in our service to your family.

The policies and procedures within are in compliance with the National Association for the Education of Young Children, The American Academy of Pediatrics, and the Georgia Department of Early Care and Learning (Bright from the Start). Your submission of supplies requested by the teacher and completion of all registration materials prior to your child's first day will prepare them for a safe and successful school year. We look forward to this opportunity to help your child become the spiritual champion they were destined to be. Please let us know if we may be of further assistance. We appreciate the opportunity to serve your family! Please contact me for further information or if I can be of further assistance, at 678.XXX.XXXX or email at YOURSCHOOL@yahoo.com.

In Christ's service,

Helping families play, learn and grow together…for God's glory!

Forming Christian character as we prepare students for future works of service… "For the perfecting of the saints, for work of the ministry, for the edifying of the body of Christ." Ephesians 4:12

Mission Statement

Our mission is to provide a Bible-based, Christian education which excels in teaching the whole child, considering multiple intelligences, the way they learn and support families' efforts to fulfill Deuteronomy 6:4.

Philosophy of Education

It is our desire to provide a Christian environment which will afford the opportunity for your child to receive a Bible based education, from a Christian staff. It is our prayer that this will complement the Christian training you are providing in your home.

1) Jesus is preeminent in our instruction: We believe the fear of the Lord is the beginning of knowledge and all the treasures of wisdom and knowledge are in Christ, thus true learning cannot be achieved apart from Christian education. Proverbs 1:7; Colossians 2:3; Psalm 111:10

2) God has a plan and a purpose for you and your child's life: We Believe a Bible based education is necessary to enable the children to reason from the Bible and discern the perfect will of God. Enabling both parent and child to understand they are created in Christ Jesus to perform works, which were appointed before the foundation of the world. Proverbs 4:20-22; Acts 17:28; Psalm 78:6,7; Ephesians 2:10

3) We are committed to being led by the Word and Spirit of God: We believe the Holy Spirit is the Teacher and the Revealer of all knowledge (spiritual and academic) and by His instruction and guidance; we will cultivate and encourage the development of God given gifts and talents within each child. John 14:26; Romans 12:1-8

4) The great commandment and the great commission are revealed in our instruction: The love of God is manifested as we teach the whole child (spirit, soul and body) considering their unique learning styles. We also share the gospel of Jesus Christ with the children in obedience to the scripture. Matthew 22:37-40; 28:16-20 We believe children should be encouraged to develop Christ like character qualities. Romans 8:28, 29 See FAITH BASED PRESCHOOL student outcomes.

Methodology

The Principle Approach ® method of education is the manner of consistent and ordered teaching and learning that produces Christian character and self-government, Christian scholarship and Biblical reasoning for lifelong learning and discipleship.

The notebook method is an essential component to the Principle Approach ® that governs the teacher and student in their participation in each subject. It establishes a consistent tool and standard of Christian scholarship. The learners are producers as they build their own daily record of a subject, taking ownership of the learning process. The notebook method embraces the four steps of learning: research, reason, relate and record. It aids in the Biblical purposes of education by "enlightening the understanding, correcting the temper, and forming the habits of youth that fit him for usefulness in his future station." (excerpted from the Webster's 1828 Dictionary definition of education) The notebook method is the product of the student's creativity and a permanent record of his productivity. It assists parents and teachers in overseeing progress and visually demonstrates the character development, diligence, and responsibility of the student.

4-R'ing—in every subject at every grade level, the student is required to actively participate in his learning by:
1. Researching the subject, word, or study
2. Reasoning through identifying the leading idea and basic principles
3. Relating it to other areas of study and the world around them
4. Recording what he has learned in his notebook using his writing skills and his own ideas, conclusions and creativity. Each child's notebook is a reflection of his unique individuality!

Reasoning from recurring Biblical principles and leading ideas—every study draws out a leading idea that relates to one or more of the seven basic principles built on God's Word.

The Seven Principles
Each Principle Builds on the One Before
Where the Spirit of the Lord is, there is Liberty.   2 Corinthians 3:17

God's Principle of Individuality
I will praise thee; for I am fearfully and wonderfully made: marvelous are thy works; and that my soul knoweth right well. Psalm 139:14
Doctrinal Application: Our God is Himself an Individual who made us in His image for a providential purpose.
Personal Application: My unique individuality has a purposeful destiny that can only be fulfilled through Christ's redemption.

The Principle of Christian Self-Government
But the fruit of the Spirit is love, joy, peace, longsuffering, gentleness, goodness, faith, meekness, temperance: against such there is no law. Galatians 5:22, 23
Doctrinal Application: Knowing God through Christ teaches me to obey Him and enjoy liberty with law.
Personal Application: I am only properly self-governed when governed by Christ.

The Principle of Christian Character
Doctrinal Application: As my character is forged by Christ, I reach my fullest expression and enjoy harmony with others.
Personal Application: My character predicts the success and happiness of fulfilling my destiny.
Conscience is the Most Sacred Property
Doctrinal Application: Righteous law protects life and property; consent is the title to conscience.
Personal Application: My stewardship of property, both internal and external, has consequences.

The Christian Form of Our Government
Doctrinal Application: The form of government proven to best protect life and property is a Christian constitutional federal republic.
Personal Application: As I learn to think governmentally, I can balance the three powers of government to avert the tyranny of self in my personal conduct.

Planting the Seed of Local Self-Government
Doctrinal Application: Education is the cause to effect multi-generational maintenance of a Christian republic.
Personal Application: I continually sow seeds in my thought, speech and action; consequently I continually reap the results.

American Political Union
Doctrinal Application: The internal gives rise to the external.

Personal Application: Internal unity spawns external union.

Reflective learning—the student internalizes principles that shape his thinking and behavior—internal to external.

Key word study—using Noah Webster's 1828 *American Dictionary of the English Language*, students study the meanings of words defined whenever possible from the Bible, their original root and etymology, and research the meaning of other words found in the definition. Through this study, students truly understand the word and gain the ability to articulate an idea, acquire mastery of the English language, and learn its application to history and today.

Fine arts and liberal arts emphasis—building the person from the inside out requires the teacher to encourage the student's creativity, talent, gifts and inherent skills—seeking each one's unique purpose in Christ.

The classroom constitution—instills Christian character and conscience by empowering the student to take responsibility for his own learning and the learning environment where he contractually agrees to practice self-government.

Mastery learning—repetition of basic recurring principles at every grade level, continually applying age-appropriate methods to enable the student to internalize and understand his subject of study.

Expected Students Outcomes

Our student(s) ….
1. Are well prepared in all academic disciplines, and are skilled in reading, writing, speaking, listening, and thinking.
2. Are proficient in mathematics and science.
3. Have a knowledge and understanding of people, events, and movements in history (including church history) and the
cultures of other peoples and places.
4. Appreciate literature and the arts and understand how they express and shape their beliefs and values.
5. Have a critical appreciation of languages and cultures of other peoples, dispelling prejudice, promoting interethnic harmony, and encouraging biblical hospitality for the "alien" or "stranger."
6. Personally respond to carrying out the Great Commission locally and around the world in a culturally sensitive manner.
7. Know how to utilize resources including technology to find, analyze, and evaluate information.
8. Are committed to lifelong learning.
9. Have the skills to question, solve problems, and make wise decisions.
10. Understand the worth of every human being as created in the image of God.
11. Can articulate and defend their Christian worldview while having a basic understanding of opposing worldviews.
12. Understand and commit to a personal relationship with Jesus Christ.
13. Know, understand, and apply God's Word in daily life.
14. Possess apologetic skills to defend their faith.
15. Are empowered by the Holy Spirit and pursue a life of faith, goodness, knowledge, self-control, perseverance, godliness,
brotherly kindness, and love.
16. Treat their bodies as the temple of the Holy Spirit.
17. Are actively involved in a church community, serving God and others.
18. Understand, value, and engage in appropriate social (community) and civic (political) activities.

19. Embrace and practice justice, mercy, and peacemaking in family and society.

20. Value intellectual inquiry and are engaged in the marketplace of ideas (open, honest exchange of ideas).

21. Respect and relate appropriately with integrity to the people with whom they work, play, and live.

22. Have an appreciation for the natural environment and practice responsible stewardship of God's creation.

23. Are prepared to practice the principles of healthy, moral family living.

24. Are good stewards of their finances, time (including discretionary time), and all other resources.

25. Understand that work has dignity as an expression of the nature of God.

Adapted from the Association of Christian Schools International Student Outcomes

Statement of Faith

The Scriptures...We believe the Bible is the inspired Word of God, the product of men of old who spoke and wrote as they were moved by the Holy Spirit. The New Covenant (New Testament), we accept as our infallible guide in all matters of life and doctrine. (2 Timothy 3:16; I Thessalonians 2:13; II Peter 1:21)

The Trinity...We believe there is one God, eternally existent in three persons - the Father, the Son, and the Holy Spirit being coequal. (I John 5:4-8; Philippians 2:6) God the Father is the sender of the Word. (John 16:28; John 1:14) The Son is the Word made flesh and has existed with the Father from the beginning. (John 1:1; John 1:18; John 1:14) The Holy Spirit proceeds forth from both the Father and the Son and is eternal. (John 15:26)

Man, his fall and redemption...We believe in salvation is the gift of God to man, which we receive by faith in Jesus Christ. (Ephesians 2:8) Man is a created being, made in the likeness and image of God, but through Adam's fall, sin came into the world. "All have sinned and come short of the glory of God". Jesus Christ, came in the form of man and gave His life to restore us back to God, undoing the work of the Devil. (Romans 5:14; Romans 3:10 & 21-30; I John 3:8, Galatians 4:4-7).

Eternal life and the new birth...We believe in man's first step toward salvation is godly sorrow through repentance. The new birth is necessary for all men, and when experienced produces eternal life. (II Corinthians 7:10, I John 5:12; John 3:3-5; Romans 10:9-10)

Hell and eternal retribution...We believe in the one who dies in his sins without accepting Christ is hopelessly and eternally lost in the Lake of Fire and, therefore, has no further opportunity of hearing the Gospel or repenting. The Lake of Fire is literal, the terms "eternal" and "everlasting", used in describing the duration of the punishment of the damned in the Lake of Fire, carry the same meaning of endless existence as used in denoting the duration of joy and ecstasy of the saints in the presence of God. (Hebrews 9:27; Revelation 20:15)

Water baptism...We believe in the baptism in water by immersion as a direct commandment of our Lord, and is for believers only. The ordinance is a symbol of the Christian's identification with Christ, His death, burial, and resurrection. (Matthew 28:19; Romans 6:4, Colossians 2:12; Acts 8:36-39)

Baptism in the Holy Spirit...We believe in the promise of the baptism in the Holy Spirit as a commensurate experience is available to all believers with the evidence of speaking in other tongues as well as the demonstration of spiritual power in daily life. (Acts 2:4;Acts 10:44-46; Acts 19:6; Acts 1:8; Mathew 3:11)

Sanctification...We believe in the Doctrine of Sanctification as a definite, yet progressive work of grace, beginning at the time of salvation, and continuing until the consummation of Christ's return. The Bible teaches that without holiness no man can see the Lord. (Hebrews 12:14; I Thessalonians 5:23; II Peter

3:18; II Corinthians 3:18; Philippians 3:12-14; I Corinthians 1:30)

*Divine healing...*We believe in healing for the physical ills of the human body, mind and spirit, and it is available to us by the power of God through the prayer of faith, and/or by the laying on of hands. Jesus Christ made this available to all believers at Calvary. (Mark 16:18; James 5:14-16; I Peter 2:24; Matthew 8:17; Isaiah 53:4-5)

Resurrection of the just and the return of our Lord...We believe in the resurrection of both the saved and the lost; they that are saved unto the resurrection of life and they that are lost unto the resurrection of damnation. (John 5:24, 28, 29) The angels said to Jesus' disciples, "This same Jesus, who was taken up from you into heaven, will so come in like manner as you saw Him go into heaven." When He comes, "...the dead in Christ will rise first. Then we who are alive and remain shall be caught up together with them in the clouds to meet the Lord in the air..." (Acts 1:11; I Thessalonians 4:16-17) Following the Tribulation, He shall return to earth as King of kings, and Lord of lords, and together with His saints, who shall be kings and priests, He shall reign a thousand years. (Revelation 20:6)

*The church...*We believe in the spiritual unity of believers in our Lord Jesus Christ, and seek community together, to become more and more in every way like Christ who is the head of His body, the church. (Ephesians 4:16, Hebrews 10:25)

POLICIES AND PROCEDURES

Admission Policies

FAITH BASED PRESCHOOL admits students of any race, color, national and ethnic origin to all the rights, privileges, programs and activities generally accorded or made available to students. It does not discriminate on the basis of race, color, national or ethnic origin in administration of its admissions, educational, or employment policies, scholarship, athletic and other school administered programs. We do not make it a policy to deny enrollment on the basis of a child with special needs, however, if after talking with the parents of such a child we realize that we do not have the training, equipment, facilities, etc. to handle their child, we will not accept the child. This is in the best interest of the child, since our goal is to meet the needs of each child. If we are not sure whether or not we could handle a special needs child, we would be willing to try. The parents and we would have to evaluate whether or not this placement is capable of meeting the child. We will not deny admission to, terminate enrollment of, or otherwise discriminate against any child because of that child's disability. In addition, we will administer emergency care to any child who has asthma and needs to be treated with an inhaler in accordance with the instructions provided by the child's doctor. We will review our policies annually in order to assure that it meets the requirements of the Americans With Disabilities Act of 1990, 42 U.S.C. §§ 12181-89 and its implementing regulation, 28 C.F.R. pt. 36. All students are accepted on a trial basis, we reserve the right to dismiss any student.

Examples of why we would terminate your child include (but may not be limited to):
Failure to complete or provide required forms. (i.e. immunization certificates)
  Failure to pay tuition in a timely manner.
  Lack of mutual agreement with program philosophy and policies.
  Lack of parental involvement
  Failure of child to adjust to the program after a reasonable amount of time.
  Our inability to meet the child's needs.
  Excessive discipline challenges.

Contact the office today at (678) XXX-XXXX in order to receive admissions materials, schedule a tour and testing. For further information please request an inquirer's packet.

Waiting List

Upon visiting FAITH BASED PRESCHOOL and submitting the admissions materials, parents may reserve a space for future enrollment of their child. After your child's application is received the following fees must be submitted: registration, testing (if applicable), and the non-refundable wait list fee of $100 (per family). Your child's name will be kept of a list of prospective students in the event a space becomes. You have ten days from the date of notification to fill the slot or you are required to wait until the next open enrollment season. The date the fees are received is the date your child is added to the list.

School Tour

Tours are conducted by appointment only. Parents are encouraged to schedule a tour with the administrative staff. We encourage you to join us for a complementary observation day before your child's first full day. This will provide an opportunity for your child to meet his teacher and his/her classmates. The teacher may be able to provide transition tips during this time. Open house is held in December, March, June, and August. Parent orientation is held each August and December. **All parents or guardians are required to attend orientation to become familiar with the program's policies and procedures.**

Registration

Parents may register for enrollment at anytime. Please note the application procedures below:
1. Schedule a visit or tour of the facility
2. Complete and return the following forms with the registration and necessary testing fees
Enrollment Application
Medical Authorization Form
Certificate of Immunization
Eye, Ear and Dental Examination Form (K5)
Field trip permission forms
Family Agreement
External Preparations Form
CACFP Income Eligibility Form
Food Allergy Action Plan (if applicable)
Special Care Plan for Asthma (if applicable)
Special Care Plan for Diabetes (if applicable)
Pastor or Church Leader Reference
Request for Student Records Form (if transferring)
3. Schedule interview with administrative staff and teacher to clearly establish a mutually supportive relationship between the home and school
4. Schedule Admissions Test for K4 and K5 students
5. Notification of application acceptance or denial

Sessions and Hours of Operation

The school year begins the day after labor day and lasts 180 days in order to fulfill Department of Education requirements. Camp Destiny is held eight weeks during the summer. We are open Monday through Friday, 8 a.m. – 2:45 p.m. We are closed in observance of the following federal holidays: New Year's Day, M. L. King, Jr. Day, Labor Day, Thanksgiving Day*, and Christmas*. We are closed the day prior to the holidays indicated by an asterisk(*) and two weeks for Christmas.

TUITION, FEES AND PAYMENT PLAN OPTIONS

Our operating budget does not cover all expenses therefore we rely upon your donations and assistance in an annual fundraiser. Our program accepts employer dependent care subsidies, Georgia Child and Parent Services/Maximus subsidies and employer matching gifts.

Full Tuition: $5,400
All tuition and fees are due prior to or at registration. Full payments may also be made via credit card at or before registration. FAITH BASED PRESCHOOL reserves the right to limit credit card acceptance to specific card issuing companies.

Full Tuition: $5,150 *Save $250*
Tuition and all fees are due and paid at or before registration. All tuition and fees are due prior to or at registration. Full payments may also be made via credit card at or before registration. Credit card payment will only be accepted for the full tuition option. Credit card holder is responsible for processing fees. FAITH BASED PRESCHOOL reserves the right to limit credit card acceptance to specific card issuing companies.
9 Month Plan: $____ Tuition is paid by bank draft in nine equal installments September 2013 through May 2014:
All tuition is due September 1, the 9 payment plan permits monthly installment payments. The first payment is due by September 1. Your last payment for the 2013-14 school year will be in May 1, 2013.

Applicable Fees
Application Fee: $50.00 per student - This fee is nonrefundable unless the applicant is refused acceptance. The application fee is due with the enrollment forms.
Late Payment Fee - A $25.00 fee will be assessed for any missed or late payments. A $39.00 fee will also be assessed for any check written to FAITH BASED PRESCHOOL that is returned by the bank for any reason. Checks are accepted as a courtesy. After one delinquent payment all other payments must be processed by electronic draft from your bank account by FACTS tuition management company or paypal.com 10 days prior to the due date.
Late Pickup Fee – A $30/hour fee will be assessed per hour or portion thereof for students picked up after 1 p.m. Repeated occurrences will result in termination from the school program. If we do not hear from parents before 1 p.m. we will assume that something has happened and will contact the _____County Department of Family and Children Services.
I/We understand this contract will be in force if my/our child is accepted for admission. I/We hereby agree to make tuition payments as outlined above and on the previous page. I/We understand that delinquency in tuition and other payments may result in the termination of my/our child's enrollment. I/We further agree that if my/our child is withdrawn after October 1, 2013. I/We am responsible for the tuition owed per the Withdrawal Policy Regarding Tuition. I understand that no school records, including grades and transcripts, will be released until all obligations are paid to FAITH BASED PRESCHOOL.

Withdrawal Policy Regarding Tuition
· If a new student withdraws prior to September 1, the $50.00 non-refundable admission fee is forfeited to FAITH BASED PRESCHOOL.
· If a new or re-enrolling student withdraws between July 1, 2013 and the first day of school, 50% of the annual tuition is owed to FAITH BASED PRESCHOOL. The amount owed will be: $720.
· If a student withdraws on or after the first day of school, 100% of the annual tuition is due The amount owed will be $1,440.

Faith Based Preschool
2013-14 Calendar

The SCHOOL is open Monday through Friday with the exception of the following holidays:

Martin L. King Jr. Day   Columbus Day
Good Friday   Veteran's Day

Memorial Day   The Day after Thanksgiving
Labor Day   Christmas Eve
New Year's Day   Christmas Break

Attendance Policy

Students are expected to be on time for every class. Please notify the instructor by telephone before 8 a.m. if you will be arriving late. Students arriving repeatedly more than ten minutes after the begin time may not be admitted to class. This is an interruption of the first and most important period of the day (Bible). Students should arrive between 8:15-8:30 a.m. with all homework assignments completed and materials necessary for class. Students arriving after the first period will be counted absent for Department of Education reporting purposes (A school day is considered 4 ½ hours of attendance). Chronic tardiness and/or absence (5 or more) will result in expulsion from the program. Tuition for the remainder of the school year will be due and payable immediately.

Absences/Holidays/Vacation Credit

Please notify the office at your earliest convenience in the event your child will be late or absent for any reason. Due to the deeply discounted tuition rates, fees are not pro-rated if your child is absent due to illness or vacation. Please provide ten days notice in the event your child will be absent for vacation purposes. The teacher will provide homework if you prefer.

Meals

Current research shows that children need a variety of nutrient-dense foods that include protein, carbohydrates, oils, vitamins, and minerals, with an amount of calories that prevents hunger, fosters healthy growth, and prevents obesity. Children learn to develop lifelong healthful habits by being introduced to developmentally appropriate foods and observing healthy eating modeled by others. Parents are required to provide nutritious breakfast, lunch and afternoon snacks. All meals should be prepared according to the United States Department of Agriculture's guidelines. In the future the program may offer lunch. Menus will be posted in advance for the upcoming month. In the future we will participate in the Child and Adult Care Food Program (CACFP), a Federal program that provides healthy meals and snacks to children during the school day. Each day more than 2.6 million children participate in the CACFP across the country. Providers are reimbursed for serving nutritious meals that meet USDA requirements. Each family must submit an income eligibility form in order for students to receive the meals free of charge and the facility to qualify to participate in the program. The program plays a vital role in improving the quality of meals and making it more affordable for all families. All staff members make sure that the food offered to children meets the recommendations of the Institute of Medicine for the US Department of Agriculture (USDA) Child and Adult Care Food Program, which are posted on the USDA Food and Nutrition Service Web site.

CACFP meals requirements established by the United States Department of Agriculture.
Breakfast   Milk, Fruit or Vegetable, Grains or bread
Lunch or Supper   Milk, Meat or meat alternate, Grains or bread, Two different servings of Fruit or vegetable
Snacks (Two of the four groups) Milk, Meat or meat alternate, Grains or bread, Fruit or vegetables

Please do not bring fast food or candy with your child to school unless prior approval has been given. In the event your child's diet must be modified for health, cultural or religious purpose parents must provide all meals which meet USDA meal pattern requirements.

Please **use a permanent black marker to** label all food containers with the child's name and the current date (month and date should be sufficient), then place all food containers in a zip-loc type plastic bag. Please label the plastic bag with the child's name only.

We discourage outside homemade birthday party snacks, however a store bought birthday cake or cupcakes are permitted. The label listing all ingredients must be provided. We ask that parents provide a few days notice and the snack be served in the afternoon (2:15-2:45 p.m.). Snacks containing peanuts or other nuts may not be served at school. This includes snacks with almonds, Brazil nuts, cashews, hazelnuts, macadamias, pecans, pine nuts, pistachios, and walnuts. We cannot accept foods prepared at home.

Nutritious Snack List for morning snack, field trips or food allergy substitutions
Fruits/Vegetables
• Any fresh fruit, including oranges, apples, bananas, grapes, pears, plums, tangerines that have been thoroughly washed
• Applesauce cups
• Raisins and other dried fruits – prepackaged (except Eileen's brand)
• Fruit cups (canned)
• Any pre-packaged fresh vegetables (e.g. baby carrots) and low fat dips

Juices
• 100% fruit or vegetable juices

Dairy
• Yogurt in individual cups or tubes
• Pudding in individual cups, cans or tubes
• String cheese or other individually packaged cheeses (1 oz)
• Frozen yogurt bars

Crackers/Snack items
Nabisco/Kraft brand:
• Crackers (Wheat Thins, Triscuits or Vegetable Thins)
• Red Oval Farms Stoned Wheat Thins
• Honey Maid Graham crackers or sticks (honey, cinnamon or chocolate flavor)
• Ritz crackers (original flavor or wheat), dinosaurs or sticks (EXCEPT Ritz bits)
• Cheese Nips or Better Cheddars
• Teddy Grahams or Teddy Graham character brands
• Barnum's Animal Crackers
Keebler brand:
• Wheatables (wheat or honey flavors)
• Club Crackers
• Town House Crackers
• Graham Cracker Sticks
• Grahams
• Sunshine Cheez-Its
• Saltines and Oyster Crackers (any)
• Pepperidge Farm Goldfish Crackers (any EXCEPT Sandwich Snackers)

Cereals
• Cheerios (EXCEPT Honey Nut or Frosted Cheerios)

- Raisin bran
- Grape Nuts
- Frosted Mini-Wheats
- Wheaties
- Rice Chex, Corn Chex, Wheat Chex or Multibran Chex
- Honey Maid Soft Baked Bars
- Kellogg's Apple Jacks or Mini Wheats
- Cracklin' Oat Bran
- Corn Bran

Cereal Bars
- Kellogg's Nutrigrain Bars
- Quaker Fruit and Oatmeal Bites

Other
- Small bagels (Lenders and Thomas brand) with cream cheese (no nut types)
- Baked Tortilla chips and salsa (Tostitos brand)
- Frozen treats such as 100% fruit/juice pops
- New York bagel chips
- Handi Snacks with cheese and red sticks
- Pretzels – Rold Gold and most other brands are peanut free
- Quaker Crispins

This list is intended to provide guidance to parents about snacks that are peanut and tree nut free. Parents whose children have peanut or nut allergies should check product labels every time to be sure that the products are peanut and nut free, free from cross contamination during processing and safe for their child to eat. Please read labels carefully to make sure products are nut free. As of May 2007, some manufacturers have discontinued labeling products that may have nuts or are produced on equipment also used for products with nuts.

Withdrawal From School
If for some reason you decide to discontinue our services, we require a two-week written notice. This may provide time to fill your child's spot. Payment is due for the remaining school year whether or not the child attends. Any outstanding fees must be paid on or before the child's last day. If it becomes necessary for us to resort to legal action to collect fees, the parent(s) or guardians will be responsible for legal fees incurred.

STAFF AND CURRICULUM

Staff
All staff members of FAITH BASED PRESCHOOL are credentialed professional educators with first aid and CPR training. Each staff member has a satisfactory background check performed by the Georgia Bureau of Investigation. Teachers complete fifteen hours of professional development each year. This training is designed to enhance their knowledge and skills in child development.

Overall Curriculum
We use Christ-centered curriculum©, a Bible based intensive phonics and math instruction program, which is supplemented with Purposeful Design©, A Beka Books©, Learning Resources ® and Delta© instruction models. Our goal is optimal spiritual and moral development along with quality academic instruction.

Chapel Bible Stories

In our efforts to grow in our relationship with the Lord Chapel or devotional is held each morning from 8:15-9:00 a.m. Parents are encouraged to join the children in worship and morning devotions. Children will learn Christian character traits from Bible stories of characters such as Jesus (love), Noah (obedience), Daniel (faithfulness), and the Apostle Paul (joyfulness).

Discipline

A distinction of Christian living is a love for God and a love for people. Therefore our students are expected to respect others, especially those in authority. Our discipline policy is based upon the parent teacher partnership and the teacher child relationship. Staff members model godly character to the children in every interaction. We strive to demonstrate by the way we speak to our students and one other and by their nonverbal expressions and actions that Christian character cultivates an environment of love, acceptance and blessing. Disrespectful language, attitudes and behaviors may be grounds for dismissal. We also encourage students to respect property by being good stewards of the materials and equipment entrusted to them. The staff will provide guidelines for behavior and use praise, positive guidance, redirection, planning ahead to prevent problems, encouragement of appropriate behavior, consistent clear rules, and involving children in problem solving to foster the child's own ability to become self-disciplined. Behavioral expectations and discipline will be explained to the child before and at the time of any disciplinary action. We will encourage children to respect other people, to be fair, respect property, and learn to be responsible for their actions. Aggressive physical behavior toward staff or children is unacceptable. We will intervene immediately when a child becomes physically aggressive to protect all of the children and encourage more acceptable behavior. We will use the scripture to provide consistent, clear and understandable behavioral expectations to the child. Parents will be provided a daily report of academic and behavioral progress.

WE DO NOT:

1. Spank, shake, bite, pinch, push, pull, slap, or otherwise physically punish the children.
2. Belittle, humiliate, make fun of, yell at, threaten, make sarcastic remarks about, use profanity, or otherwise verbally abuse the children.
3. Shame or punish the children when bathroom accidents occur.
4. Deny food or rest as punishment.
5. Relate discipline to eating, resting, or sleeping.
6. Leave the children alone, unattended, or without supervision.
7. Place the children in locked rooms, closets, or boxes as punishment.
8. Allow discipline of children by children.
9. Criticize, make fun of, or otherwise belittle children's parents, families, or ethnic groups.

DAILY SCHEDULE

8:00 **Breakfast**
8:15 **Devotional:** pledge, calendar skills, psalms, scripture reading, catechism, prayer
8:45 **Language:** phonics and reading, poetry, manuscript and cursive penmanship
10:00 Restroom Break
10:15 **Arithmetic:** Number recognition, concepts, Sequences, Coins, Time, Addition, and Subtraction
11:05 **Physical Education:** Mixture of indoor and outdoor fine and gross motor skills development activities
11:50 Restroom Break

12:00 **Lunch**
12:30 **Science** M/W: plants, health and human biology, earth and space
Social Studies Tu/Th: Community helpers; children of the world, American history, geography
Music, Computer, Spanish Fr (rotating and integrated throughout the curriculum)
1:00 Restroom break
1:15-2:45 Restbreak (as needed) or Field Trip, Arts and Crafts-Centers
2:45 Dismissal for the day

PARENT-SCHOOL COMMUNICATIONS

During daily routines (e.g., eating/feeding, play, diapering/toileting, hand washing, active play indoors and outdoors), teachers/caregivers comfort children, play and socially interact with them verbally, use positive facial expressions and a pleasant tone of voice and actions, and integrate required health and safety practices. At the time transitions occur for care of the child from the family to a staff member and back again, program staff members and families will use a consistent method to receive and give communication about the child's experiences and routines at home and while in the program. Communication about any unusual event or circumstance occurs promptly no matter when it occurs.

Parent Observations/Conferences
Parents are encouraged to observe the classroom from the hallway in order to prevent the disruption of the classroom. Conferences are held each October and April to discuss your child's development. Please contact the office to schedule a conference at any other time. Parents are always welcome to drop in and visit or observe any time the center is in operation.

Change of Address/Phone
Families are responsible for updating addresses and telephone numbers for emergency purposes.

Number/Emergency Pick-up
Personal information including telephone number and address are required for all persons authorized to pick up your child in the event of an emergency. Please update these numbers as necessary. Letters, telephone or fax authorizations are unacceptable. Children will be released only to those persons listed on the enrollment application form.

Newsletters
Weekly classroom newsletters are sent home on Monday indicating teaching and learning goals for the week. A bi-monthly newsletter is published for administrative purposes to inform parents of upcoming events and relevant information regarding their child. Columns by children, teachers, parents and administrative staff are included.

Information Boards
A parent bulletin board is located in the kitchen area. Please refer to this bulletin board for calendars, menus, community resources referrals, etc..

Parent Meetings
A parent teacher fellowship and open house will be held December 21, 5-7 p.m. Parents are encouraged to attend in order to stay informed about school activities. Guest speakers may speak on topics such as childhood nutrition, safety and ways we can help our children excel.

Volunteer Opportunities
We cannot effectively serve your child's needs without your support. We need you! We welcome any parents or grandparents of enrolled children to volunteer in the school or for special events. Volunteers must meet the minimum requirements of the staff (background checks, orientation, health and safety training). Volunteers will not be left alone with children; a paid supervisory staff member will be present at all times. Parents are expected to volunteer one hour per nine week grading period. Please see the Director to schedule a time or sign in and receive the assignment for the day. Please indicate on your application for enrollment areas you are interested in and join us at a parent meeting for more information.

Some examples of ways to be involved include:
Chaperoning on field trips.
Lending objects for units of study.
Volunteering as class parent.
Coming and talking about your job when asked.
Helping your child at home with the concepts we are studying here.
Helping your child prepare for "Show and Tell" or "Mystery Box."
Helping to provide treats or other items for our parties.
Participating in "National School Lunch Week", "Dads and Books", "Parent Appreciation" (come and eat with your child).
Serving on the parent advisory committee.

HEALTH

Medication
If your child is on medication and it needs to be administered while he/she is at school, the medicine must be in the original container and labeled with the child's name, doctor's name, name of medication, dosage, and when to be taken. Medication cannot be administered unless there is a signed medication authorization form on file. Medication will be administered at the time or with the meal you specify and a written record kept. All medication is to be stored at home when the period of use is ended. We keep medications in a locked cabinet or refrigerator. Children may not store medication in a cubby or backpack, nor may they assist the teacher in administration.

Recalled Over the Counter Medications List
We cannot administer any of the following over-the-counter cold medications for children under the age of six years:
• Dimetapp Decongestant Plus Cough Infant Drops
• Dimetapp Decongestant Infant Drops
• Little Colds Decongestant Plus Cough
• Little Colds Multi-Symptom Cold Formula
• Pediacare Infant Drops Decongestant (containing pseudoephedrine)
• Pediacare Infant Drops Decongestant & Cough (containing pseudoephedrine)
• Pediacare Infant Dropper Decongestant (containing phenylephrine)
• Pediacare Infant Dropper Long-Acting Cough
• Pediacare Infant Dropper Decongestant & Cough (containing phenylephrine)
• Robitussin Infant Cough DM Drops
• Triaminic Infant & Toddler Thin Strips Decongestant
• Triaminic Infant & Toddler Thin Strips Decongestant Plus Cough
• Tylenol Concentrated Infants' Drops Plus Cold
• Tylenol Concentrated Infants' Drops Plus Cold & Cough

Please request your pediatrician prescribe an extended release medication or keep your child in the comfort of your home until he/she feels better.

Immunization Check List
Every child attending[Insert your school name] Christian Academy is required by law to have a Georgia Certificate of Immunization, Form 3231. The rules of DHR public health require the following immunizations of children as a prerequisite to admission to school:
• Diphtheria
• Pertussis (whooping cough)
• Tetanus (lockjaw)

- Poliomyelitis
- Measles
- Mumps
- Rubella
- Pneumococcal
- Varicella (chicken pox)
- Haemophilus influenzae type B
- Hepatitis A and B
- Pneumococcal conjugate vaccine (PCV)

Once the Certificate of Immunization is declared "Complete for School Attendance,"" no other forms are needed if a child receives additional shots. Parents or guardians that desire to take an exemption for religious reasons must provide a notarized letter.

OPERATIONAL POLICIES

Attendance

Our staff members possess specialized training in recognizing communicable diseases and common childhood illnesses. We rely upon our training, National health and safety guidelines and State rules and regulations to determine exclusion policies. We follow strict handwashing and disinfection procedures.

We ask that you have a back-up person you can call if we have an emergency or if your child is sick. If we have an emergency, the Director will contact you by telephone as quickly as possible so that you can make other arrangements for your child. If your child has a fever of 100 degrees, vomited or had diarrhea within the last 24 hours state guidelines require that they be excluded from group settings. If your child has a green discharge from his/her nose, he/she must be on an antibiotic for 24 hours before he/she can attend. If your child is not feeling well, do not give him/her Tylenol to mask his/her symptoms. If your child vomits the night before and seems fine the next day, he/she is more than likely still contagious to the others. You must wait 24 hours to return to the center. All the children use the same restroom and play with the same toys. They are often very affectionate with each other and it is very difficult to keep a sick child from infecting everyone else. A child shall not be accepted nor allowed to remain at the center if he/she has a fever of 100 degrees or higher oral temperature and another contagious symptom/illness, such as, but not limited to, a rash or diarrhea or a sore throat.

Illnesses are defined as:
Fever.
Conjunctivitis (pink eye) or "cold in the eye".
Flu.
Unusual rash.
Severe cough.
Rapid breathing or labored breathing.
Severe cold.
Vomiting.
Yellowish skin or eyes.
Diarrhea.
Head lice.
Contagious illnesses (i.e. ringworm, strep throat, impetigo, chickenpox, scabies, etc.)

Illness of any sort which results in your child being too ill to participate in daily activities or that requires additional attention from the teacher. We will not accept a child if any of the above symptoms are present or have been present within the last 24 hours. If your child exhibits symptoms during the schooldays, we will remove him/her from the group and notify the parent or authorized adult to pick up the child. Parents have *one hour from time of notification* to pick up the child. The child may return 24 hours after a temperature has returned to normal, 24 hours after the child is no longer vomiting, or 24-48 hours (depending on the illness) after the first dose of an antibiotic. If a child receives an antibiotic for an ear infection that child may return to school immediately if he/she has been free of other symptoms mentioned for at least 24 hours. The child is welcome when he/she has only a mild cold, and is able to participate in the day's activities.

Arrival and Departure

Each day upon arriving, the parent or guardian is required to sign the child in, noting the time arrived. A time clock or sign-in/out pad, pens, and a clock are all located in the entry. This is to be followed by signing the child out when they leave. This gives us a written record of the child's attendance, hours, and who brought/picked up the child. Parents and staff are asked not to admit unfamiliar people or visitors into the school without escorting them to sign in and receive assistance from the teacher.

Children are released to parents and persons authorized on the appropriate form. Verbal notice and handwritten notes are unacceptable. The emergency contact list you are required to complete designates who may pick the child up if there is an emergency and you cannot contact us. Those on the list should also be people we could call in the event something happened and you did not arrive to pick up your child.

Please inform your emergency contacts that we will make a copy of their state issued identification. We do not mean to offend them. This is simply a measure taken for the child's protection. Children will be released to either parent unless there is a restraining order or legal documents outlining the custody arrangement on file.

Clothing

Teachers/caregivers and children wear clothing that permits easy and safe movement as well as full participation in active and messy play. Children are not allowed to wear clothing that has strings or decorations that can get caught on equipment. Children and staff members must have suitable clothing at the facility for going outdoors when it is raining or snowing to allow children to use these opportunities to learn about the natural world and how to function in it. Children are required to wear uniforms. Girls and boys are permitted to wear red, white or navy blue polo shirts and khaki or navy blue pants, skirts or jumpers. Each student is required to wear black or brown covered toe shoes for outdoor play safety. Footwear must be the equivalent of gym shoes that are not slippery, will not twist or come off the feet while running, and stay firmly on the feet while climbing, jumping, skipping, and crawling. Footwear is not permitted that provides insufficient support for or limits active play, such as shoes with heels, flip-flops, loose boots, or dress shoes. Several stores carry school uniforms at reasonable prices (Target, Wal-Mart, or JCPenney) Please provide a spare set of clothing and shoes to wear in the event clothing becomes heavily soiled or wet or is in contact with blood or other body fluids during the program day. Program staff members remove clothing or shoes that are badly soiled or damaged or that interfere with active play or comfort. Such articles are exchanged with the spare set of clothing and shoes.

Share Items/Toys

Toys from home may pose a safety hazard or not be developmentally appropriate for group settings, therefore we prohibit toys from outside the school, esp. party favors. Other toys may be recalled by the Consumer Products Safety commission. The only times toys are permitted is for show and tell or homework assignments. Action figurines (Hulk, Fantastic Four, Spiderman, Superman, etc.) encourage violent behavior and are prohibited altogether including on backpacks, shoes, clothing.

Lost and Found

The lost and found Container is in the classroom. Please see the Director or Administrative Assistant for items.

Naps

Children need sleep for health and growth. Sleep provides the opportunity for the brain and other body tissues to repair and prepare body tissues to manage the active parts of the day. On average, children younger than 5 years sleep between 10 and 12 hours as the combined daily total of nighttime and nap time sleep. Insufficient sleep is a risk factor for overweight/obesity and behavior problems. Young children sleep and rest best at routinely scheduled times, in a relatively less stimulating place, and with consistent supervision by trusted adults. Some children are ready to nap, while others just need a quiet activity time to rest. Predictable routines help children feel comfortable. Spacing of children 3 feet apart during sleep is necessary to reduce the risk of droplet spread of infectious diseases through the air from one child to another. For infants, safe sleep practices must follow the national recommendations to reduce the risk of sleep-related deaths, including sudden infant death syndrome (SIDS) and suffocation. While swaddling of infants may help them sleep better, this practice is not recommended in child care. Swaddling can be associated with an increased risk of abnormal hip development and, if the swaddling cloth becomes loose bedding, with SIDS. National and state health and safety guidelines require that all children be provided a rest period each day. In the event a child does not fall asleep a quiet toy or other activity will be provided.

Birthdays

Please provide three days notice if you would like to celebrate your child's birthday with his/her class. We have reserved the 2:15-2:45 p.m. period for birthday games and snacks (cake and juice). Balloons and party favors are not permitted. Please speak with your child's teacher about appropriate games or crafts which can be incorporated in the celebration. All special event celebration plans require prior approval from the Director, including approval of the activities, materials, and any food involved (e.g. themed partyware, etc.). Staff members encourage parents to celebrate their child's birthday or other special occasions with an alternative to food, such as sharing favorite stories, music, dancing, games, crafts, or other activities. What is important to children is that their families planned something special. Using food as the focus of celebrations is discouraged. If perishable food is brought from home to be shared with other children, it must be store bought, in its original package, and in a quantity sufficient for all of the children. Children may not share food provided by the child's family unless the food is intended for sharing with all of the children. This is discouraged due to food allergies and the risk of food poisoning.

Accidents/Injury

Minor cuts and abrasions suffered while at school will receive proper care -- specifically, they will be washed with soap and warm water, an antiseptic and properly bandaged. Treatment will be documented and the Director will contact you by telephone to tell you how and when the injury occurred. You will be asked to sign an incident report form upon arrival to pick up your child. The form indicates you have been informed of the incident and does not waive any rights. We are also required to log any injuries we observe on your child which have occurred outside of our care.

In the event of a medical emergency requiring medical attention, the Director, the teacher will telephone a parent first, unless doing so endangers the child's life. In that case we will take necessary steps, putting the child first (calling emergency medical services, hospital, doctor, poison control, etc.). If need be, we or emergency medical services will transport your child to [Name and address of the nearest urgent care facility for children] or the child's pediatrician listed first. We will try to call you in route or when we arrive. If a parent is unable to be reached, we will keep trying until he or she is available.

Emergency Preparedness

We practice fire evacuation and severe weather drills each month. In the event of a fire or physical plant problems we would evacuate the school immediately and gather at the back of the building. If severe weather arises and a tornado or hurricane alert is issued, we will proceed to the center of the school, where the children will crouch and cover their heads. Parents will be notified by telephone. In the event our property is unsafe, the children will be evacuated to [name and address of a facility more than 100 yards away]. Emergency plans are posted for parent viewing

School Pictures

School pictures are taken each winter for the annual yearbook. Picture packages and yearbooks may be purchased at that time.

Testing

We assess students for the following reasons at our school:
1. To guide instruction
2. To monitor progress

We use the Developmental Indicators for the Assessment of Learning – Third Edition (DIAL-3) to assess students for admissions placement. This provides an indication of developmental levels, which assists the teacher in planning instruction. We use informal assessment instruments throughout the year. The DIAL-3 identifies any special needs the child has before placement in the classroom. We do not deny admission based on a test. The test includes a questionnaire for the parent. Both the test results and questionnaire are reviewed and discussed with the parent to set learning objectives. Each family is required to identify goals for development as well.

In the Spring all K4 and K5 students are assessed using the Preschool SAT-10 and (K5) Otis Lennon School Ability Test. The Testing and scoring fee of $50 is due December 1, 2010. The *Stanford Achievement Test* Series is a multiple-choice assessment that measures student progress and helps teachers determine what students know and are able to do. It provides very detailed parent reports with ways to help in areas of weakness. The Otis-Lennon School Ability Test®, Eighth Edition evaluates student's performance in the following tasks: detecting likenesses and differences, recalling words and numbers, defining words, following directions, classifying, establishing sequence, solving arithmetic problems, and completing analogies. This test helps us to measure a child's ability to reason logically and thereby helps us to understand their perceptions of school related tasks. Modifications are made to accommodate students with learning difficulties and language barriers.

Our teachers use informal observation forms, curriculum based checklists, rating scales and portfolios to complete parent conference note sheets which are discussed with parents on a quarterly basis. Student work is compiled in a portfolio from day one and is reviewed with parents during conferences and open house nights. Records are maintained for students that are referred for evaluations by intervention specialist. These specialists meet with the teacher (and parents) periodically to review progress.

Five year old students applying for admission may take The Wide Range Achievement Test *3rd edition*. The WRAT 3 is normed by age not grade level for greater accuracy. Its standard scores and percentiles compare an individual's performance with others of the same age. Its grade levels are rough clues to instructional levels. There are three subtests contained on each of the alternate forms. The reading subtest includes the recognition and naming of letters and pronunciation of words out of context. In the spelling subtest, the examinee is asked to write his or her own name, and then to write letters and words as they are dictated. The Arithmetic involves counting, reading number symbols, solving oral problems, and doing written computations.

School Events

Parents are asked to join us for the following opportunities for Christian fellowship and mutual support: the annual Christmas production, St. Valentine's Day party, Parent Appreciation luncheons, Dad's Day, and Mother's Day.

Peer Group/Family Member Visits
We welcome grandparent and extended family classroom visits. Please schedule them with in advance in order not to disrupt the class. For safety reasons siblings or other children or not permitted to visit class unless pre-approved.

Supplies
5 2" 3-ring binders
 4 #2 pencils
24 Count package of crayons
1 Set washable, broadline markers, 8 colors
1 Dry erase marker, any color - low odor please
1 Set of water color paints (Crayola or Prang is best)
1 Pair of scissors -- Fiskars, please
1 Bottle of school glue
4 Glue sticks
1 Pencil box
4 Two-pocket folder
2 Reams of white photocopy paper
Book bag or backpack
1 Large box of facial tissues
2" naptime mat from Walmart
1 box Ziploc (or other brand) Easy Zipper Storage Bags, Gallon Size, 15-pack
<u>monthly</u>
4 boxes snack crackers (teddy grahams, butter cookies, or other crackers)
2 8-pack kid's essentials chocolate milk
2 8-pack juicy juice 100% 6.75 oz. juice boxes
1-40 count Container of Wet Ones Moist Towelette antibacterial wipes (for hands)
1-75 count pop-up Clorox wipes
1 roll of Bounty brand select-a-size paper towels
(Optional) A blank video/DVD or disposable camera to document your child's growth throughout the year.

Parents are responsible for replenishing wipes and diapers/pull-ups. Teachers will inform parents when refills are needed. Please label all items with a permanent marker.

Please do not bring the following items from home: toys of any type without prior approval from the administration (esp. violence (guns, swords, action figures, etc.), candy, toys, electronic devices, jewelry, chewing gum, "jellies", sandals, anything unlabeled, a frown or bad attitude.

ALL I REALLY NEED TO KNOW I LEARNED IN KINDERGARTEN
All I really need to know about how to live and what to do and how to be I learned in kindergarten. Wisdom was not at the top of the graduate school mountain, but there in the sand pile at school.
These are the things I learned:

- Share everything.
- Play fair.
- Don't hit people.
- Put things back where you found them.
- Clean up your own mess.
- Don't take things that aren't yours.
- Say you're sorry when you hurt somebody.
- Wash your hands before you eat.
- Flush.
- Warm cookies and cold milk are good for you.
- Live a balanced life - learn some and think some and draw and paint and sing and dance and play and work every day some.
- Take a nap every afternoon.
- When you go out in the world, watch out for traffic, hold hands and stick together.
- Be aware of wonder. Remember the little seed in the Styrofoam cup: the roots go down and the plant goes up and nobody really knows how or why, but we are all like that.
- Goldfish and hamsters and white mice and even the little seed in the Styrofoam cup - they all die. So do we.
- And then remember the Dick-and-Jane books and the first word you learned - the biggest word of all - LOOK.

[Source: "ALL I REALLY NEED TO KNOW I LEARNED IN KINDERGARTEN" by Robert Fulghum. See his web site at http://www.robertfulghum.com/]

Train up a child in the way he should go: and when he is old, he will not depart from it.
Proverbs 22:6

(Your school's name) Early Learning Center

[Street Address]
[City, state and zip]
[Telephone]
[Web address]
[Email address]

Medical Illness Log

Date	Child/Staff Member Name	Symptoms	Diagnosis	Class	Days Exc.	* Action Taken

*Report more than 3 cases to the Board of Health for your county.

(Your school's name) Early Learning Center

[Street Address]
[City, state and zip]
[Telephone]
[Web address]
[Email address]

Medical Injury Log

Date	Child/Staff Member Name	Location	Injury type	Time	Reported to parents	* Action Taken

*Report more than 3 cases to the Board of Health for your county.
http://www.dekalbhealth.net/PDFs/Common%20Communicable%20Diseases%20of%20Childhood.pdf

Montessori Program Handbook Materials

Mission statement

Our mission is to support each child's drive for independence by implement an inspiring, energizing program where the children learn the skills necessary to reach their full potential. We encourage your child's natural desire to be creative and helpful by nourishing the whole child's development (socially, emotionally, intellectually, spiritually, creatively, and physically).

Vision statement

[Your school's name] Montessori School offers an individualized learning environment that responds to a child's unique abilities, learning styles, and interests; through excellent teachers and a specially prepared and fully equipped Montessori classroom. The school is guided by its vision to respect an ingenious combination of learning theories, principles, skills, ethics, and ideas.

Philosophy

Dr. Maria Montessori (August 31, 1870 – May 6, 1952) was an Italian educator, scientist, physician, philosopher, and humanitarian. She believed that "education should no longer be mostly imparting of knowledge, but must take a new path, seeking the release of human potentialities." What followed worldwide has been called the "discovery of the child" and the realization that: "...mankind can hope for a solution to its problems, among which the most urgent are those of peace and unity, only by turning its attention and energies to the discovery of the child and to the development of the great potentialities of the human personality in the course of its formation."

The effectiveness of Montessori teaching methods has most recently been demonstrated by the results of a study published in the U.S. journal, Science (29 September 2006) which indicates that Montessori children have improved behavioral and academic skills compared with a control group from the mainstream system. The authors concluded that, "when strictly implemented, Montessori education fosters social and academic skills that are equal or superior to those fostered by...other types of schools."

The Montessori Method of education is distinctive in the following ways:
- Instruction of children in 3-year age groups, corresponding to sensitive periods of development (example: Birth-3, 3-6, 6-9, and 9-12 year olds)
- Children as competent beings, encouraged to make maximal decisions
- Observation of the child in the environment as the basis for ongoing curriculum development (presentation of subsequent exercises for skill development and information accumulation)
- Small, child sized furniture and creation of a small, child-sized environment (microcosm) in which each child can be competent to produce overall a self-running small children's world
- Parent participation to include basic and proper attention to health screening and hygiene as a prerequisite to schooling
- Defining of a scale of sensitive periods of development, which provides a focus for class work that is appropriate and uniquely stimulating and motivating to the child (including sensitive periods for language development, sensorial experimentation and refinement, and various levels of social interaction)
- The importance of the "absorbent mind," the limitless motivation of the young child to achieve competence over his or her environment and to perfect his or her skills and understandings as they occur within each sensitive period.
- Self-correcting "auto-didactic" materials
- The teacher serves as an enthusiastic guide in the child's progress from simple to complex, rudimentary to refined, outer to self-control. Next to learning from one's own experience, the child learns best from other children. Therefore, children are grouped in three-year age groups to give children a series

of models for imitation and older children the opportunity to reinforce their own knowledge by helping younger children. Competition has no place in Montessori education until after the child has gained confidence in his or her own abilities.

Dr. Montessori's research indicated that children have fantastic powers of concentration if properly stimulated, far exceeding that of most adults. Children would rather work than play when given a choice between toys and stimulating work. Montessori educators have a responsibility to train children's character to achieve self-discipline and self-direction which result from the mastery of firsthand experience and fulfillment of the inner urge to expand and grow in one's own way. This growth is achieved without jeopardizing the rights of others to have this same privilege.

Benefits

Montessori education offers children opportunities to reach their full potential as they engage the world as competent, responsible, and respectful citizens with an understanding and appreciation that learning is a lifelong process.

🔹 **Each child is valued as a unique individual.** [Your school's name] educators recognize that each child learns differently and accommodate all learning styles. In addition, students learn at their own pace, advancing through the curriculum as he is ready, guided by the teacher and an individualized learning plan.

🔹 **Montessori students develop order, coordination, concentration, and independence.** Classroom design, materials, and daily routines support the individual child's emerging "self-regulation" (ability to educate one's self, and to think about what one is learning).

🔹 **Students form a caring community.** The multi-age classroom—typically spanning 3 years— resembles a family structure. Competence is fostered as older students assume leadership by serving as mentors and role models; younger children feel supported and gain confidence through social interactions. Teachers model respect, loving kindness, and a belief in peaceful conflict resolution.

🔹 **Montessori students enjoy freedom within limits.** Working within parameters set by their teachers, students are active participants in deciding what their focus of learning will be. Montessorians understand that intrinsic motivation drives the child's natural curiosity and interests, resulting in joyous learning that is sustainable over a lifetime.

🔹 **Students are supported as active seekers of knowledge.** Teachers provide developmentally appropriate environments where students have the freedom and the tools to pursue answers to their own questions.

🔹 **Self-correction and self-assessment are an integral part of the Montessori classroom approach.** As students mature they learn to look critically at their work, and become adept at recognizing, correcting, and learning from their errors.

🔹 Given this freedom and support to question, to probe deeply, and to make connections, Montessori students become confident, enthusiastic, self-directed learners. They are able to think critically, work collaboratively, and act boldly—necessary skills for the 21st century.

Toddler program (18 months-3 years old):

Under the nurturing guidance of our teachers, toddlers learn to care for themselves and their environment (self-help skills such as potty training, dressing themselves, cleaning up toys, etc.). Hands-on activities and games refine motor skills, teach basic concepts and expose children to art and music. Socialization is also an integral part of each moment in the classroom with children learning from each other.

Primary program (3-6 year old):

🔹 Practical Life exercises instills care for self, others and for the environment.

🖐 Sensorial Materials serve as tools for development. Children build cognitive skills and learn to order and classify impressions by touching, seeing, smelling, tasting, listening and exploring the physical properties of their environment.

🖐 Language development is vital to human development. The Montessori environment is rich in oral language opportunities, allowing the child to experience conversations, stories and poetry. They will be learning the phonic skills necessary to develop their reading. The children are also exposed to the study of grammar.

🖐 Geography, Biology, Botany, Zoology, Art and Music are presented as extensions of the sensorial and language activities.

🖐 Mathematical activities help give children a solid understand of basic mathematical principles, prepares them for later abstract reasoning and helps to develop problem-solving capabilities.

Classroom Guidelines

The Montessori Environment is a prepared environment designed to assist your child in their search for independence, concentration and happiness. Children need an interactive, hands-on, educational environment to become self-motivated and successful learners. Here, children are free to explore with their senses in order to fully understand the world around them. They are free to learn at their own pace. We never push a child academically; the child learns through their own explorations and from others in their environment. Interaction with their peers in a real life community is necessary. Children require ample time and space to practice and perfect their abilities.

The Montessori materials provide children with a variety of interactive experiences including learning activities of practical life, sensorial, language, math, science, history, culture, art, etc. Dr. Montessori found that children need more than just academics; they need to be allowed to explore their world and society.

Our classrooms are communities. The children care for the environment they learn in, along with the people within. Children will have a job within their community. Our school and classrooms only have one rule and that is the rule of respect. Respect fulfills so many needs within an environment. When a child follows the rule of respect, they will never say or do anything to hurt another child. With respect, the child will care for everything within their environment. Most importantly, with respect, the child will care for their own self. Respect will carry a child confidently and happily through the rest of their life. We ask that you help in fostering this self-respect. Respect comes in many forms. We respect people by listening attentively. We respect people by giving them common courtesies (e.g. saying "Excuse me", "Please", "Thank you" and "You're Welcome". We respect the environment by not throwing trash on the floor, by not harming animals, by caring for books we read, etc. These small considerations show respect and model respect for our children. This leads to a child feeling appreciated and cared for. Once a child feels respect, they will in turn give that respect to their immediate environment, including the animals and people within it.

Classroom procedures

The children of each classroom learn through special lessons or presentations given individually by the teacher. There is a process that the child should follow in their classroom. Please go over these procedures with your child before the first day of school.

1. You may only take work from a shelf that you have had a lesson on.
2. Please take your work to a table or a mat and sit down.
3. You may practice work that you have had a lesson on, as often as you would like, any day that you are in school.
4. Please place all of the material back in order and where it belongs on the shelf.
5. Please remember to push in your chair or store your mat.

6. If you are observing a child at work, please stand with your arms at your sides, or behind your back and please do not speak, as we do not want to distract the child working.

7. If while observing a child work, that child asks you to leave, please respect their wishes and go choose your own work.

8. When you need to speak to a teacher or another child who may be busy, please rest your hand on that person's arm or shoulder and wait patiently for them to call upon you.

Thank you for helping your child in adjusting to this new environment with these rules. We appreciate any consistency that can be offered at home.

Discipline and Guidance Policy

Discipline and guidance are opportunities to teach students how to make correct choices regarding their own behavior and in their interactions with others. Our discipline procedures are individualized and consistent for each child; appropriate to the child's level of understanding; and directed toward teaching the child acceptable behavior and self-control. We employ positive methods of discipline and guidance that encourage self-esteem, self-control and self-direction (e.g. redirection, time away, and positive guidance). Corporal and other forms of physical punishment are not permitted on the school property.

Daily schedule 36 months to 6 years

7:30-8:00	Morning meet and greet activities (Calendar Skills)
8:00-8:30	Individual chores (Folding personal laundry, sweeping, etc.)
	Grace and Courtesy Lesson (e.g. Table manners, etc.)
	Snack Preparation (Wash and chop fruit)
	Teacher's Helper
8:30- 9:00	Bathroom break (wash hands and prepare snack) and Snack
9:00-10:30	Individual work time (Practical life, Sensorial, Mathematics, Science, Geography, Language, Critical Thinking, and/or Art)
10:30-11:15	Outdoor activities (weather permitting - gardening, nature walks, etc.) or Indoor Gross Motor Activities
11:00-11:30	Bathroom and hand washing
11:30-12:00	Lunch
12:00-12:30	Clean up, bathroom, hand washing, and tooth brushing
12:30-1:00	Dismissal for half day, other students Story time
12:30-1:30	Rest or nap time
1:30-2:00	Hand washing, bathroom, and tooth brushing
2:00-2:15	Snack
2:15-2:45	Music and movement
2:45-3:00	Dismissal

Disclaimer: Although the author embraces many aspects of Montessori education (hands on learning experiences, leadership skills development through age groupings, project based learning, teaching adapted to learning styles, self correcting materials, and the like), inclusion of this material is not a complete endorsement of the teaching method for every child or demographic.

Early Childhood Checklist

Student _____ **Year entered** _____

Practical Life Activities		Practical Life Continued		Sensorial Activities		Geography	
Sitting on a chair		Nuts and bolts		Touch Boards		Body awareness	
Walking on a line		Funnel pouring		Touch Tablets		Cardinal Directions	
Silence		Tonging		Fabric sorting		Town Map	
Shaking hands		Scissors		Mystery bag		Land/Air/ Water	
Walking around obstacles		Watering plants		Sorting		Globe – land and water	
Sitting on a line		Flower arranging		Cylinder blocks		Globe – continents	
Saluting and pledging the flag		Folding		Pink Tower		Hemisphere Map	
Watching		Dressing frames		Brown Stair		Land and Water Forms	
Interrupting		Polishing		Red Rods		Maps	
Walking in the class		Rock scrubbing		Knobless Cylinders			
Opening and closing doors		Hand washing		Color Box 1			
Blowing nose		Table washing		Color Box 2			
Using the toilet		Dish washing		Sound Basket			
Restoring the environment		Food preparation		Sound Cylinders			
Hanging up a coat		Sewing		Thermic Bottles		**Science**	
Dusting				Thermic Tablets		Solar System/Planets	
Sweeping				Baric Tablets		Weather	
Table top cleanup				Cylinder Grid		Non living/ living	
Floor clean up				Geometric Solids		Plant/Animal	
Carrying a tray				Geometric Solids Bases		Leaves/Trees	
Carrying a box				Geometric Cabinet		Fish	
Carrying a table				Geometric Cards		Amphibians	
Carrying a chair				Color Box 3		Birds	
Carrying a pitcher				Bells		Reptiles	
Carrying a pail				Smelling Bottles		Mammals	
Rolling and carrying a rug				Tasting Bottles		Flowers	
Putting on a folding aprons				Tasting Party		Life Cycles	
Handling and carrying scissors				Constructive Triangles		Magnetism	
Puzzles				Monomial Cube		Sink/Float	
Bead Stringing				Binomial Cube		Temperature	
Peg Board				Trinomial Cube		Color	
Nesting barrels							
Popup Beads							
Dry pouring							
Transfer with hand/scoop							
Wet Pouring							
Lids and containers							

Early Childhood Checklist continued

Student _____ **Year entered** _____

Language Activities		Language Activities Continued		Mathematics Activities		Mathematics Activities Continued	
Conversations with objects		Reads phonetic readers – blends		Cover it all up		Linear Counting – Long chains	
Conversations with pictures		Reads phonetic readers - digraphs		Matching		Subtraction Introduction	
Matching object to object		Grammar - nouns		Put and take		Linear Counting – 1000 chain	
Matching object to picture		Grammar – articles		Number rods – red and blue		Subtraction w/ number rods	
Matching picture to picture		Grammar – adjectives		Discrete Rods		Subtraction strip board	
Rhyming with objects		Grammar – farm		Sandpaper numerals		Bank Game Sub. w/o exchange	
Rhyming with pictures		Writing – Morning Message		Wooden numeral cards		Bank Game Sub. w/ exchange	
Language Experience Stories		Creative Writing – invent spelling		Bridging sp and wooden numerals		Bank Game Mult. w/o exchange	
Line Time Activities		Writing - Research		Number rods with numerals		Bank Game Mult. w/ exchange	
Songs, Fingerplays, Poems				Spindle Box		Multiplication Bead Board	
Read Aloud				Zero Game		Multiplication Bead Box	
Books				Card and counters (odd and even)		Division Introduction	
I Spy – initial consonants				Memory Game		Bank Game Division	
I Spy – ending sounds				Bead Stair		Division Bead Board	
I Spy – medial sounds				Decimal System – introductory tray		Addition Stamp Game	
Sandpaper letters				Linear counting – teen numbers		Fractions – equivalent	
Composes words with SL				Decimal System – building tray		Measurement w/ Discrete Rods	
Composes words with MA/objects				Linear counting – teen board		Measurement w/ Discrete centimeter	
Composes words with MA/pictures				Addition w/ number rods		Measurement w/ meter stick	
Reads labels for objects				Decimal system – 45 layout		Measurement w/ balance scale	
Reads sight words				Decimal System – Crisis of 9		Time Introduction	
Read phrases & matches w/ pict.				Linear Counting – Tens Board		Time – calendar	
Metal insets				Addition with dice		Time – days/months	
Traces letters				Decimal system – Fetch and exch.		Time – standard calendar	
Writes class names				Positive snake game		Time – Seasons	
Copies sentences				Addition strip board		Time – First Time Line	
Reads command card and performs				Decimal System – Bank Dice Game		Time – intro to the clock	
Reads sentence cards				Decimal System – Change game		Coin Identification	
Reads non phonetic words				Decimal System – Dice Game			
Reads environmental labels				Linear Counting – Hundred's Chain			

Reads silent E words			Linear Counting – Hundred's Board			
Reads phonograms/ match to obj.			Coin Exchange for Pennies			
Read phonogram booklets			Linear Counting – short chains			
Reads phonetic readers – short v.			Bank Game Addition – no exchange			
Reads phonetic readers – long v.			Bank Game Addition – w/ exchange			

Early Childhood Narrative Assessment

Student _____

Teacher _____ **School** _____

Grading Period _____ **Year** _____

Area of Learning	Teacher Assessment
Practical Life Activities	
Sensorial Activities	
Mathematics Activities	
Language Activities	
Cultural Activities	
General Comments	
Parent's Signature/Date	Signature:
Parent's Comments	

(Your school's name) **Early Learning Center**
Infant/Toddler Daily Report
To be completed by childcare provider/teacher.

Name _____   Date _____

Disposition: Cooperative Cheerful Tired Talkative Energetic Obedient Mischievous

Appetite: Good Fair Poor   **Rest time:** Good Fair Poor

I enjoyed: _____

_____

I need: a change of clothing other supplies: _____

_____

✂---

Parent's Daily Report

My child has experienced the following: runny nose cough sneezing wheezing sore throat earache rash stomachache vomiting diarrhea behavior change scratch bruise other:

_____

Disposition: Cooperative Cheerful Tired Talkative Energetic Obedient Mischievous

Appetite: Good Fair Poor

Last meal/feeding (list time and foods): _____

_____

Rest time: Good Fair Poor

(Your school's name) Early Learning Center
Preschool Daily Report

For the week of: _____

Monday

Homework: ___ Completed ___ Missing _____

All forms signed and returned: ___ Yes ___ No

Work habits: 1-Independent 2-Needed Some Assistance 3-Needed Constant Assistance/Redirection

___ Following directions

___ Paying attention/following along

___ Working Independently

___ Working cooperatively with others

___ Completing classwork on time

Comments:

Parent Signature _____ Date _____

Tuesday

Homework: ___ Completed ___ Missing _____

All forms signed and returned: ___ Yes ___ No

Work habits: 1-Independent 2-Needed Some Assistance 3-Needed Constant Assistance/Redirection

___ Following directions

___ Paying attention/following along

___ Working Independently

___ Working cooperatively with others

___ Completing classwork on time

Comments:

Parent Signature _____ Date _____

Wednesday

Homework: ___ Completed ___ Missing _____

All forms signed and returned: ___ Yes ___ No

Work habits: 1-Independent 2-Needed Some Assistance 3-Needed Constant Assistance/Redirection

___ Following directions

___ Paying attention/following along

___ Working Independently

___ Working cooperatively with others

___ Completing classwork on time

Comments:

Parent Signature _____ Date _____

Thursday
Homework: ___ Completed ___ Missing _____
All forms signed and returned: ___ Yes ___ No
Work habits: 1-Independent 2-Needed Some Assistance 3-Needed Constant Assistance/Redirection
___ Following directions
___ Paying attention/following along
___ Working Independently
___ Working cooperatively with others
___ Completing classwork on time
Comments:

Parent Signature _____ Date _____

Friday
Homework: ___ Completed ___ Missing _____
All forms signed and returned: ___ Yes ___ No
Work habits: 1-Independent 2-Needed Some Assistance 3-Needed Constant Assistance/Redirection
___ Following directions
___ Paying attention/following along
___ Working Independently
___ Working cooperatively with others
___ Completing classwork on time
Comments:

Parent Signature _____ Date _____

Sample Experiential Learning Program Overview

Our programs are a synergistic system of systems that:
• Provides multi-sensory and experiential instructional strategies utilizing all learning style preferences, and is conducive for the academic success of students with exceptional learning;
• Provides opportunities to implement innovative assistive technology;
• Provides individualized and authentic real world learning opportunities;
• Promotes the teaching and learning of 21st century skill outcomes (critical thinking and problem solving, collaboration, communication, creativity, and innovation);
• Enables students to master the multi-dimensional skills and abilities (work readiness, financial literacy, and entrepreneurship) required of them in the 21st century;
• Emphasizes high academic standards, community service, and social responsibility.

Excerpt from Disorder Fact Sheet Resource Booklet:
For parents and teachers of exceptional learners

ATTENTION DEFICIT DISORDER
SIGNS /SYMPTOMS
- Problems with paying attention
- Being very active (called hyperactivity)
- Acting before thinking (called impulsivity)

Three types of AD/HD
- Inattentive type (student can't seem to focus or stay focused on task/activity)
- Hyperactive-impulsive type (student is very active and often acts without thinking)
- Combined type (when the student is in-attentive, impulsive, and too active)

SIGNS TO LOOK FOR IN THE CLASSROOM
- Denies events or misattributes blame or responsibility
- Temper tantrums due to overstimulation (sensory or affective)
- May break things due to carelessness, accidental
- On first meeting someone generally pleasant toward others
- May have difficulty settling down at night and may awaken early
- Even with interest and motivation have significant difficulty staying fully involved in academic tasks
- Symptoms often improve as the child gets older
- Stimulant medication may cause an improvement in symptoms

STRATEGIES FOR INSTRUCTION
- Determine which specific tasks are difficult for the student. Example: Student may have trouble starting a task-Another may have trouble ending one task and starting the next- each student needs different help.
- Review rules, schedules, and assignments. Clear rules and routines will help a student with AD/HD
- Teach study skills and learning strategies and reinforce regularly
- Help student channel his/her physical activity (let student do some work standing up)
- Provide regularly scheduled breaks
- Make sure directions are given step by step, and that student is following the directions
- Give directions both verbally and in writing. ADHD students benefit from doing the steps as separate tasks.
- Work with student's parents to create and implement an educational plan tailored to meet the student's needs
- Regularly share information about how the student is doing at home and at school
- Be willing to try new ways of doing things.
- Be patient and maximize the student's chances for success.

The Disorder Fact Sheet Booklet: For parents and teachers of exceptional learners is available http://www.amazon.com or www.barnesandnoble.com.

The Shepherd's Christian School
___ Grade Teaching and Learning Goals Newsletter
Semester 1, Week(s) 7-12, October 17-November 25, 2011

Bible: (8:15-9:00) The student will develop an understanding of God's Word; understand how to use the Bible as a practical and spiritual resource; and understand the different stories in the Bible as being a part of history. Answer 5 W's and a H. Test each Monday
Wk. 7 Memory Verse: Eph. 4:32 Lessons Jacob blesses his children, Genesis 48-49, Moses and the Exodus
Wk. 8 MV: Proverbs 20:11 Lessons: Exodus 2-15 Moses and the burning bush, the plagues, the Passover, crossing the Red Sea
Wk. 9 MV: Psalm 106:1 Lessons: Exodus 15-16 Israel in the Wilderness, God provides quail and manna, the Ten Commandments
Wk. 10 MV: Ephesians 5:20 Lessons: The Ways of God, The twelve Spies, The Bronze Serpent Numbers 1-2
Wk. 11 MV: Psalm 100 Good bye Moses, Promised Land, Rahab Believes Joshua, The Fall of Jericho
Wk. 12 MV: Psalm 100 Christian Heritage Thanksgiving week

Language Arts: (9:00-10:00) Developing Christian character through the reading of God's Word. Eccl. 12:12-14, Phil. 4:8 The student writes clear and coherent sentences and paragraphs that develop a central idea. His writing shows he considers the audience and purpose. He will progress through the stages of the writing process (e.g., prewriting, drafting, revising, editing successive versions). Create readable documents with legible handwriting. Understand the purposes of various reference materials (e.g., dictionary, thesaurus, atlas). Student writes compositions that describe and explain familiar objects, events, and experiences. Student writing demonstrates a command of standard American English and the drafting, research, and organizational strategies. Student will distinguish between complete and incomplete sentences and identify and correctly use various parts of speech, including nouns and verbs, in writing and speaking. Use commas in the greeting and closure of a letter and with dates and items in a series. Use quotation marks correctly. Capitalize all proper nouns, words at the beginning of sentences and greetings, months and days of the week, and titles and initials of people. Spell frequently used and irregular words correctly (e.g., was, were, says, said, who, what, why). Spelling word list (vocabulary): Test Mondays. Speech Club 1st and 3rd Fridays at Crossroads Presbyterian Church: Student delivers brief recitations and oral presentations about familiar experiences or interests that are organized around a coherent thesis statement. Describe story elements (e.g., characters, plot, setting). Journal 3 times each week.
Reading: The Children's Treasury of Virtues (HONESTY/LOYALTY/FRIENDSHIP)
The Pasture, George Washington and the Cherry Tree, God Make My Life a Little Light, The Indian, Cinderella, Little Boy Blue, The Boy Who Cried "Wolf", The Honest Woodman, Why Frog and Snake Never Play Together, Heroes, Opportunity About Angels, A Prayer at Valley Forge, Only a Dad, The Sphinx, Jackie Robinson, Sail On! Sail On!

Arithmetic: (10:15-11:05) In second grade mathematics the student is taught to see that the addition and multiplication tables are part of the truth and order that God has built into reality. Student counts, reads, and writes whole numbers to 1,000 and identifies the place value for each digit. The student uses words, models, and expanded forms (e.g., 45 = 4 tens + 5) to represent numbers (to 1,000); Orders and compares whole numbers to 1,000 by using the symbols <, =, >. Student estimates, calculates, and solves problems involving addition and subtraction of two-and three-digit numbers (inverse relationships between addition and subtraction (e.g., an opposite number sentence for 8 + 6 = 14 is 14 - 6 = 8) to solve problems and check solutions); Finds the sum or difference of two whole numbers up to three digits long; Uses mental arithmetic to find the sum or difference of two two-digit numbers; Recognizes, names, and compares unit fractions from 1 /12 to 1 /2; Solves problems using combinations of coins and bills; Know and use the decimal notation and the dollar and cent symbols for money; Uses the commutative and associative rules to simplify mental calculations and to check results; Relates problem situations to number sentences involving addition and subtraction; Solves addition and subtraction problems by using data from simple charts, picture graphs, and number sentences; Measures the length of an object to the nearest inch and/or centimeter; Tells time to the nearest quarter hour and know relationships of time (e.g., minutes in an hour, days in a month, weeks in a year); and Records numerical data in systematic ways, keeping track of what has been counted. Calendar skills in Spanish.

Science: (12:00-1:50 Wednesday and Thursday) The student will be aware of the importance of curiosity, honesty, openness, and skepticism in science and will exhibit these traits in their own efforts to understand how God's creation (the world) works. Earth is made of materials that have distinct properties and provide resources for human activities. As a basis for understanding this concept: we will compare the physical properties of different kinds of rocks and know that rock is composed of different combinations of minerals; smaller rocks come from the breakage and weathering of larger rocks; soil is made partly from weathered rock and partly from organic materials and that soils differ in their color, texture, capacity to retain water, and ability to support the growth of many kinds of plants; fossils provide evidence about the plants and animals that lived long ago and that scientists learn about the past history of Earth by studying fossils; and rock, water, plants, and soil provide many resources, including food, fuel, and building materials, that humans use. The student will: Make predictions based on observed patterns and not random guessing; Measure length, weight, temperature, and liquid volume with appropriate tools and express those measurements in standard metric system units; Compare and sort common objects according to two or more physical attributes (e.g., color, shape, texture, size, weight); Write or draw descriptions of a sequence of steps, events, and observations; Construct bar graphs to record data, using appropriately labeled axes; Use magnifiers or microscopes to observe and draw descriptions of small objects or small features of objects; and Follow oral instructions for a scientific investigation.

Social Studies: (12:00-1:50 Monday and Tuesday) To inspire each student that he has a divine place and purpose in Christ. His Story. Student understands the importance of providence, individual action and character and explains how heroes from long ago and the recent past have made a difference in others' lives (e.g., from biographies of Abraham Lincoln, Louis Pasteur, Sitting Bull, George Washington Carver, Marie Curie, Albert Einstein, Jackie Robinson, Sally Ride). You Can Change the World: Learning to Pray for People Around the World (Volume II) Working with Maps, Globes, and Other Geographic Tools: Name specific continent, country, state, and community; Understand that maps have keys or legends with symbols and their uses; Find directions on a map: east, west, north, south; Identify major oceans: Pacific, Atlantic, Indian, Arctic; The seven continents: Asia, Europe, Africa, North America, South America, Antarctica, Australia (Oceania); Locate: Canada, United States, Mexico, Central America; Locate: the Equator, Northern Hemisphere and Southern Hemisphere, North and South Poles. Reading: The Story of the World history from ancient times until the present. Africa, China, Europe, the Americas—world's civilizations (nomads to the last Roman emperor).

Integrated Art: To develop the disciplined use of God-given talents to produce visual are for the glory of God and to encourage creative expressions thereby building self-esteem.
Integrated Music: To recognize music as a gift from God to mankind. To participate in music making, praise and worship as technical abilities and understanding increase. Singing, moving, playing and understanding instruments, appreciation, hearing, and music theory.
Computer: Students use technology tools to enhance learning, increase productivity and promote creativity all to God's glory. Accelerated Reader software will be used to assess students' reading with four types of quizzes: reading practice, vocabulary practice, literacy skills, and textbook quizzes. This will build a lifelong love of reading and learning

Physical Education (Daily): To develop and strengthen the child in both body and spirit through conditioning (skill, coordination, endurance, and health). Wednesday Hiking with Hiking Exploring Group

Homework:
Practice memory verse 10-15 minutes and Spelling Words
Complete worksheets (if applicable) and get communication folder signed
Monthly Christian Home school Group Meeting
1st Thursday 7 p.m. at Word from Above Ministry and Church

DIFFERENTIATED LEARNING PLAN

Subject   Date

Standards: What should students know, understand, and be able to do? (Grade Level Expectations, Depth of Knowledge, Show Me Standards, Common Core State Standards)

Assessment/Criteria for Success: How will you know students have gained an understanding of the concepts? (Identify tools for data collection, logs, checklists, journals, agendas, observations, portfolios, rubrics, contracts, etc.)

Essential Questions:

Content: (Bible Truths, Concepts, Vocabulary, Facts)

Developmental Domains Addressed:
(Check all that apply to the lesson(s) Notes:

Spiritual

Ethical

Cognitive

Psychological

Language

Physical

Social

Cultural

Skills Development:

Monday

Tuesday

Wednesday

Thursday

Friday

Materials:

Procedures:

Engagement (Activate or Motivate): How will you pre-assess, gain, and maintain students' attention?

Process/Acquire: (How will the lesson be taught?)

Lesson Segment 1 (Explain-Model):

Activities (Explanation):

Lesson Segment 2 (Explore-Guided Practice):

Activities (Explanation):

Lesson Segment 3 (Elaboration and Extension-Independent Practice):

Activities (Explanation):

Evaluate (Feedback or Closure)

Instructional Strategies Employed:

1. Identifying similarities and differences
2. Summarizing and note taking
3. Reinforcing effort and providing recognition
4. Homework and practice
5. Nonlinguistic representations
6. Cooperative learning
7. Setting objectives and providing feedback;
8. Generating and testing hypotheses
 9. Cues, questions, and advance organizers)

Grouping Decisions: Check selection or identify activity in space provided. Apply and adjust as needed.
TAPS: Total-whole, Alone, Partner

Small Groups

Random

Heterogeneous

Homogeneous

Interest

Task

Constructed

Brain Compatible Strategies: Which will you use to deliver the content?

Brainstorming/Discussion

Drawing/Artwork

Fieldtrips

Games

Mnemonic Devices

Music/Rhythm/Rhyme/Rap

Reciprocal Teaching/Cooperative Learning

Storytelling

Technology

Graphic Organizers/Semantic Maps/Word Webs/Thinking Maps

Humor

Work study/Apprenticeships

Manipulative/Experiments/Labs/Models

Role play/Drama/Charades/Metaphor/Analogy/Simile

Movement

Writing/Journals

Visuals

Project/Problem-based Instruction

Visualization/Guided Practice

Evaluation: (report, quiz, test, performance, products, presentations, demonstrations, logs, journals, checklists, portfolios, rubric, meta-cognition)

Teacher's Lesson Reflection:
Describe

Analyze

Reflect

Instructional supervisor or peer observer suggestions:

Initials

Daily Observation Form

Record any symptoms, scratches, bruises, illnesses, injuries, infections, physical conditions, etc., that are observed.

Date	Child's Name	Observation Upon Arrival/Explanation	Staff Initials

[Your school's name]   Date _____

Attendance Record

Child's Name	Arrival Time	Signature	Departure Time	Signature

2 STAFF RECORDS

[Your School's name]
[Your school's address]

APPLICATION FOR EMPLOYMENT

Date _____   Date available to work _____

_____

Name: Last   First   Middle   Home phone

_____

Street Address   City   State   Zip

Position desired _____ Hours desired _____ Full time__ Part time __ Substitute __

Are you at least 18 years old? ___ Yes ___ No   Birthdate _____ (required in GA)

Have you applied with us before? ___ Yes ___ No If so, when _____

Do you have relatives that are currently working for our program? ___ Yes ___ No

Education and Training

Name and address of school   Degree, Diploma
High School _____

College _____

Other _____

Have you completed courses providing specific training for early childhood education? Provide details.

_____

_____

List any languages you can speak fluently (other than English):

_____

List any other educational training experiences that you have had including opportunities to experience cultures other than your own.

_____

List any books or articles that you have read recently that have helped you to grow professionally.

_____

Are you certified by _____ Professional Standards Commission or do you hold any teaching credential? If so, please list

_____

_____

What level(s): early ed, grade level, primary, secondary? _____ Remains valid for _____ years.

Endorsement(s)

_____

List semester hours in endorsement area(s)

_____

_____

✓Please request a sealed official transcript from each school be mailed to the school.
If you do not hold a certificate, what requirements do you need to complete?
* Please attach photocopies of any certificates held.
Have you had any courses in Philosophy of Education? If so, which philosophies, where and when?

_____

If not, would you be willing to take such a course? Yes ___ No ___

List any conferences or seminars that you have attended, led or participated in the past three years.

_____

_____

Name the curriculum(a) you are most familiar with:

_____

_____

_____

How has teacher evaluation impacted you or your students.

_____

_____

_____

_____

References
DO NOT INCLUDE PREVIOUS EMPLOYERS OR RELATIVES

Name	Address	Phone #	Occupation

Ten Year Employment Record

Begin with your most current or last employer. If you have been unemployed during any time within the past ten years, list how you spent your time, e.g. student, home with your children, unemployment, etc.
May we contact previous employers? _____ Yes _____ No

Month/Year	Name, Address, Phone # of Employer	Position/Duties	Reason for Leaving
From_____ To_____			
From_____ To_____			
From_____ To_____			
From_____ To_____			
From_____ To_____			
From_____ To_____			
From_____ To_____			
From_____ To_____			
From_____ To_____			
From_____ To_____			
From_____ To_____			
From_____ To_____			
From_____ To_____			
From_____ To_____			
From_____ To_____			

Background Information

Have you ever been convicted of a crime, including misdemeanors, other than traffic violations? _____
If yes, explain in detail

_____

_____

_____

_____

_____

Have you ever been shown by credible evidence, e.g., a court order or jury, a department investigation or other reliable evidence, to have abused, neglected, or deprived a child or adult or to have subjected any person to serious injury as a result of intentional negligent misconduct (as evidenced by oral or written statement)? _____

If yes, explain in detail _____

_____

_____

Do you have a valid driver's license? If yes, give license no., state, and expiration date

_____

_____

Do you currently hold a valid CPR card? ___ Yes ___ No If yes, list expiration date _____

Do you currently hold a valid First Aid card? ___ Yes ___ No If yes, list expiration date _____
Please read the attached "Duties and Responsibilities". Are you in all respects able to adequately perform the duties as described? ____ Yes ____ No If no, explain

_____

_____

_____

Please not any accommodations that may be neccessary _____
The state requires annual childcare training and we encourage additional hours of professional development .

Are you willing to participate? _____

Applicant's Certification And Agreement

I understand that **[Your school's name and address]**does not discriminate in its employment practices against any person because of race, color, national or ethnic origin, gender, age, or qualified accommodate individuals with a disability. The reasonable accommodation requirement applies to the application process, any pre-employment testing, and actual employment. but <u>only </u>if the program supervisor is made aware that an accommodation is required. If you are disabled and require accommodation, you may request it at any time during the interview process. Under the Americans with Disabilities Act of 1991, this program is required to reasonably accommodate individuals with a disability. You are obligated to inform the program director of your needs if it will impact your ability to perform the job for which you are applying. All paid and volunteer staff members must have a health appraisal before their first involvement in child care work. The appraisal should identify any accommodations required for the staff person to carry out assigned duties per that person's job description. I hereby certify that I have read the job description for the position for which I am applying, and am in all respects, able to adequately perform the essential functions and duties as described.

The pre-employment staff health appraisal must include
i. Health history.
ii. Physical examination.
iii. Dental examination.
iv. Vision and hearing screening.
v. Results and appropriate follow-up of tuberculosis (TB) screening using the tuberculin skin test or interferon-gamma release assay once on entry into the child care field with subsequent TB screening as determined by a history of high risk for TB thereafter (eg, foreign born, history of homelessness, HIV infected, contact with a prison population or someone with active TB).
vi. Review and certification of up-to-date immune status per the current adult immunization schedule on the CDC Web site at www.cdc.gov/vaccines. Any staff person who is not up to date with current recommended vaccines will be reminded that this is a job-related requirement. Unless an under-immunized employee or volunteer person has a medical exemption for a specific type of vaccine, failure to obtain the vaccines recommended by the CDC is grounds for termination.

I hereby certify that the facts set forth in this application process are true and complete to the best of my knowledge. I understand that falsification of any statement or a significant omission of fact may prevent me from being hired, or if hired, may subject me to immediate dismissal regardless of the time elapsed before discovery. If I am released under these circumstances, I further understand and agree that I will be paid and receive benefits only through the day of release.

I authorize **[Your school's name and address]** to thoroughly interview the primary references which I have listed, any secondary references mentioned through interviews with primary references, or other individuals who know me and have knowledge regarding my testimony and work record. I also authorize the school to thoroughly investigate my work records and evaluations, my educational preparation, and other matters related to my suitability for the position.

I authorize references and my former employers to disclose to the school any and all employment records, performance reviews, letters, reports, and other information related to my life and employment, without giving me prior notice of such disclosure. In addition, I hereby release the school, my former employers, references, and all other parties from any and all claims, demands, or liabilities arising out of or in any way related to such investigation or disclosure. I waive the right to ever personally view any references given to the school.

Since I will be working with children, I understand that I must submit to a criminal record check and possibly other federal and state authorities. I agree to fully cooperate in providing and recording as many sets of my fingerprints as are necessary for such an investigation. I authorize the school to conduct a criminal record check. I understand and agree that any offer of employment that I may receive from the school is conditioned upon the receipt of background information, including criminal background and other pre-employment screening information. The school may refuse employment or terminate conditional employment if the school deems any background information unfavorable or that it could reflect adversely on the facility or on me as a role model for the students. I understand that this is only an application for employment and that an employment position is not being offered at this time.

I am aware that before awarding the position, the **[Your school's name and address]** will conduct the following pre-employment background check on all candidates:
- Social Security Verification;
- Prior Employment Verification;
- Education Verification all levels);
- Residence Verification;
- Criminal Background Investigation – Local, State, & Federal;
- Sexual Offender Database Search.

In addition, candidates for designated positions may also be subject to the following additional types of checks, depending on the requirements of the position:
- Motor Vehicle Record (drivers for field trip or other student transportation);
- Professional Reference Checks;
- State/Federal Civil Litigation, Lien & Judgments (administrative, finance and business office, etc.);
- Credit Verification (administrative, finance and business office, etc.);
- Corporate Filing and Status Search (administrative, consultants, etc.);
- Media Search;
- Professional Licensing Check (instructional, consultants, trainers, and the like).

[Your school's name and address] will maintain a summary of job classifications and applicable categories of inquiry that may be amended as necessary by the school as needs and requirements may evolve.

I certify that all information on this application is correct. It is understood and agreed that any misrepresentation by me on this application will be sufficient cause for cancellation of the application process and/or separation from the company if I have been employed.

Applicant Signature _____ Date _____

PERSONAL PHILOSOPHY ESSAY QUESTIONS

* On separate paper please label and succinctly answer in one or two paragraphs three of the questions below.

Instructional staff

A. What are your top three reasons for becoming a teacher?

B. Why do you wish to teach at [your school's name]?

C. What do you consider to be the most optimal environment for learning?

D. What is your philosophy and practice of discipline?

E. How much do you want to know about your students in order to be most helpful to them?

F. What is your philosophy and practice regarding learning styles?

G. What areas do you feel are your strengths? Weaknesses?

H. What do you believe the role of the parent is in a child's education? How does your belief affect your interaction with parents?

I. What are the four key components of an effective lesson plan?

J. Please summarize any additional information that you would like to present regarding your candidacy for this position.

Support staff

A. What are your top three reasons for going into this line of work?

B. Why do you wish to work at [your school's name]?

C. What are the THREE most important qualities you would want a school leader to recognize in you as a potential staff member? Please focus on personal and professional qualities, talents, or experiences unique to you and provide examples and other evidence to support these.

D. As you search for employment, what are the top THREE characteristics you are looking for in a job or school?

E. Please summarize any additional information that you would like to present regarding your candidacy for this position.

Your address
Your website
Your telephone number

[Enter Your School Name]
Personnel Manual
2013-2014

Revised [enter date]

[YOUR SCHOOL'S NAME]

Forward

This handbook is a basic reference concerning policies and procedure, privileges and opportunities, and obligations and responsibilities affecting the employees, volunteers, student workers, work study students, and enrolled families of the [YOUR SCHOOL'S NAME] Child Development Center. Information contained in this handbook does not create any contractual rights for employees, volunteers, student workers, or enrolled families. Policies contained in this handbook do not increase or diminish the legally enforceable rights of the school or center and its employees. The misapplication or failure to follow any specific provision in this handbook should not be grounds for setting aside or modifying any employment or enrollment decision when it has been determined by appropriate administrative authority that the decision was fairly made and in the best interest of the [YOUR SCHOOL'S NAME] Child Development Center. Because the [YOUR SCHOOL'S NAME] Child Development Center is the initiator of change and is subject to various external legal and regulatory forces requiring change, the information in this handbook will be revised as the [YOUR SCHOOL'S NAME] Child Development Center, federal or state laws determine that conditions warrant.

The contents of this handbook are presented as a matter of information only and are not intended to cover all policies, plans and procedures of [YOUR SCHOOL'S NAME]. The plans, policies and procedures described are not conditions of employment. [YOUR SCHOOL'S NAME] reserves the right to modify, add, revoke, suspend, terminate, or change any or all plans, policies, or procedures of the company, in whole or in part, at any time with or without notice. The language in this booklet is not intended to create, nor is it to be construed, a contract between [YOUR SCHOOL'S NAME] and any one or all of its employees. Your employment with [YOUR SCHOOL'S NAME] is employment-at-will. That is, your employment can be terminated at any time by you or [YOUR SCHOOL'S NAME]. The information contained in this Personnel manual is confidential and proprietary to [YOUR SCHOOL'S NAME]. The information is for internal use only and may not be distributed outside of [YOUR SCHOOL'S NAME]. Copies of this document are not to be made. Circulation of this document must be restricted to only those who have a need to know in their official capacity. This document must remain secured when not in use. Upon completion of use of this document, it shall be returned to [YOUR SCHOOL'S NAME].

Table of Contents

Mission and Vision Statement	
Philosophy	
Welcome	
Upon Hire	
Schedule	
Pay Scale	
Pay Schedule	
Staff benefits	
Hours	
Illness	
Change of Schedule	
Babysitting	
Staff Corrective Action	
Adverse Performance Action	
Non Discrimination	
Workplace Harassment	
Code of Ethics	
NAEYC Statement of Commitment	
Confidentiality and Security of Records	
Abuse and Neglect	
Grievance	
Personal Items	
Smoking and Tobacco Products	
Prohibited Substances	
Drug Free Workplace	
Dress Code	
Communication	
Electronic Communications	
Facility Maintenance	
Health	
Staff Meetings	
Staff Development	
Continuing Education	
Daily Schedule	
Daily Activity Report	
Incident Report	
Permission to Photo/Video/Audio	
Diaper Changing	
Infection Control and Disease Prevention	
Rest time	
Feeding	
Bottle and Breast Feeding	
Foods from Home	
Foods to Avoid	
Meal Guidelines	
Guidance	
Limits of Behavior	
Biting	

Outdoor Play	
Water Play	
Off-site Activities	
Transportation	
Departure	
Emergency Procedure	
Closings	
Assignment of Employees	
Work Schedule	
Substitute Employees	
General Job Descriptions	

Mission Statement

The mission of [Your school's name] is to provide quality care and education for the children of [name] community.

Vision Statement

Our goal is to provide accessible, affordable, high-quality early education by keeping the learner's needs at the center of decision-making and working in partnership with families and our dynamic, multicultural community.

Philosophy

We believe in the value of human diversity and the fair treatment of all people. Our primary goal is to provide a nurturing environment that supports all children as they become creative, independent, responsible, fully-functioning, self-directed individuals who have a strong sense of self and accomplishment. Secondly, as adults, we must strive to continue learning and growing in our relationships with others to role model a peaceful environment and surround the children with understanding and warmth.

Welcome

Welcome to the [YOUR SCHOOL'S NAME] Child Development Center Staff! The following staff policies and procedures will guide you through your daily routines and enable the center to be a safe and smooth running center. All employees serve as character role models through their actions, words, and deeds for the children for which the center cares.

Upon Hire

Immediately upon hire, all forms must be completely filled out and all supporting documents must be provided. The [YOUR SCHOOL'S NAME] CDC requires that medical physical documentation must be turned in no later than one week after hire. All Georgia Department of Early Care and Learning: Bright from the Start (BFTS) requirements for staff must be met. All new staff members are considered on probation for the first four weeks. At the end of this period, the Director will review and evaluate your performance. If your performance is satisfactory you will become a regular member of our staff.

Upon hire you will participate in orientation that will cover BFTS rules and regulations in addition to the National Health and Safety Standards, this staff handbook containing policies and procedures, and the Parent handbook. Your responsibility is to read through each document upon receipt so that you are familiar with the guidelines that govern the center.

Schedule

Staff shall not regularly be scheduled to perform child care duties for more than twelve (12) hours within any twenty-four (24) hour period. Lead staff (non student staff) will be scheduled 9 hours per day. This includes two 15 minute breaks and a 30 minute lunch break. Employees may roll their break and lunch together for a total of one hour. This hour can be taken during an employee's shift or at the end of the shift depending on staffing. Please notify the director of your preference at the beginning of employment (when you will use your breaks and lunch), so that staffing can be determined for your room. Once all staff schedules are made for the school year your work schedule does not change each week you will work the same time and days throughout the year.

Pay Scale

The Lead fulltime staff of the [YOUR SCHOOL'S NAME] Child Development Center pay scale is based on education level and certifications and employee annual reviews. Assistant staff pay scale begins at minimum wage and each year of employment the staff member will be evaluated by the administrator and their supervising teacher. If they are awarded "acceptable" then they will receive a .25 raise for the upcoming semester.

Pay Schedule
All payroll checks are direct deposit. If you do not have a checking account, Capital One, the school or center partner can open up a free checking account for you. Upon direct deposit to your account, the funds will be available on the check disbursement date. Employee time sheets will be placed in you mailbox. The date due and instructions will be attached to the time sheets. Timesheets submitted late will be held until the next scheduled payroll period for processing.

Staff benefits
The following staff benefits are available to all Lead Staff; Employee Health Insurance, paid annual leave, paid sick leave, child care benefit of $1200 per year (if an employee does not use the child care benefit then the $1200 rolls into their salary), Retirement, bonuses based on merit/achievement or education, tuition reimbursement to the school or center in the form of a BFTS scholarship (employees are eligible for this benefit when they have been employed by the school or center for two years), and paid membership to the Georgia Association of Young children or the Association of Christian School International.

Hours
Time: 7:00 a.m. – 6:00 p.m.
The center is closed in conjunction with [local county Department of Education (DOE)]'s scheduled holidays and semester breaks.

Illness
Staff, or any other persons being supervised by the staff, shall not be allowed in the center who knowingly have, or present symptoms of a fever, vomiting, or diarrhea. If illness occurs overnight that prevents you from working the next day, you should call the Director at (77) XXX-XXX any time day or night. Emergencies will be handled on a case by case basis. **YOU** must report in personally unless your condition is so grave that you cannot physically do so yourself.

Change of Schedule
If you need a one time request to have a schedule changed, you will need to fill out the Request for schedule change located in box next to office. Requests must be placed in the Director's box one week prior to requested change. Note if your schedule change leaves only one staff member at the center, your request will be denied. However if you are trading work time with another staff member for this time fill out the bottom of the form and the person you are trading with must sign by his/her name so that I know the person is aware of and has agreed to the change. Upon review of schedule, the request will be approved or denied and posted on the staff board to the left of the office door.

Babysitting
As sometimes happens, because of your specialized experience as a caregiver, you will be asked to care for children of family or friends outside of your obligations in working with the [YOUR SCHOOL'S NAME] Child Development Center. [YOUR SCHOOL'S NAME] Child Development Center faculty and staff members are prohibited from providing any babysitting or other childcare services to any families enrolled. In the event a family approaches you to provide nanny services you shall immediately inform the family that you are prohibited under your non-compete agreement to provide such services and direct the family to discuss this issue with your director. You shall then immediately inform your director of this conversation. Failure to do so may result in termination of your employment. In the event you breach your non-compete and provide such nanny services, you agree that you (unless the family requesting such services agrees to pay) shall be obligated to pay [YOUR SCHOOL'S NAME] the sum of $3,000, the

estimated cost of damages to [YOUR SCHOOL'S NAME] for recruiting, hiring, and training a new staff member. Your signature on the Employee Acknowledgement form at the back of this Personnel manual constitutes your agreement to this section.

Staff Corrective Action

From time to time, all of us make mistakes or have an oversight. When this occurs, the director will bring the issue to your attention; discuss the error, and how to avoid it in the future. This will solve most problems. If problems repeat, or are sufficiently severe in their first occurrences, more serious discipline, up to and including discharge, is warranted. The decision as to the level of discipline will be determined by the director. If we strive to use common sense and good judgment on the job, we can avoid this situation.

Adverse Performance Action

During the duration of your employment, your responsibility is to learn, know, and adhere to, at all times, the rules and regulations of all the agencies that affect our center. Any violation that harms a child or other staff member may result in immediate termination and a report to the authorities for further action. All violations of policy are documented and will result in a disciplinary conference, possible probation, corrective action, and/or termination.

Non-Discrimination

All employees will be treated in a fair manner to ensure that matters do not discriminate on the basis of race, age, sex, national origin, or disability. Employees are hired on the basis of their merit and ability to perform the essential duties assigned to their job. Positions will be filled without regard to race, sex, national origin or disability. This policy extends to all employment practices including but not limited to recruitment, hiring, training, promoting, compensation, and benefits for all employees.

The [YOUR SCHOOL'S NAME] Child Development Center does not discriminate against children based on race, color, creed, sex, national origin, handicapping condition, ancestry or children being breastfed.

Workplace Harassment

Employees are entitled to work in an environment that is free of harassment from fellow employees, supervisors, parents, vendors, or others. Failure to comply with this policy will result in immediate employment termination. If you feel you are treated unfairly, an appointment with the center director should be scheduled.

Code of Ethics

Those of us who have selected Early Childhood Education as our profession follow the National Association for the Education of Young Children (NAEYC) code of ethics that guides our involvement with children. We expect each of the staff, students, and volunteers who work in our center to be similarly committed to maintaining ethical behavior. The following guidelines relate particularly to staff, students', and volunteers' involvement in the child care center.

1.   Remember to have these children and parents to talk with and observe is a privilege; they are people who deserve respect. This respect is conveyed by a variety of behaviors, including active and sincere valuing, patience, tolerance, and acceptance. Please remember that while children may respond in ways that are "funny" to adults, to smile or laugh is appropriate only when expressing happiness or delight. In other words, laugh with them, not at them.

2.   That we protect the confidentiality of all personal information concerning our children and their families is essential. Therefore, use the children's names in discussions occurring during lecture and lab only, but not in situations other than these. Such conversations can be very beneficial. Observations can be discussed in light of others' experiences and the knowledge and experience of your instructors.

3. During staff meetings, an observation or discussion of a child's behavior is acceptable: "Sarah has been hitting several children today," or "Joe has been playing by himself a lot today." To make evaluative comments is not acceptable: "Sarah is little toot," or "Joe is really a wallflower."

4. Evaluative comments are unprofessional in nature, and, if overheard by the child or parents, can have serious consequences for the child and the program.

5. Remember that children are people who deserve respect. This respect is conveyed by a variety of behaviors, ranging from sensitive to "active" listening to protecting children from their own impulses or the aggression of others.

6. Remember to maintain your own self-respect. You can be a kind," friendly adult without allowing children to abuse or manipulate you: "I'm tired of running, I'd like to rest now," will help children understand the limits of their expectations of others.

7. Maintaining a professional attitude includes being responsive to the needs of teachers, peers, and children. Staff continually serve as role models for children, as well as for other adults, thus such qualities as patience, tolerance, cooperation, and enthusiasm are highly desirable.

Staff, students, and volunteers adherence to these ethical principles is truly appreciated. Professional behavior is essential to providing a quality program for young children, and we believe that it will enhance staff, students', and volunteers' learning experience.

NAEYC Statement of Commitment to Professional Ethics

As an individual who works with young children, I commit myself to furthering the values of early childhood education as they are reflected in the ideals and principles of the NAEYC Code of Ethical Conduct. To the best of my ability I will:

* Never harm children
* Ensure that programs for young children are based on current knowledge and research of child development and early childhood education.
* Respect and support families in their task of nurturing children.
* Respect colleagues in early childhood care and education and support them in maintaining the NAEYC Code of Ethical Conduct.
* Serve as an advocate for children, their families, and their teachers in community and society.
* Stay informed of and maintain high standards of professional conduct.
* Engage in an ongoing process of self-reflection, realizing that personal characteristics, biases, and beliefs have an impact on children and families.
* Be open to new ideas and be willing to learn from the suggestions of others.
* Continue to learn, grow, and contribute as a professional.
* Honor the ideals and principles of the NAEYC Code of Ethical Conduct.

Signature: _____ Date: _____

This Statement of Commitment is not part of the Code but is a personal acknowledgement of the individual's willingness to embrace the distinctive values and moral obligations of the field of early childhood care and education. It is recognition of the moral obligations that lead to an individual becoming part of the profession.

Confidentiality and Security of Records

The Director will supervise the maintenance and have custody of all records for staff and children. Records may be released only to custodial parents. All records are the property of the center and will be in a locked cabinet to secure them against loss; tampering or unauthorized use.

The center shall maintain the confidentiality of all children's records. Employees of the center shall not disclose or knowingly permit the disclosure of any information concerning the child or his/her family; directly, or indirectly, to any unauthorized person.

The center shall obtain written informed consent from the parent prior to releasing any information or photographs from which the child might be identified, except for authorized agencies.

Abuse and Neglect

As a staff member if you suspect abuse or neglect of any child at our center immediately notify the center director. The director will call and report this action to **Georgia Department of Family and Children Services.** As mandated reporters, all center staff shall report any suspected abuse and or neglect of a child in accordance with [OCGA 19-7-5(c)(1)] to the Local Child Protection Agency. If you have reasonable cause to believe that a child has been abused, you *must* make a report, immediately but no later than 24 hours, to your local DFCS office or law enforcement and are subject to criminal penalty for failing to do so. The following chart on "Recognizing Child Abuse and Neglect in the Classroom Setting" will provide guidelines, which should be helpful.

Recognizing Child Abuse and Neglect in the Classroom Setting	
Physical Abuse	
Physical Indicators	**Behavioral Indicators**
Unexplained Bruises and Welts: • On, face, lips, mouth • On torso, back, buttocks, thighs • In various stages of healing • Clustered forming regular patterns • Reflecting shape of article used to inflict (electrical cord, belt buckle) • Aggressiveness or withdrawal • On several different surface areas Regularly appear after absence, weekend or vacation **Unexplained Burns:** • Cigar, cigarette burns, especially on soles, palms, back or buttocks • Immersion burns (sock-like, glove-like, doughnut shaped on buttocks, genitalia • Rope burns on arms, legs, neck, torso **Unexplained Fractures:** • To skull, nose, facial structure • In various stages of healing • Multiple or spiral fractures **Unexplained Lacerations or Abrasions:** • To mouth, lips, gums, eyes • To external genitalia	• Wary of Adult Contacts • Apprehensive when other children cry • Frightened of parents (extreme) • Afraid to go home (extreme) • Reports injury by parent
Physical Neglect	
Physical Indicators	**Behavioral Indicators**
• Consistent Hunger, Poor Hygiene, Inappropriate dress • Constant lack of supervision, especially in dangerous activities of long periods • Unattended physical problems or medical needs • Abandonment	• Begging, stealing food • Extended stays at school (early arrival and late departure) • Constant fatigue, listlessness or falling asleep in class • Alcohol or drug abuse

• States there is no caretaker	• delinquency

Sexual Abuse	
Physical Indicators	**Behavioral Indicators**
• Difficulty in walking or sitting • Torn or stained, or bloody underclothing • Pain or itching in genital area • Bruises of bleeding in external genitalia, vaginal or anal areas • Venereal disease, especially in pre-teens • Pregnancy	• Unwilling to change for or participate in physical education class withdrawal, fantasy, or infantile behavior • Bizarre, sophisticated, unusual sexual behavior or knowledge • Poor peer relationships • Delinquent or run-away • Reports sexual assault by caretaker • Child doesn't feel safe where he lives • Change in eating habits, sleeping habits (nightmares, sleepwalking, etc.) • Depressed crying episodes • Seductive or promiscuous behavior which is not age appropriate

Dynamics that may indicate a sexually abusive family: Isolated either socially or physically, Inappropriate sleeping arrangements, poor supervision, rigid rules, children forced into adult roles, family members don't communicate, no limit setting, inability to empathize, emotional deprivation, neglectful situation, unrealistic expectations, history of drug or alcohol abuse, absent parent, prior sexual offenses involving family members, a large number of surrogate parents in and out of the family, parent with personality disorder or mental illness, adults with special needs as caretakers, and adults who expect immediate gratification/have no impulse control. **Why do children keep sexual abuse secret? They fear: blame, rejection, punishment, loss of parental love, that adults won't believe them, parents will divorce, parent will go to jail, child will go to foster home or institution, retaliation, pregnancy, disease, and what friends will say, etc.**

Emotional Maltreatment	
Physical Indicators	**Behavioral Indicators**
• Speech disorders • Lags in physical development • Failure to thrive	• Habit disorders (sucking, biting, rocking, etc.) • Conduct disorders (anti-social, destructive, etc) • Neurotic traits (sleep disorders, inhibition of play) • Psychoneurotic reactions (hysteria, obsession, compulsion, phobia, hypochondria) • Behavior extremes (complaint, passive, aggressive, demanding) • Overly adaptive behavior (inappropriately adult, inappropriately infant) • Developmental lags (mental, emotional) • Attempted suicide

Grievance
Employees shall state their grievances in writing and submit them to the Director. The Director is

responsible for addressing the grievance. If the employee does not feel that the director has resolved their grievance then they will need to submit your grievance in writing to the president of the Board of Directors.

Personal Items
Personal items such as purses and backpacks must be stored in the designated locked area in the cubby room before you enter the classroom. Except in the case of an emergency, the use of personal cell phones in the classroom is not permitted. *Medication required during work hours must be locked in the designated closet in the director's office, and consumed away from the children.*

Smoking and Smokeless Tobacco
Caregivers serve as role models for young children. Staff or other persons shall not smoke or use tobacco products within the center premises, on the center playgrounds or in any vehicle being used to transport children. (Note: Current Fire Safety laws prohibit smoking on the premises of the child care center.)

Prohibition of Alcohol, Firearms, Tobacco or Other Toxic Materials
[YOUR SCHOOL'S NAME] Child Development Center prohibits the use of alcohol, tobacco, and use or possession of illegal substances or unauthorized potentially toxic substances, fireworks, firearms, pellet or BB guns(loaded or unloaded) in the center, on the playground, and on any sponsored field trip.

Substance Abuse and Drug-Free Workplace
The use or possession of illegal or controlled substances is not permitted in the center, on the grounds of the center or in the center vehicle. Employees of the [YOUR SCHOOL'S NAME] Child Development Center will be subject to alcohol and controlled substance testing at any time under the following conditions: post hire pre-employment, reasonable suspicion, post accident, random, return to duty, driving duties, and follow up testing. Violation of this policy, including refusal to submit to drug testing when properly ordered to do so, will result in actions up to and including termination of employment.

Dress Code
As an employee of the [YOUR SCHOOL'S NAME] Child Development Center, you are to present a professional image. You are expected to be neatly groomed and clean. You must dress for easy movement and the potential of being engaged in messy activities comfortably.
The following clothing is prohibited, short shorts, cut off shorts, low cut blouses or blouses with spaghetti straps. Shirts should be tucked in. Skirts must be no shorter than 3" above the knee. Low heals, flats and casual shoes are much more comfortable and safer than high heels when working with children; high heel shoes are not appropriate and are prohibited.
Many people find tattoos and unusual body piercing (i.e. nose, lips, or tongue) objectionable. visible body piercing, other than that of the ear are not acceptable. Visible tattoos are not acceptable. All of these can be frightening for children.
Staff must have appropriate clothing for outdoor wear at all times. A person who is cold or uncomfortable cannot focus adequately on their assignments and care giving of the children. Prepare for weather.
[optional: As this is a non-profit facility, no attire may be worn that supports persons running for any political office.]
Caps, hats, hoods and nylon head wraps are prohibited inside the building. These can be frightening to children and can obscure supervision visibility. Winter hats are permitted on the playground.
Certain dress standards may be reflective of an individual's religious beliefs. Reasonable accommodations will be provided as needed.

Communication
Caregivers are hired for their skills in the classroom, and their ability to communicate with others. Good

communication skills are essential in dealing with parents, and other staff.

Electronic Communication

The [YOUR SCHOOL'S NAME] Child Development Center provides telephones for business use and computers for office use. The office computer may not be used to conduct on-line commercial transactions.

Occasional personal telephone calls are necessary. These calls should be held to a minimum both in frequency and duration. If an emergency phone call is received for you, you will be contacted immediately. In all other cases, a note of the call will be made and posted on employee board or given to you. Please ask children, family, and friends not to contact you by phone at work unless absolutely necessary.

Cellular phones and pagers present many workplace problems. They are distracting to both employees and students, and their use during work time interferes with our responsibility. All devices of this nature must be turned to the silent mode and remain in cubbies. We ask that no personal calls be placed while you are responsible for children so that supervision will not be a lapse in supervision.

Facility Maintenance

Before leaving the center, drink cups, eating utensils, and any materials used, must be placed in their appropriate location. To keep the classroom space and outdoor play area orderly and well maintained is important. Cleaning and sanitizing procedures must be completed daily and throughout the day as needed.

Health Requirements

Upon offer of employment all center staff shall be required to obtain a statement of good health signed by a physician or designee. A health statement dated within three months prior to offer of employment or within one month after date of employment is acceptable (Note: The [YOUR SCHOOL'S NAME] Child Development Center requires this statement to be on file one week following hire date) . A health statement is required every three years.

Staff Meetings

Attendance at staff meetings is mandatory .The Director shall conduct, at a minimum, one staff training session each three-month quarter. Documentation shall consist of dated minutes of the training sessions including topics and signatures of all staff in attendance. Staff members may be asked to attend other meetings and workshops during the year. Some training events may occur after work hours or on weekends. Advance notice will be given regarding upcoming workshops and meetings. Staff meetings and training requirements are considered work responsibilities and will be detailed further in the next two sections.

Staff Development

Orientation is typically completed within *one week* of employment and prior to having sole responsibility for a group of children, each staff member, including substitutes, shall review the following materials:
1. Center policies and procedures including health and safety procedures,
2. Emergency and evacuation plan
3. Supervision of children
4. Discipline policy
5. Job description
6. Individual needs of the children enrolled (ADA, IDEA)
7. Curriculum and lesson planning
8. Confidentiality of information regarding children and their families
9. Review of State's Health and Safety Requirements regarding:
a. Operations, health, safety, activities

b. Physical environment and equipment
c. Emergency situations
d. Food service and nutrition
10. Reporting Requirements for:
a. Suspected Child Abuse, Neglect or Deprivation
b. Communicable Diseases
c. Serious Injuries
d. Missing/Lost Children
11. Childhood Injury Control
a. The Administration of Medication
b. Reducing the Risk of Sudden Infant
c. Death Syndrome (SIDS)
d. Hand Washing
e. Fire Safety
f. Water Safety
g. Prevention of HIV/Aids and blood borne pathogens
h. Transportation
12. Approved Child Care Training Requirements

This training shall be followed by 4 days of supervised orientation and work with children. The director or lead teacher may conduct this supervision. On the employees 5th day of employment an orientation with the center director will be conducted to review the centers policy and procedures, employee and parent handbook. All staff, including substitutes, shall annually review information provided at orientation training.

Documentation shall consist of a form that is signed and dated by the employee and Director attesting to having received such orientation training.

Continuing Education

The Director shall provide opportunities for continuing education of staff through attendance at BFTS approved childcare workshops or conferences to enhance the ability of staff to meet the individual needs of children enrolled. This training is mandatory.

1. The childcare staff shall obtain 12 clock hours of training per center's anniversary year in job-related subject areas. (BFTS approved CDA training or renewal hours and college courses in child development can count toward this)
2. Infant/child CPR, and first aid
3. State approved health and safety training –6 clock hours (injury control, infection diseases, child abuse/neglect); 5 hours fire safety, 4 hours nutrition, 2 hours transportation (CDA state approved health and safety training hours can count for this)
4. Training required by Bright from the Start Quality Rating System.

Documentation shall consist of attendance records and certificates received by staff which will be kept on file in the director's office.

Daily Schedules and Lesson Plans

Schedules and lesson plans shall reflect Developmentally Appropriate Practices. Plans and schedules are important in helping to give each class structure and organization. Weekly lesson plans will be posted, allowing for flexibility and change. Lesson plans and schedules shall be adhered to with reasonable closeness, but shall meet both the individual needs and the differences among the children. The schedule shall provide time and materials for both vigorous and quiet activity, for children to share or to be alone, indoor and outdoor play, and rest. Time shall be scheduled for routines such as washing hands, lunch, rest, snacks, and putting away toys. Active and quiet periods shall be alternated so as to guard against over-stimulation of the child.

Daily Activity Report

Activity reports are a very important part of our program. Reports must be completed daily in infant/toddler classroom and sent home. Daily reports allow families to feel like they have been a part of their child's day. Reports reassure parents that the staff are caring for and interacting with the child.

Incident Reports

The incident log must be filled out each time a child is involved in an accident/incident. Any accident/incident should be immediately reported to the Director or the on-duty designee. This will assure that appropriate child intervention and family notification is initiated.

Permission to Photograph/Video/Audio Tape

By joining our staff, you are agreeing to give permission for the [YOUR SCHOOL'S NAME] Child Development Center to photograph, video, or audio tape following purposes:

1. To display on bulletin boards, use in activities, label items at the CDC.
2. To illustrate a child or children participating with caregiver in a particular activity or the Child Development Center at meetings/training/conferences.
3. To use for public relations and student recruitment.
4. To use for individual assessments of employee.
5. To use in [YOUR SCHOOL'S NAME] Child Development Center weekly newsletter or on the [YOUR SCHOOL'S NAME] Child Development Center web site.

Diaper Change Procedure

The following diaper changing procedure shall be posted in the changing area, shall be followed for all diaper changes, and shall be used as part of staff evaluation of caregivers who do diaper changing. Child caregivers shall never leave a child alone on a table or countertop, even for an instant. A safety strap or harness shall not be used on the diaper changing table. If an emergency arises, caregivers shall put the child on the floor or take the child with them.

Step 1: Get organized. Before you bring the child to the diaper changing area, wash your hands, gather and bring what you need to the diaper changing table:
1. Fresh diaper, clean clothes (if you need them);
2. Wipes for cleaning the child's genitalia and buttocks removed from the container or dispensed so the container will not be touched during diaper changing;
3. A plastic bag for any soiled clothes;
4. Facial tissue or wipe with ointments applied in order to avoid contamination of the tube or container;
5. Disposable gloves

Step 2: Carry the child to the changing table, keeping soiled clothing away from you and any surfaces you cannot easily clean and sanitize after the change.
Always keep a hand on the child;
If the child's feet cannot be kept out of the diaper or from contact with soiled skin during the changing process, remove the child's shoes and socks so the child does not contaminate these surfaces with stool or urine during the diaper changing;
Put soiled clothes in a plastic bag and securely tie the plastic bag to send the soiled clothes home.

Step 3: Clean the child's diaper area.
Place the child on the diaper change surface and unfasten the diaper but leave the soiled diaper under the child.

If safety pins are used, close each pin immediately once it is removed and keep pins out of the child's reach.

Never hold pins in your mouth.

Lift the child's legs as needed to use disposable wipes to clean the skin on the child's genitalia and buttocks. Remove stool and urine from front to back and use a fresh wipe each time. Put the soiled wipes into the soiled diaper or directly into a plastic-lined, hands-free covered can.

Step 4: Remove the soiled diaper without contaminating any surface not already in contact with stool or urine.

Fold the soiled surface of the diaper inward.

Put soiled disposable diapers in a covered, plastic-lined, hands-free covered can. If reusable cloth diapers are used, put the soiled cloth diaper and its contents (without emptying or rinsing) in a plastic bag or into a plastic lined, hands-free covered can to give to parents.

Remove gloves rolling them inside each other and put them into a plastic-lined, hands-free covered can.

Use a disposable wipe to clean the surfaces of the caregiver's hands and another to clean the child's hands, and put the wipes into the plastic-lined, hands-free covered can.

Check for spills under the child and clean as needed.

Step 5: Put on a clean diaper and dress the child.

Slide a fresh diaper under the child.

Note and plan to report any skin problems such as redness, skin cracks, or bleeding.

Fasten the diaper. If pins are used, place your hand between the child and the diaper when inserting the pin.

Step 6: Wash the child's hands and return the child to a supervised area.

Use soap and water, no less than 60 degrees F and no more than 120 degrees F, at a sink to wash the child's hands, if you can.

· If a child is too heavy to hold for handwashing or cannot stand at the sink, use commercial disposable diaper wipes or follow this procedure:

· Wipe the child's hands with a damp paper towel moistened with a drop of liquid soap.

· Wipe the child's hands with a paper towel wet with clear water.

· Dry the child's hands with a paper towel.

Step 7: Clean and sanitize the diaper-changing surface.

· Clean any visible soil from the changing surface with detergent and water; rinse with water.

· Wet the entire changing surface with the sanitizing solution (e.g. spray a sanitizing bleach solution of 1/4 cup of household liquid chlorine bleach in one gallon of tap water, mixed fresh daily).

· Put away the spray bottle of sanitizer. If the recommended bleach dilution is sprayed as a sanitizer on the surface; leave it in contact with the surface for at least 2 minutes. The surface can be left to air dry or can be wiped dry after 2 minutes of contact with the bleach solution.

Step 8: Wash your hands according to the procedure and record the diaper change in the child's daily log.

· In the daily log, record what was in the diaper and any problems (such as a loose stool, an unusual odor, color, or consistency, blood in the stool, or any skin irritation).

Infection Control Practices and Disease Prevention

1. SITUATIONS THAT REQUIRE HANDWASHING

All staff, volunteers, and children shall follow this procedure for handwashing at the following times:

a) Upon arrival for the day or when moving from one child care group to another;

b) Before and after:
· Eating, handling food, or feeding a child;
· Giving medication;
· Playing in water that is used by more than one person.
c) After:
· Diapering;
· Using the toilet or helping a child use a toilet;
· Handling bodily fluid (mucus, blood, vomit), from sneezing, wiping and blowing noses, from mouths, or from sores;
· Handling uncooked food, especially raw meat and poultry;
· Handling pets and other animals;
· Playing in sandboxes;
· Cleaning or handling the garbage.

2. HANDWASHING PROCEDURE
Children and staff members shall wash their hands using the following method:
a) Check to be sure a clean, disposable paper towel is available.
b) Turn on warm water, no less than 60 degrees F and no more than 120 degrees F, to a comfortable temperature.
c) Moisten hands with water and apply liquid soap to hands.
d) Rub hands together vigorously until a soapy lather appears, and continue for at least 20 seconds. Rub areas between fingers, around nailbeds, under fingernails, jewelry, and back of hands.
e) Rinse hands under running water, no less than 60 degrees F and no more than 120 degrees F, until they are free of soap and dirt. Leave the water running while drying hands.
f) Dry hands with the clean, disposable paper towel.
g) If taps do not shut off automatically, turn taps off with a disposable paper towel.
h) Throw the disposable paper towel into a lined trash container. Use hand lotion to prevent chapping of hands, if desired.

ASSISTING CHILDREN WITH HANDWASHING
Caregivers shall provide assistance with handwashing at a sink for infants who can be safely cradled in one arm and for children who can stand but not wash their hands independently. A child who can stand shall either use a child-size sink or stand on a safety step at a height at which the child's hands can hang freely under the running water. After assisting the child with handwashing, the staff member shall wash his or her own hands.

If a child is unable to stand and is too heavy to hold safely to wash the hands at the sink, caregivers shall use the following method:
· Wipe the child's hands with a damp paper towel moistened with a drop of liquid soap. Then discard the towel.
· Wipe the child's hands with a clean, wet, paper towel until the hands are free of soap. Then discard the towel.
· Dry the child's hands with a clean paper towel.

3. Staff is responsible for teaching children appropriate hand washing procedures.
   Assist children in adjusting warm water temperature.

4. The Director will monitor hand washing procedures on a weekly basis.

5. Noses shall be blown or wiped with disposable, single-use tissues. After use,

tissues are to be disposed of in lined, covered trash can. *Children are to be encouraged to be independent in this process. Hands must be washed afterward. Tissues are on the shelf by backdoor for use during outdoor play. After use they must be placed in the trash can on the playground that is lined and covered.*

6. Any oozing cuts or sores on children or staff must be covered.

7. A solution of ¼ cup household bleach dilutes in 1 gallon of water made fresh every 24 hours will be used to clean any surfaces contaminated by bodily fluids.

8. A child who manifests symptoms of illness will be separated from the group and taken to the Director's Office. An adult will remain with this child until a parent comes to take the child home. The cot used for this child will be cleaned and sanitized after use (using the bleach solution).

9. Gloves will be worn when treating an open sore or when cleaning areas soiled with body fluids. Gloves will be discarded after single use (in covered trash can).

10. Blood-containing clothing or other material shall be wrapped or disposed of in plastic bag with a secure tie.

Policies Regarding Safety Procedures
Healthy children require a safe physical environment in, which to eat, sleep, and play.
1. Check rooms and outdoor play area for hazards before children arrive and/or play in the area daily.
2. Damaged equipment or broken toys must be removed from the classroom and reported to the Director.
3. Keep objects smaller than one and one quarter inches in diameter away from young children who are likely to mouth objects. Avoid toys, stuffed animals, and dolls with parts that could break off or be pulled off by little hands.
4. Watch children at all times.
5. Always attend a child on a diaper changing table. Strap children in high chairs, swings, and bouncy seats.
6. Walk around and keep ears and eyes alert to monitor children when playing outside.
7. Only custodial parents and designated adults listed on the *Release Form* can pick up a child at the center. If a caregiver is unfamiliar with a designated adult, a photo ill must be checked before the child can be released. Parents and designated adults must sign the child in and out on the *Daily Sign In & Out Sheet*.
8. All cleaning materials and supplies shall be stored in original containers and kept in locked cabinet.
9. Electrical outlets shall be covered.
10. Smoking is not permitted on premises.
11. Any pesticides, including fire ant treatment, shall be applied when children are not on the premises.
12. Open containers such as mop bucket shall not be left unattended.
13. One staff member must be supervising the playground any time it is in use. The staff member will be charged to take periodic head counts of the children. The staff member also must take 2nd phone handset outside with them to intercom with other staff personal inside the building.
14. Only regular staff members only may release children.
15. Outdoor equipment will be formally monitored on a monthly basis by Director. Any staff member identifying broken, splintered, or otherwise hazardous equipment must notify Director immediately. Children will be permitted to use equipment only after repair has been verified by Director.
16. All backpacks and purses must be stored away in locked cabinet in the cubby room.
17.   Before any soap, wet wipes, lotion, toothpaste, etc. or any commercially purchased materials are set out you must read label to determine if it is hazardous, toxic, or not to be left in the reach of children.

18. Verify the parents have signed an Authorization to Dispense External Preparations form before application of lotions, ointments, insect repellant, sunscreen, wipes, or diaper ointment.

Hygiene
1. Follow diapering procedures.
2. Watch for any signs of sick children and report to the Director.
3. Noses shall be blown or wiped with disposable, single-use tissues. After use, tissues are to be disposed of in lined, covered trash can. *Children are to be encouraged to be independent in this process. Hands must be washed afterward. Tissues are on the shelf by backdoor for use during outdoor play. After use they must be placed in the trash can on the playground that is lined and covered.* Wash hands between wiping noses. Wipe noses frequently.
4. Dispose of all Kleenex in trash containers.
5. A solution of ¼ cup household bleach dilutes in 1 gallon of water made fresh
   every 24 hours will be used to clean any surfaces contaminated by bodily fluids.
6. Clean and disinfect toys touched by infants, toddlers, and 2-year-olds daily.
7. Clean toys touched by 3 & 4-year-olds weekly or when soiled daily.
8. Avoid soft, non-washable toys in the infant/toddler rooms. Place toys that can be washed in the Germ bucker or washer hamper for your classroom.

Health
1. Conduct a daily evaluation on each child for any indication of illness, injury or abuse and record on *My Daily Health Check Form.* Submit forms to the director at the end of each week. Forms will be filed on each child in the Director's office for one year.
2. Report any case or suspected case of a communicable disease to the Director.
3. A child will be sent home if:
a. the child does not feel well enough to participate comfortably in the usual activities of the center
b. the caregiver cannot care for the sick child without interfering with the care of the other children
c. keeping the child in the center poses an increased risk to other children or staff in the center, as determined by the Director or, if necessary, a local health official
d. the child has a fever of 100° or higher within the previous 24-hour period
4. A parent or designated adult shall be notified immediately if a child becomes ill, has an accident or exhibits unusual behavior while at the center. Notification shall be documented on the *Parent Contact Log* in the child's folder.
5. A staff member will supervise the child in the sick room, or another area of the center separate from other children, until the parent arrives to pick up the child.

Medication
Written consent is required for ANY medication. All prescriptions must be in original containers labeled with the child's name. Children should be observed closely once medication is given, to see if any noticeable adverse reactions are happening. Should any adverse reactions be noticed, parents will be notified immediately by the Director (phone call) to pick up their child. All non-prescription medications must be in the original containers bearing the original label, child's name and age, expiration date and directions for dosages. Parents should drop off and pick up any medication with the director or staff present in the office. The medication will be given according to the times on the prescription. [School name] will not administer medication to a child longer than two weeks, unless there is written authorization from your physician.

At least fifty percent (50%) of the caregiver staff and the director shall have current evidence of training in first aid and cardiopulmonary resuscitation (CPR). There must always be an employee with evidence of current First Aid training and CPR on the center premises whenever children are present, on any center-sponsored field trip, and on any center vehicle transporting children.

Universal Blood Precautions

Universal blood precautions must be observed as follows:

1. Disposable latex gloves must be immediately available and worn whenever there is a possibility for contact with blood, including but not limited to:

a. changing diapers where there is blood in the stool

b. touching blood-contaminated body fluids

c. treating cuts that bleed

d. wiping surfaces stained with blood

e. any other situations where there is: potential or actual contact with blood

2. Disposable gloves must be discarded after each use.

3. If blood is touched accidentally, the exposed skin must be thoroughly cleansed with soap and running water.

4. Surfaces that have been blood stained must be wiped with Bleach solution.

5. In an emergency, a child's well-being must take priority. A bleeding child must not be denied care because gloves are not immediately available.

6. Any oozing cuts or sores on children or staff must be covered.

7. Blood-containing clothing or other material shall be wrapped or disposed of in plastic bag with a secure tie.

8. A face mask and/or eyewear should be worn when available.

Illness

A child who manifests symptoms of illness will be separated from the group and taken to the Director's Office. The Director or other administrative staff member will call the parents immediately. An adult will remain with this child until a parent comes to take the child home. The cot used for this child will be cleaned and sanitized after use (using the bleach solution). All illnesses, accidents, unusual behavior, etc. must be logged.

Please review the procedures below or the communicable disease chart for further information:

Illness/Infection Symptom	Should child/staff stay home?	When can child/staff return to center?
Chicken Pox	Yes	When all the blisters/pox have scabbed over
Cold	No (without fever) Yes (with fever)	Refer to fever
Coxsackie (hand, mouth and foot disease)	No	
Diarrhea (two or more stools or over and above what is normal for child	Yes	Diarrhea is resolved
Ear Infection	NO (with doctors diagnosis)	
Fever of unknown origin (100 degrees) and some behavioral signs of illness	YES	Free of fever for 24 hours and reducing medications have not been given in the past 8 hours or on prescribed medication for 24 hours.
Fifth Disease	No (without fever) Yes (with fever)	Refer to fever
Giardia	Yes	When diarrhea subsides or Doctor approves readmission

Hib Disease		Well and proof of non-carriage or cleared by physician
Hepatitis A		One week after illness started and fever is resolved
AIDS (or HIV infection)		Until child's health, neurological development, behavior, and immune status is deemed appropriate (on a case by case basis)by qualified persons, including the child's physician chosen by the child's parent or guardian and the Director.
Impetigo	Yes	When treatment has begun
Lice	Yes	When 1 treatment has been given
Meningococcal disease		Well and proof of non-carriage (Neisseria Meningitis)
Pink Eye	Yes	24 hours after treatment has begun
Undiagnosed generalized rash		Well or cleared by child's physician as non- contagious
Ring Worm	No (keep area covered)	
Roseola	Yes (with fever)	See fever
Rota virus	Yes	24 hours after treatment has begun and fever free
Severe Cold (with fever, sneezing, and nose drainage)	Yes	Refer to fever
Thrush	No (should seek treatment)	
Any child with a sudden onset of vomiting, irritability or excessive sleepiness	Yes	Evaluated and cleared by physician

Rest Time
During rest time:
1. Each child is assigned a cot or crib.
2. Teachers rest infants on demand.
3. To reduce the risk of Sudden Infant Death Syndrome (SIDS), always place infants on their back to sleep. Do not place blankets, stuffed toys or pillows in the crib with the infant. If a child is swaddled or placed on a boppy pillow there must be a doctor's orders to do so.
4. Space cots at least 36 inches apart when in use with a head/toe arrangement so that no two children's heads are adjacent.
5. Place cribs 36 inches apart.
6. Sit with children who are resting and/or sleeping on their cots. Adult presence may be important to their comfort. Gently massaging their backs may also help.
7. Staff ratio is maintained at nap time.
8. Record time child rested on Daily Activity Report.
9. Diapers are checked before and after naps.
10. Wash infant's bedding daily or label with the child's name and launder weekly or as soiled.
11. During rest, write charts and family notes, empty trash, check for children's belongings, disinfect and/or dust cubbies, shelves, toys, etc., prepare materials for afternoon activities but remember as you perform these tasks you must maintain visual contact with all areas of the classroom.

Feeding

Staff will:

1. Hold infants in arms while feeding.
2. Cover food label with child's name if a child is sleeping during lunch, and keep in a refrigerator.
3. Be prepared for some fussiness at lunchtime since it occurs right before rest time. Some children may need to sleep now and eat later.
4. Give children spoons and encourage them to use the utensil. Be patient.
5. Children's food and bottles do not need to be hot –warm is best.
6. Provide milk at lunchtime for those children who are able to have it.
7. Sit at the table and eat the meal or snack with the children. This is a great time for talking and relaxing. Talk with the children about the concepts of color, quantity, number, temperature, texture and taste of the food. Talk about acceptable eating behaviors and the events of the day.
8. Encourage, but do not force children to eat any food.
9. Monitor children closely to be sure that food is not being shared.
10. Provide younger children cups with a lid, but work towards drinking without the lid by putting smaller amounts of liquid so that spilling is not a problem.
11. Not allow children to eat when walking, running, playing, lying down, or riding in vehicles.
12. Not allow children to bring food from home to be eaten at the center unless on special diet. A doctor's statement may be required.

Bottle and Breast Feeding

Staff will:

1. Feed infants on demand unless the parent provides written instructions otherwise.
2. Follow current feeding instructions provided to the center by the parent. These instructions, from the parent or physician, shall be kept on file and posted in the infant room.
3. Infants shall either be held or be fed sitting up for bottle-feeding. Infants unable to sit shall always be held for bottle-feeding. We do not prop bottles or allow children to carry bottles around with them.
4. We do not place an infant/toddler who can hold a bottle in a crib with the bottle.
5. Warm bottles for feeding with a bottle warmer or under warm running water. Staff check temperature of milk on your wrist.
6. Bottles of breast milk and formula that are left at the center over night are dated.
7. All bottles shall have caps and shall be labeled with the child's name and date formula is prepared and used only for the intended child. All pacifiers should be labeled also.
8. See that all filled bottles of breast milk or iron fortified formula shall be refrigerated until immediately before feeding. Any contents remaining after a feeding (1 hour) shall be discarded.
9. Keep expressed breast milk can be kept in the refrigerator for 48 hours and in the freezer for 2 weeks. Frozen breast milk shall be thawed under running cold water or in the refrigerator.

Foods to Avoid

Food that are round, hard, small, thick and sticky, smooth, or slippery shall not be offered to children less than 4 years of age. Examples of such foods include hot dogs (sliced into rounds), whole grapes, hard candy, nuts, seeds, raw peas, dried fruit, pretzels, chips, peanuts, popcorn, marshmallows, spoonfuls of peanut butter, and chunks of meat larger than can be swallowed whole.

Food from Home

Georgia Department of Early Care and Learning: Bright from the Start and the United States Department of Agriculture Child and Adult Care Food program do not allow any homemade or fast food products to be brought into the center at any time. Sack lunches must meet the USDA guidelines for food service (meal patterns, portion sizes, etc.). Exceptions are granted for special occasions such as birthdays and holidays, with prior approval from the director in the preschool building. When foods are brought to the facility from home or elsewhere, these foods shall, to the extent reasonable, be limited to whole fruits (like apples, oranges, or pears) and commercially packaged foods.

Meal Guidelines – Ages 1-12 *Updated 8/03/05* Source: Child and Adult Care Food Program, USDA Food and Nutrition Service See infant menu patters at: www.usda.gov

BREAKFAST

Food Components	Ages 1-2	Ages 3-5	Ages 6-12[1]
1 milk fluid milk	1/2 cup	3/4 cup	1 cup
1 fruit/vegetable juice,2 fruit and/or vegetable **1 grains/bread3** bread or	1/4 cup 1/2 slice	1/2 cup 1/2 slice	1/2 cup 1 slice
cornbread or biscuit or roll or muffin or	1/2 serving	1/2 serving	1 serving
cold dry cereal or	1/4 cup	1/3 cup	3/4 cup
hot cooked cereal or	1/4 cup	1/4 cup	1/2 cup
pasta or noodles or grains	1/4 cup	1/4 cup	1/2 cup

LUNCH OR SUPPER

Food Components	Ages 1-2	Ages 3-5	Ages 6-12
1 milk fluid milk	1/2 cup	3/4 cup	1 cup
2 fruits/vegetables juice,2 fruit and/or vegetable **1 grains/bread3** bread or	1/4 cup 1/2 slice	1/2 cup 1/2 slice	3/4 cup 1 slice
cornbread or biscuit or roll or muffin or	1/2 serving	1/2 serving	1 serving
cold dry cereal or	1/4 cup	1/3 cup	3/4 cup
hot cooked cereal or	1/4 cup	1/4 cup	1/2 cup
pasta or noodles or grains	1/4 cup	1/4 cup	1/2 cup
1 meat/meat alternate meat or poultry or fish4 or	1 oz.	1½oz.	2 oz.
alternate protein product or	1 oz.	1½ oz.	2 oz.
cheese or	1 oz.	1½ oz.	2 oz.
egg7 or	½	¾	1
cooked dry beans or peas or	1/4 cup	3/8 cup	1/2 cup
peanut or other nut or seed butters or nuts and/or seeds5 or yogurt6	2 Tbsp. 1/2 oz. 4 oz.	3 Tbsp. 3/4 oz. 6 oz.	4 Tbsp. 1 oz. 8 oz.

SNACK: *Choose 2 of the 4 components*

Food Components	Ages 1-2	Ages 3-5	Ages 6-12
1 milk fluid milk	1/2 cup	1/2 cup	1 cup
1 fruits/vegetables juice,2 fruit and/or vegetable **1 grains/bread3**	1/2 cup	1/2 cup	3/4 cup
bread or	1/2 slice	1/2 slice	1 slice
cornbread or biscuit or roll or muffin or	1/2 serving	1/2 serving	1 serving
cold dry cereal or	1/4 cup	1/3 cup	3/4 cup
hot cooked cereal or	1/4 cup	1/4 cup	1/2 cup
pasta or noodles or grains	1/4 cup	1/4 cup	1/2 cup
1 meat/meat alternate meat or poultry or fish4 or	1/2 oz.	1/2 oz.	1 oz.
alternate protein product or	1/2 oz.	1/2 oz.	1 oz.
cheese or egg7 or	1/2 oz. ½	1/2 oz. ½	1 oz. ½
cooked dry beans or peas or	1/8 cup	1/8 cup	1/4 cup

peanut or other nut or seed butters or nuts and/or seeds5 or yogurt6	1 Tbsp. 1/2 oz. 2 oz.	1 Tbsp. 1/2 oz. 2 oz.	2 Tbsp. 1 oz. 4 oz.

Guidance

The purpose of guidance in our center is to help children learn acceptable behavior and develop inner controls. When redirecting or guiding a child's behavior, the age, intellectual development, emotional make-up and past experiences will be considered, and consistency will be maintained in setting limits for each child.

Corporal punishment is prohibited in the center. No child shall be subject to verbal abuse, threats, cruel, severe and/or unusual punishment. Derogatory remarks shall not be made in the presence of children about family members or about the children themselves. No child or group of children shall be allowed to discipline another child. No child shall be deprived of meals or any parts of meals for disciplinary reasons.

The following is a list of alternate forms of positive guidance that will be used in the Center:

1. Tell the child what they CAN do.
2. Establish eye contact when speaking with the child.
3. Give choices whenever possible, but only when the child really has a choice.
4. Encourage children to solve their own problems, and work out conflicts whenever possible.
5. Redirect the child to another activity.
6. Hold a child until they gain control of themselves.
7. Remove a child from the situation.

Action steps for all [YOUR SCHOOL'S NAME] Child Development Center staff to use in guiding behavior to a desirable level of self control.

Step 1 – Give verbal reminder by asking student what type of behavior they should be exhibiting.

- *Example: What type of voice do we use inside? Child replies "Good, we need to remember to use our inside/indoor/ voice."*

Step 2 – Give verbal warning and state that they will be redirected to another area to work if desired behavior is not exhibited.

- *Example: "Sophia, Mr. Penn asked you to lower your voice and use an inside voice – are you doing that?" Child replies. "Sophia, I am giving you a **"warning"** if you choose to continue to use your outside voice in the building you will have to clean up this center and move to ___ (name a center, you may want to choose a quiet center or one that is not being used.)"*

Step 3 - If Sophia continues to talk in a loud outside voice redirect her to another area.

- *Example: "Sophia, Mr. Penn asked you with my words to use an inside voice. Did you do that?" Child replies. "What did Mr. Penn say would happen when he gave you a warning?" Child Replies. "I need for you to clean up this area and move to the (name another center). If you continue to use an outside voice you will have to come and sit with me and discuss how we can correct this behavior."*

Step 4 – If Sophia moves to another center and continues to talk in an outside voice then she will need to come and talk about the behavior and motive with the caregiver.

- *Example: "Sophia, Mr. Penn asked you to use an inside voice, I have given you a warning and moved you to another area. What did Mr. Penn say we would have to do if you continue to talk with an outside voice?" Child replies. "I need for you to clean up and come sit with me at the round table." Seated at the table ask," Sophia, why did you have to come and sit with me at the table?" I want you to think about what you need to do so that you can use your inside voice. Wait a minute or two. "Sophia, what do you need to do?" Child replies. "Tell me how you will do that." Wait a minute or two. "Sophia, do you think you can work in centers without using your outside voice?" Child replies. "Show me that you can use your inside voice. You may return to work."*

Limits of Behavior
Limits of behavior for the children in your care:
1. You may not hurt others.
2. You may not hurt yourself.
3. You may not damage equipment.

Biting

If a bite occurs, remove the child who was the biter. Provide first aid for the child that was bitten. Wash the bite wound with soap and water and cover with a bandage if necessary. When you are finished administering first aid, check the child's immunization records to see if the child that bit or was bitten has an up to date tetanus shot. Neither AIDS nor hepatitis A testing of the biter or bite victim is recommended. Ordinary mouth germs can cause local bacterial infection from bites, but viral infections rarely result. The incident will be documented and parents of both children will be notified by the Director or teacher. Remember to comfort both the biter and the bitten student. Fact sheet should be provided for all parents at orientation and again in the event an incident occurs.

Outdoor Play

Weather permitting, all children, including infants, will spend from one to two hours per day in daily outdoor play. It is necessary that children have freedom of movement, so it is requested that children are dressed accordingly. Closed toe shoes and socks are required. As we encourage children to explore, there may be times when he/she may become messy or rumpled. For this reason, we request that parents send one complete change of clothing to remain at the center. Parents are to be sure to label all articles of belongings.

Children will be outside unless weather conditions prohibit safe play or walking. Accommodations cannot be made for children to remain indoors if they are feeling "under the weather." A child too sick to be outside, is probably too sick to be around other children. Children with asthma or airborne allergies may be assigned to another class for poor air quality days.

Water Activities

Water Activities are defined as a water-related activity in which children, under adult supervision, are in, on, near, or immersed in a body of water such as swimming pools, wading pools, water parks, lakes, rivers or beaches, etc. Wading pools with a depth of less than 2 feet shall not require staff to have Water Safety training. The [YOUR SCHOOL'S NAME] Child Development Center does not participate in the above listed activities.

Water activities used at the [YOUR SCHOOL'S NAME] Child Development Center include the use of water tables, sprinklers, and water spraying devices.

Off-Site Activities

Occasionally we will take official field trips approved by parents. Each family will be notified about the trip, the price (if any), and how the child will be transported. Each child will be required to have a signed permission slip. Walking field trips may be taken on campus, the family will be asked to sign a blanket permission slip during the enrollment process to cover campus based walking field trips.

Off site activities will include at least one staff member in attendance and accessible to children at all times who has documented current certification in infant/child/adult CPR and pediatric first aid. In addition to the adult/child ratio regularly employed by the center, an additional adult shall be added for off-site activities.

Children shall be under the direct supervision of staff at all times, during the off site activity.

Transportation

The [YOUR SCHOOL'S NAME] Child Development Center does not transport children from home to center, center to home, or from school to center. Occasionally we will take official field trips approved by parents. Each family will be notified about the trip, the price (if any), and how the child will be transported. Each child participating in the trip will have to have e a signed permission from parent. Permission may not be given over the telephone to participate in a field trip.

Transportation will be provided for field trips or vehicles owned by staff and parents will be used. The following rules regarding transportation vehicles must be adhered to:

1. All drivers and vehicles shall be covered by liability insurance.
2. The driver shall hold a valid appropriate driver's license.
3. The vehicle shall have evidence of a current safety inspection.
4. There shall be first aid supplies and a fire extinguisher in the vehicle.
5. There shall be information in each vehicle identifying the name of the Director and the name, telephone number and address of the center for emergency situations.
6. Transportation arrangements must conform to state laws, including seat belts and child safety restraints.
7. At least two staff, one of whom may be the driver, shall be in each vehicle unless the vehicle has a communication device and child/staff ratio is met in the vehicle.
8. Staff members should take the class roster, BFTS transportation forms, special care plans, authorization forms, and other necessary maps.
9. Children must be under the direct supervision of staff at all times. Staff shall not leave the children unattended in the vehicle at any time while transporting children.
10. Each child shall board or leave the vehicle from the curbside of the street and/or shall be safely escorted across the street.
11. Good order shall be maintained on the vehicle.
12. The staff shall check the vehicle at the completion of each trip to ensure that no child is left on the vehicle and document their boarding and exiting.
13. The vehicle shall be maintained in good repair.
14. The use of tobacco in any form, use of alcohol and possession of illegal substances or unauthorized potentially toxic substances, firearms, pellet or BB guns (loaded or unloaded) in any vehicle while transporting children is prohibited.
15. Children shall not be transported in the back of a pickup truck.

Documentation shall consist of a checklist that all transportation rules were followed along with a copy of the driver's license, and proof of insurance, signed and dated by the driver and /or staff member in vehicle and the Director.

Departure Time/Third Party Release Procedure

Parents should escort children into and from the center each day. Children can only be released to those people listed on the consent form. If an adult you do not recognize or someone other than those on the list comes to pick up a child, ask for state issued photo identification and get the director. **If parents ask assistants or other staff a question concerning their child, please refer the parents to the director/lead teacher**. The teacher has been with the child the whole day while you have only been with the child for a short period of time.

Only those persons listed on the Emergency Information Sheet as "Persons authorized to pick up child at any time" can pick a child up from the center. If anyone other than those authorized on the Emergency Information Sheet is to pick up a child, written permission must be given to the center by the registering parent/guardian. In an extenuating circumstance, when an authorized person cannot pick up the child, another individual may pick up a child from child care if that person is authorized to do so by the parent/guardian in authenticated communication, such as a witnessed phone conversation in which the caller provides written consent (fax) from the parent/legal guardian with pre-specified identifying information, and confirmed by a return call to the parent/legal guardian before release of the child.

In case of an emergency, persons listed in the "To be called in an emergency' list can pick up a child if the center cannot reach the parent/guardian and the center calls these persons to pick up a child. In a non-emergency situation, persons on the "To be called in an emergency" list cannot pick up a child without written permission from the parent guardian.

Every child enrolled in the center must have an Emergency Information Sheet on file. It is the responsibility of the family to inform the center of any changes on this form.

The center will not release a child at <u>any time </u>to a designated individual who is visibly impaired due to alcohol consumption or substance abuse (either prescribed or illegal). In the event that a parent or designated individual is impaired, the center's administrative staff will telephone individuals from the third party release form to arrange for an alternative adult to pick up the child. If a parent or designated individual is impaired and insists that their child be released in his or her custody, the center's administrative staff will immediately telephone the appropriate law-enforcement officials. A judge's order must be on file for custody issues. Contact law enforcement whenever there is a dispute in such instances.

Emergency Procedures
Emergency Procedures: These procedures are posted in each classroom and reviewed during orientation. Emergency phone numbers are posted next to every telephone.

In the event a child becomes ill: *This policy applies for children with a temperature of 100 degrees or higher or another contagious symptom.*
1)The sick child will be brought to the office. The Director, teacher, or administrative staff will call the parents to pick up the child. After the child has been moved to a separate area, the child must be supervised until his/her parents arrive for him.

2)The Director will determine after reviewing the child's condition and a physician's statement, whether or not he/she can be readmitted to class based upon State Board of Health standards regarding common childhood illnesses. She will notify the parents by telephone of injuries or illnesses immediately.

In case of a serious injury to a child: *A serious injury shall include but is not limited to bleeding, broken bones, fractures, head injuries, bites, and objects in the ear, eye, nose, or absence of breathing.*
1)The office staff will call EMS or contact poison control. The teacher will administer first aid.
2)Determine the seriousness of the injury by information gathered from the victim, his/her appearance and responses. Your child will be transported by EMS to [name, address, telephone, of nearest hospital]
3)Remove all other children and adults with the exception of two persons certified to perform CPR or First Aid.
4)Perform First Aid or CPR until emergency paramedics arrive.
5)The Director will notify the parents/guardians or emergency contact by telephone.
6)Complete an incident report form (describe in detail the activity in which the child was engaged) and submit to the Director and parents (for signature) within 2 hours.
7)The Director will follow up on the report & notify Bright from the Start within 24 hours by fax.

In the event of a minor injury: *Minor injuries include minor cuts, burns, scrapes and bruises.*
1) Remove the child to a separate area and alert the office staff,
2) Treat the wound by washing with clear water as needed. Follow basic first aid instructions.

Complete an accident report (obtain parent signature) and submit it to the Director within 2 hours. The teacher shall contact the parents immediately. Please do not permit children to administer first aid. Staff members will wear gloves.

Severe Weather (Tornado and Hurricane) Drills
Severe weather drills will be practiced in December and June at various times of the day. No alarm will sound in the school. The command "TAKE COVER" will be issued verbally. As soon as the command is sounded you must take immediate action. These actions may save your life and the children's life.
Procedures:
1. Children and staff are to move to the hall in an orderly fashion.
2. Children with all adults will sit down on knees and cover heads.
3. EVERYONE will stay down and covered until the all clear is given.
4. Head teacher or student teacher is to hold the roll book while in the
   covered position.
5. REMINDER: stay away from windows, outside walls and all doors.

In case of severe weather:
1) Seek inside shelter. Stay away from windows! If you're caught outside in case of a tornado, travel at right angles to path of funnel, or lie flat in ditch and protect your head.
2) If inside, take your students to the large hallway and be seated along the wall.
3) The office personnel will shut off electricity and fuel lines.
4) The telephone will only be used in cases of an emergency.
5) The following basic supplies will be stored: water, non-perishable food, first aid kid, battery powered radio, & flashlights.
6) The Director will notify the parents by telephone to pick up their children when safe.

In case of loss of electrical power (heating or cooling):
1) The Director will contact [name of power company] after switching the breaker switch in the electrical room to determine length of lack of service.
2) The Director shall notify parents by telephone (to pick up children) if the center/school will be without power for more than one hour.
3) In the event of failure of the emergency lighting equipment, evacuate the building.

In case of fire or structural damage-Emergency Evacuation Procedures:
Teachers are to stop activities immediately.
Line students up and follow practiced exit route if possible. Infants should be placed in an evacuation crib.
Count each student and take attendance as you leave the building.
Take your **attendance record** and **medical permission form** file. Teachers will test the doors for danger before opening to exit. Feel the door and the knob for heat, with the back of your hand. If the doorknob is hot, look for an alternate exit.
Exit building and go to the designated meeting place beneath the sign out front.
Check your attendance records. Notify the Program Director if all children are not present or if someone is missing.
The Director retrieves attendance records, visitor records, emergency records/cards from office and cellular phone. Calls 911
The Director checks each room and closet or bathroom in the building for students; Closes each door and window; Upon arrival of fire department notify them of attendance and/or unaccounted staff or students; Approves re-entry of the building after giving approval by the firemen.
If unable to re-enter the Director and administrative staff will notify parents of need to pick up students.

Parents or authorized pick up persons will be allowed to retrieve their children from the designated Lead teacher or other staff member. Do not leave children unattended for any reason, nor send a child back into the building. If danger is eminent, students may be taken to [List Secondary evacuation location less than 3 miles away]

In the event of a bomb threat:
Make note of caller's comments on the report form, recording conversation if possible.
the Director or Administrative Assistant will dial *69 to obtain caller's number, then dial 911 and report the call.
Notify teachers and staff.
Team members will follow emergency evacuation plan above.

In case of gas outage/leak:
Notify office personnel. The Director will shut off gas at switch outside and contact the Gas Company. Students will be evacuated as above. Parents will be advised to pick up the children (by telephone) if service is not restored within the hour.

In case of loss of Water:
Notify office personnel. The Director will contact the water company.
Parents will be notified to pick up students if service is not restored within an hour.

In case of loss of child:
1) Notify the Director, security and any other accompanying staff members. Search for 5-10 minutes depending upon location. Notify parent or guardian, and call 911.
2) The Director will also notify BFTS, by faxing an incident form to the consultant.

In case of the death of a child:
When a child is presumed to have expired from natural or accidental causes, take the following steps;
1) Notify the Director or office personnel.
2) Remove all other children to a separate area.
3) Contact emergency medical assistance (call 911) in order to verify the presence or absence of vital life signs.
4) The Director or office personnel will notify the parents & the police immediately, and notify BFTS within 24 hours.

Emergency Telephone Numbers
        Georgia Poison Control Center   1-800-282-5846
        Utilities   1-XXX-XXX-XXXX
        County EMS/Fire/Police   911

Address: [address]
Nearest Crossroads: [name streets in intersection]

First Aid Kits will be replenished after use and checked monthly for expiration dates. The following first aid supplies, along with a manual of instructions, shall be maintained in a central location inaccessible to the children: scissors, tweezers, gauze pads, thermometer, adhesive tape, syrup of ipecac (to be used upon the advice of a physician or poison control center), band-aids, insect-sting preparation, antiseptic cleaning solution, antibacterial ointment, bandages, disposable rubber gloves, and cold pack. Syrup of Ipecac will only be administered under the direction of the child's pediatrician or the poison control center.

Closings

In the event of structural damage, flooding, snow, ice or other unusual weather please listen for announcements from the media about school closings. The director will telephone parents immediately and BFTS within 24 hours.

Assignment of employees
Staff with diaper changing responsibilities shall not be simultaneously assigned to kitchen food preparation duties.

Substitute Employees
The center shall provide for substitute staff when regular staff is absent from work. All substitute employees shall be at least eighteen (18) years of age. Substitute caregiver staff shall be informed of these rules and the center's policies for the age group for which they will be providing care. Substitute service staff shall be informed of the center's policies and procedures necessary to the proper performance of their job duties in compliance with these rules.

General Job Description
1. Keep all toys out and at children's level at ALL TIMES -Children learn through play, and playing children are happier.
2. Transition times between activities are difficult *for* children and staff, so be creative and be prepared for the next activity before you tell the children. They want things to happen instantly and waiting is very difficult. Always tell children when you are going to diaper them or change activities, they want to know.
3. While awake, infants and toddlers **shall not remain** in a crib, swing, highchair, carrier, playpen, etc. for more than 15 consecutive minutes.
4. Have children diapered, cleaned up, and all their belongings ready before families arrive. This helps to make families, children, and teachers have a happy closing to the day.
5. Limit the use of words such as stop, no, and don't.

You have been selected for your position because of special qualities, talents, or skills, which are needed to make up a well-balanced administrative, teaching, and support staff of our center. Each member is part of the total staff, and all are dependent upon one another. Relationships are circular and what affects one affects all. Although specific responsibilities may vary according to you primary job description and your list of individual responsibilities, all staff persons are charged with the total responsibility of working together in a united manner. The goal is to achieve harmony and mutuality throughout the center with respect, tolerance, patience, honesty, trust, and friendship.

We want you to be proud of your role in this center. You are hereby charged with the responsibility of seeing that the reputation of our center is maintained as a caring and outstanding educational environment for children and their families.

Personal Qualifications of Each Staff Member
1. *Friendliness* - Maintains a positive attitude towards others, acknowledges the presence of others with a greeting, and is alert to the moods and needs of others.
2. *Honesty* - Is truthful about hours, sick and personal leave, and other school matters. Takes responsibility for own errors, is trustworthy, and respects the property of others.
3. *Voice modulation* – Refrains from use of an abusive, sarcastic, or uncontrolled tone of voice.
4. *Punctuality* – Arrives at work at the agreed-to specified time, and honors the time limits of relief and lunch periods, knowing that others are dependent on one's promptness.
5. *Dependability* – Performs responsibilities as promised. Does not require constant reminders. Utilizes working hours to do actual work for the center, seeking out tasks to be done if necessary, rather than using a lax period to take care of personal obligations.

6. *Integrity* – Cooperates in the maintenance of wholesome interpersonal relationships, free of gossip about one another or about center families. If there are questions about the actions of a particular staff member, talks directly with that person or discusses the matter, in confidence, with the director.

7. *Positive Attitudes* – Refrains from complaining attitudes. Brings complaints to the director or other supervising staff member.

8. *Present ability* – Is poised, well mannered, neatly and appropriately dressed, well groomed, and clean. Follows guidelines of staff handbook.

9. *Patience* – Maintains self-control in dealing with others.

10. *Active and energetic* – Maintains an evident interest in job.

Relationship with Children

1. *Individualization* – Demonstrates respect for the personal differences between individuals in relationship to their needs, interests, development and capabilities.

2. *Knowledge ability* – Plans age-level developmentally appropriate activities.

3. *Resourcefulness* – Demonstrates creativity and resourcefulness in planning programs and in use of materials.

4. *Flexibility* - Is able to work with both individuals and groups of children.

5. *Personal Manner* – Bends to eye level frequently when talking with a child. Is able to help each child build self-esteem and healthy self-concept.

6. Professionalism – Uses appropriate language, and relates behavior to growth and development.

7. *Discipline* – Uses non-punitive methods of discipline, and offers guidance in a positive manner.

8. *Knowledge ability* – Keeps the program operating smoothly with a variety of activities, fostering exploration, investigation, and creativity.

9. *Responsibility* – Assesses each child's growth, development, and performance, recording some observations for each child, taking special note of changes, and maintaining appropriate records as have been requested.

10. *Relaxation* – Utilizes stress-reduction techniques in helping children and adults to an inner awareness and calmness.

11. *Tolerance* – Treats all children equally, with respect and empathy. Avoids prejudicial attitudes.

Relationship with Adults, Including Parents in the center community

1. *Friendliness* – Maintains a friendly, yet at the same time, professional relationship with parents and coworkers.

2. *Respect* – Respects others' rights to their individual points of view and Ideas.

3. *Integrity* – Maintains confidentiality of information.

4. *Tolerance* – Treats all parents equally, not showing favoritism, accepting all at their individual levels. Supports cultural differences in extending the curriculum.

5. *Helpfulness* – Works in a comfortable manner with parent helpers, volunteers, and assistant teachers, offering guidance in positive ways.

6. *Receptiveness* – Is respective to the idea of home visits.

Demonstrates Concern for an Awareness of the Total Center

1. *Safety and Health Consciousness* – Gives primary consideration to the safety and health of the students when planning the environment.

2. *Knowledge ability* – Prepares environments that are appropriate for the particular children involved, both individually and in cooperation with one another. Is able to justify the presentation of a particular environment, material, or activity by explaining its relationship to the educational or personal growth of a child or children.

3. *Orderliness* – Keeps materials, supplies, and equipment well organized to present an attractive, orderly, and inviting appearance to the classroom or any other area being used.

4. *Carefulness* – Respects the use and care of materials and equipment; is not wasteful.

5. *Responsibility* – Assumes personal responsibility for small problems in the environment which others have neglected or have not been aware of (i.e. trash, lack of water, and so forth).

Demonstrates Professionalism

1. *Personal growth* – Is committed to the idea of continued personal and professional growth as an educator. Maintains a professional membership
in a job related organizations (LAECA, SECA, NAEYC, etc.) Pursues personal or formal study and/or formal study and/or reading in the field of child development education.

2. *Loyalty* – Supports the philosophy of the school and the director.

3. *Realism* – Is able to look at self-behavior as a possible cause of the problem when things do not always go smoothly.

4. *Confidentiality* – Avoids malicious gossip at all times; respects confidentiality of both written, oral, and observed information.

5. *Cooperation* – Is committed to the concept of team spirit, recognizing the Center as one total group rather than a series of separate groups. Generously shares ideas, materials, time, and services, thereby helping other persons to achieve their very best.

6. *Responsibility* – Is always ready to share responsibilities with others, to assume others' responsibilities in emergencies, and to put the needs of the center as a whole over petty differences of opinion.

7. *Supportiveness* – Is aware of the school policies and supports them. If not in agreement, knows that policies can be discussed with the Director and at staff meetings, and reserves those times for doing so rather than spreading discontent among coworkers.

Professional Qualifications

Effective December 1, 2012, a copy and/or written verification of the credential or degree awarded to directors and lead teachers (see BFTS qualification requirements) must be on file. Each employee must have a satisfactory criminal background check on file. Can be done locally and must reference GCIC or NCIC. Employees must have current infant/child first aid/CPR certification.

Applicable for all employees

1. All staff members are to complete housekeeping duties including: sweeping, cleaning, and sanitization of toys, mats, changing areas, and food preparation surfaces after every use; by wearing gloves when handling urine, feces, vomit, blood, saliva, or nasal secretions in any form.
2. All children must be supervised at all times
3. Maintain a clean, safe and attractive classroom
4. Repair or remove damaged toys or materials
5. Use only positive guidance techniques
6. Keep your personnel files up to date
7. Limit phone use to breaks or emergencies
8. Remain with your assigned group during work hours
9. Complete all required forms and daily reports
10. Free play is time to interact with the children not sit and chat
11. Remain alert and attentive during naptime
12. Adhere to all licensing regulations
13. Maintain confidentiality, avoid gossip
14. Assist children during rest time by providing a peaceful, tranquil environment with soft music and assist resting children by rubbing their backs.
15. Supervise sleeping children at all times.
16. Assist children in eating lunch, if needed

17. Change diapers or assist children in the bathroom. Assist potty training those children who show an interest.
18. Infant, toddler, and 2 year-old teachers must accurately document diaper changes, rest periods, and food experiences and send home daily.
19. All [YOUR SCHOOL'S NAME] child development center staff must park in areas designated by the Child Development Center.

Organization Chart

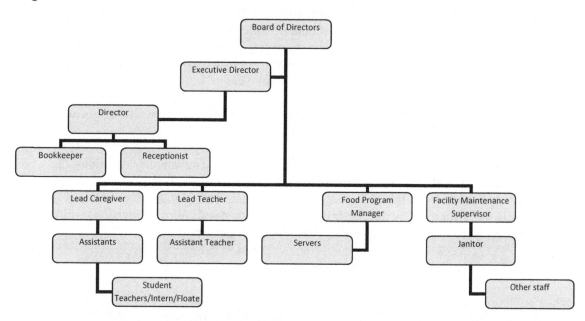

Non-Compete And Non-Solicitation Agreement
During your employment with [YOUR SCHOOL'S NAME] and for a period of ninety (90) days after terminating your employment with [YOUR SCHOOL'S NAME], you may not solicit [YOUR SCHOOL'S NAME]'s customers or staff for any purpose related to child care. For a period of ninety (90) days after termination of your employment with [YOUR SCHOOL'S NAME], you may not provide any type of child care for children that were enrolled at [YOUR SCHOOL'S NAME] during the thirty (30) days prior to your termination of employment. In the event you violate this non-compete, you agree to pay [YOUR SCHOOL'S NAME] the sum of $3,000, the estimated cost of damages to [YOUR SCHOOL'S NAME] for recruiting, hiring, and training a new staff member. I have read, understand, and agree to abide by the Confidentiality, Non-Disclosure, Non-Solicitation and other provisions of [YOUR SCHOOL'S NAME]'s personnel manual.

Date: _____ Signature: _____

Sample Personnel Handbook Policies

NATURE OF EMPLOYMENT
This Manual is only a statement of the general guidelines used by [Your school's name] and it is not intended to create, nor is it construed to constitute a contract between [Your school's name] and anyone or all of its employees.

Employment is at the mutual consent of the employee and the center. Accordingly, the center may terminate the employment relationship at will, i.e., at any time, with or without notice, and for any reason or for no reason at all. Instructional staff members should provide two week's notice of resignation. No supervisor or office manager other than the [Your school's name] Board of Directors/Owners/Director, has any authority to enter into any agreement for employment. Any such agreement must be in writing and signed by [Your school's name] Management and the Employee.

[YOUR SCHOOL'S NAME] realizes that all circumstances cannot be foreseen, therefore, this manual is purposefully flexible and adaptable to unusual circumstances.

To preserve the ability of the [Your school's name] to meet its needs under changing conditions, the center may, in its sole discretion, add, modify, augment, delete, or revoke any or all policies, procedures, practices and statements contained in this manual at any time without prior notice. Such changes shall be effective immediately upon approval by the center unless otherwise stated. Written revisions will be made available to employees at the earliest possible time after any revision.

Job Announcement and Application/Selection Process

It is the center's policy to employ, retain, promote, terminate and otherwise treat all employees and job applicants on the basis of merit, qualifications and competence. This policy shall be applied without regard to any qualified individual's sex, race, color, religion, national origin, ancestry, citizenship, pregnancy, age, marital status medical condition, physical disability, mental disability, gender, sexual orientation, or other characteristic protected by federal, state and/or local laws.

It is our policy to fill by recruitment only those vacancies that cannot be more properly filled within the center. Employees are requested to make their job position desires known in writing to their supervisor for consideration. All employees are encouraged to refer qualifies applicants for employment consideration for all job categories. The center will also utilize various forms of the media, internet and Department of Labor.

Job announcements will include a brief job description, education and experience needed, salary, how to apply and deadlines. Applicants will be asked to pick up the employment application at the center. Upon submission of the application, the selection process will continue with reference and background checks. Potential candidates will be interviewed and further documentation (official transcripts, drug test for drivers, physical examination, etc.) may be required.

Employment Categories and Classifications

The [YOUR SCHOOL'S NAME] provides definitions of employment classifications so that you understand your employment status. These classifications do not guarantee employment for any specified period of time. The employee categories and classifications are:

1. Full-time Permanent Employees are those who are regularly scheduled to work a full time schedule of 35 or more hours per week.
2. Part-time Permanent Employees are those who are regularly scheduled to work 20 – 25 hours per week
3. Intermittent Employees are those hired as interim replacements to temporarily supplement the work force or to assist in the completion of a specific project.
4. Salaried/On-Call Employees are those who work 32-50 hours per week on various shifts, i.e., 10 hour, 7.5 hour, etc

Hours of Work: The center pays wages comparable to those paid by other employers in the area to workers who perform the same or similar work. No wage shall be less than that designated by federal/state laws as the minimum wage. Deviations from the normal work week or normal work day may be required on a regular basis. Adjustment may be made with respect to any employee's schedule by the director so that the total hours worked per week do not exceed forty. Overtime must be approved by the director in advance.

All center employees are expected to adhere to the stated working hours. Frequent unexcused absences shall be grounds for discharge. It is the responsibility of the employee to notify his or her supervisor if he or she will be late or absent. Such notices should be given as early as possible, two hours before starting time except in extenuating circumstances as determined by the director.

Time Off: Staff members must submit written requests for time off 10 days in advance. The Program Director will notify you of approval or denial within three days.

Job descriptions:
Preschool and School Age Teacher

PURPOSE OF THE POSITION
The Preschool teacher is responsible for providing a safe and developmentally appropriate preschool program in accordance with all relevant legislation, policies and procedures.

SCOPE
The Preschool Teacher will be responsible for planning and implementing a program to teach young children. They must ensure the development and safety of these children in accordance with relevant federal and state policies. The Preschool Teacher will be respectful of children and parents, and ensure that equipment and facilities are clean, safe
and well maintained. Failure to provide adequate services may place children at risk.

RESPONSIBILITIES
1. Develop and implement a developmentally appropriate preschool program for young children
Main Activities
- Plan and implement activities to meet the physical, emotional, intellectual and social
- needs of the children in the program
- Provide nutritious snacks and lunches
- Provide adequate equipment and activities
- Ensure equipment and the facility are clean, well maintained and safe at all times
- Provide weekly and monthly schedules of activities
- Develop culturally appropriate programs and activities
- Develop activities that introduce math and literacy concepts
- Follow policies and procedures including acceptable disciplinary policies

- Be familiar with emergency procedures

2. Supervise children in the Center
Main Activities
- Ensure children are supervised at all times
- Provide various experiences and activities for children including songs, games and
- story telling
- Build children's esteem
- Comfort children
- Establish routines and provide positive guidance
- Provide a safe and secure environment for children to feel comfortable
- Implement positive guidance/discipline techniques when required
- Clearly and effectively communicate in a manner that children understand
- Observe children and make note of progress
- Integrate special needs children in a positive and respectful manner

3. Communicate with parents and members of the community
Main Activities
- Discuss children's development with parents
- Discuss identified problems and needs with professionals as appropriate
- Participate in community activities
- Promote literacy and early education

4. Maintain program administration
Main Activities
- Keep parents informed of program expectations, program activities and their child's progress
- Develop and maintain current, accurate and confidential client files
- Develop daily activity plans
- Monitor the program budget
- Perform other related duties as required

KNOWLEDGE, SKILLS AND ABILITIES
Knowledge
The incumbent must have proficient knowledge in the following areas:
- child development and early education theories and practices
- safe and appropriate activities for children
- relevant legislation, policies and procedures to ensure that children are supervised and safe at all times
- an understanding of the cultural environment

Skills
The incumbent must demonstrate the following skills:
- team building skills
- supervisory skills
- analytical and problem solving skills
- decision making skills
- effective verbal and listening
- communications skills
- stress management skills

- time management skills
- teaching skills

Personal Attributes
The incumbent must maintain strict confidentiality in performing the duties of a teacher.
The incumbent must also demonstrate the following personal attributes:
- be respectful
- possess cultural awareness and sensitivity
- be flexible
- demonstrate sound work ethics
- be consistent and fair
- be compassionate and understanding
- be able to build esteem while ensuring a safe and secure environment

Professional Qualifications
First Aid/CPR Training
Satisfactory Criminal Records Check
1 year experience minimum working with children
Must be 18 years of age
High School Diploma or GED

The incumbent would normally attain the knowledge, skills and attitudes required for the
position through completion of a post-secondary Early Education Program combined with related day
care and/or preschool teaching experience. Equivalencies (i.e. the Child Development Associates
Credential, Technical College Diplomas, experience, etc.) will be considered.

WORKING CONDITIONS
Physical Demands
Caring for children can be physically demanding. The Preschool Teacher may be lifting and carrying
children and equipment (up to 50 lbs. or more), and must spend time sitting on the floor or child sized
furniture.
The Preschool Teacher will be expected to clean and maintain equipment and facility, and may move
throughout the community with children The Preschool Teacher may come in contact with children who
are ill and/or contagious, and must take precautions to ensure the health and safety of all children, parents,
staff and themselves.
Environmental Conditions
The Preschool Teacher will be working in a busy and occasionally noisy environment. There may be a
number of activities and situations happening at once, and the Preschool Teacher will have to supervise
all children at all times.
Sensory Demands
The Preschool Teacher may experience smells associated with toileting, cleaning products and children
who are ill.
There may be times that the environment is noisy and busy.
Mental Demands
Caring for children can be stressful. The Preschool Teacher must ensure that children are
supervised at all times, and that children are involved in safe and appropriate activities. There may be a
number of situations happening at once, and the Preschool Teacher must be prepared to handle accidents
and emergencies at any time.

The above statements are intended to describe the general nature and level of work being performed by the incumbent(s) of this job. They are not intended to be an exhaustive list of all responsibilities and activities required of the position.

Child care worker and Teacher's Aide
Purpose of the position
To nurture and care for children. These workers play an important role in children's development by caring for them when parents are at work or away for other reasons.

Responsibilities
1.   In addition to attending to children's basic needs, child care workers organize activities and implement curricula that stimulate children's physical, emotional, intellectual, and social growth.
2.   They help children explore individual interests, develop talents and independence, build self-esteem, and learn how to get along with others.
3.   Child care workers maintain contact with parents or guardians through informal meetings or scheduled conferences to discuss each child's progress and needs.
4.   Maintain records of each child's progress and suggest ways in which parents can stimulate their child's learning and development at home.
5.   Child care workers recognize the importance of learning through play and capitalize on children's play to further language development (storytelling and acting games), improve social skills (working together to build a neighborhood in a sandbox), and introduce scientific and mathematical concepts (balancing and counting blocks when building a bridge or mixing colors when painting).
6.   Greet young children as they arrive, help them with their jackets, and select an activity of interest. When caring for infants, they feed and change them and record their activities each day.
7.   Prepare lesson plans (daily and long-term schedules of activities) as directed. Nursery and Toddler classroom activities balance individual and group play, as well as quiet and active time. Children are given some freedom to participate in activities in which they are interested. As children age, child care workers may provide more guided learning opportunities, particularly in the areas of math and reading.
8.   Supervision of school age children during the summer and extended care program ensures they constructively spend their time. Workers help students with their homework or engage them in other extracurricular activities. These activities may include field trips, sports, or learning about computers, painting, photography, or other fun subjects. Child care workers may be responsible for taking children to school in the morning and picking them up from school in the afternoon.
9.   Helping to keep children healthy is another important part of the job. Child care workers serve nutritious meals and snacks and teach good eating habits and personal hygiene. They ensure that children have proper rest periods. They identify children who may not feel well and follow state guidelines regarding exclusion
10. Child care workers watch for children who show signs of emotional or developmental problems and discuss these matters with their supervisor and/or the child's parents. Early identification of children with special needs—such as those with behavioral, emotional, physical, or learning disabilities—is important to improve their future learning ability.
11. Ensure children are supervised at all times
12. Use developmentally appropriate practices to comfort children
13. Establish routines and provide positive guidance
14. Provide a safe and secure environment for children to feel comfortable
15. Implement positive guidance/discipline techniques when required
16. Clearly and effectively communicate in a manner that children understand
17. Integrate special needs children in a positive and respectful manner

Qualifications
Teacher's aides must be 16 years of age.

Child care workers must be 18 years of age.

Minimum education requirements are a high school diploma and/GED or 1 year of experience.

A national Child Development Associate (CDA) credential or a college degree in child development or early childhood education is preferred.

Personal Attributes

The incumbent must maintain strict confidentiality in performing the duties of a teacher.

The incumbent must also demonstrate the following personal attributes:

- be respectful
- possess cultural awareness and sensitivity
- be flexible
- demonstrate sound work ethics
- be compassionate and understanding
- be able to build esteem while ensuring a safe and secure environment
- be fair and provide firm discipline and positive guidance.
- be enthusiastic and constantly alert.

WORKING CONDITIONS

Physical Demands

Caring for children can be physically demanding. The Child care worker or Teacher's Aide may be lifting and carrying children and equipment (up to 50 lbs. or more), and must spend time sitting on the floor or child sized furniture.

The Child care worker or Teacher's Aide will be expected to clean and maintain equipment and facility, and may move throughout the community with children The Child care worker or Teacher's Aide may come in contact with children who are ill and/or contagious, and must take precautions to ensure the health and safety of all children, parents, staff and themselves.

Environmental Conditions

The Child care worker or Teacher's Aide will be working in a busy and occasionally noisy environment. There may be a number of activities and situations happening at once, and the Child care worker or Teacher's Aide will have to supervise all children at all times.

Sensory Demands

The Child care worker or Teacher's Aide may experience smells associated with toileting, cleaning products and children who are ill.

There may be times that the environment is noisy and busy.

Mental Demands

Caring for children can be stressful. The Child care worker or Teacher's Aide must ensure that children are supervised at all times, and that children are involved in safe and appropriate activities. There may be a number of situations happening at once, and the Child care worker or Teacher's Aide must be prepared to handle accidents and emergencies at any time.

Child care workers must anticipate and prevent problems. Deal with disruptive children.

They must communicate effectively with the children and their parents, as well as with teachers and other child care workers. Workers should be mature, patient, understanding, and articulate and have energy and physical stamina. Skills in music, art, drama, and storytelling also are important.

The Preschool Director at [Your school's name] has many responsibilities including, but not limited to, the following:

☺ Regular meetings with the staff, including but not limited to, morning gathering time for prayers and announcements, staff meetings as scheduled at the beginning of the school year (monthly) and teacher work day activities.

☺ Communicating clearly performance expectations to the staff through both conversation and written notices.

☺ Acknowledging staff performance and work both individually and as a group. Acknowledgement will occur through written notes, verbal praise, appreciation treats, breakfasts, etc.

☺ Being available to the staff to ensure they have the necessary resources to teach, which will include, but is not limited to, assisting with the gathering, locating and/or purchasing of supplies and equipment; discussing and suggesting lesson plans and activities.

☺ Visiting the classrooms as often as necessary, to include but not limited to, formal observations no less than twice per year.

☺ Listening and acknowledging staff concerns as well as obtaining staff input when changes to the school are needed. If a concern arises that the Director is not able or qualified to help with, the Director must assist in locating an appropriate resource.

☺ Discussing the special needs of specific children and families with the teachers and assisting the teacher in solving problems, communicating with parents, identifying procedures for referrals, and communication with resource persons.

☺ Evaluating staff performance on an ongoing basis with written evaluations which include positive and constructive suggestions for modifying behavior and/or procedures. Formal observations with a written evaluation and follow-up discussion with the teacher must occur twice a year at a minimum. Teachers must receive a yearly self-evaluation form which is to be discussed with the Director. Individual and professional development goals must also be discussed.

☺ Sharing information with staff in a timely fashion.

☺ Encouraging and inviting teachers to share ideas and concerns in staff meetings and in individual conferences.

Lead teachers

In order to provide an environment of consistent, thoughtful learning, it is the policy of NSUMC Preschool to hire a Lead Teacher for every classroom. The Lead Teacher has the following responsibilities, including but not limited to:

☺ Preparing lesson plans that are thorough and understandable by a substitute if necessary. The Lesson Plan Book that is provided **must** be used. All lesson plans are due the Thursday before the next week's lesson. Lesson plans must include the area of the curriculum that each part of the daily lesson plan is geared. The curriculum provided by ABeka Book Publishers, Handwriting without Tears, McGraw-Hill, Carson Delosa, Christ Centered Publications will contain all of the learning and developmental objectives appropriate for the ages of the children in the class. If the teacher follows the curriculum as it is written, it is not necessary to note which objectives are being met by an activity. **However, any supplemental activities must have a notation signifying which objectives are being met with the activity.** The following abbreviations will be used: LA - language arts; S- science; SS- social studies; M- math; C- colors; Sh- shapes; SC- spatial concepts. If in doubt, ask the Director. It is not expected that each area of the curriculum be covered *every* day, but must be a part of the total weekly plan. It is important that teachers don't just think up crafts or activities for the children to do without a concrete plan/goal behind it.

Lesson plans must be kept in the classroom in an easily accessible place (in the event of absence) and must be out during the school day.

☺ Supervising children within the class and remaining at the end of the school day at least until all of your students have been picked up by a parent.

☺ Preparing assessment portfolios/progress reports twice a year and arranging for parent conferences during the fall and spring as noted in the school calendar. Additional conferences will be scheduled as needed. The Director must be made aware of any concerns or reasons for additional conferences prior to scheduling.

☺ Completing "Ouch!" reports and/or incident reports as needed and making sure that the Director receives a copy on the day of occurrence. Completed incident reports are required by BFTS and must be submitted within 24 hours of the incident.

☺ Discussing with the Teaching Assistant (TA) any expectations of the TA in the classroom, including, but not limited to, what tasks he/she will be expected to fulfill on a daily basis, methods of discipline preferred, upcoming needs, etc.

Teaching Assistants:

It is the policy of [Your school's name] that all classrooms must be staffed with 2 adults. In many cases there will be a Lead Teacher and a Teaching Assistant. In instances where there is a Lead Teacher and a Teaching Assistant, the TA must be responsible for the following duties (this will not be a complete and totally inclusive list):

☺ Following the direction of Lead Teachers with regards to classroom management, discipline, activities, etc.

☺ Completing specific tasks on a daily basis without reminder, such as: gathering snack, cleaning tables, attendance slips, get bags ready at the end of the day, get supplies for the day and replace at the end of the day, carpool, etc.

☺ Disciplining children in accordance with school policies and in a like manner of the Lead Teacher.

☺ Taking an active part in the classroom, assisting the children as the Lead Teacher does.

☺ Discussing with Lead Teacher what responsibilities are expected on a daily, weekly and ongoing basis.

The above statements are intended to describe the general nature and level of work being performed by the incumbent(s) of this job. They are not intended to be an exhaustive list of all responsibilities and activities required of the position.

STAFF RECORDS:

Bright from the Start: Georgia Department of Early Care and Learning requires the following staff records:

Employment Application including: Name, Date of Birth, Current address, Current telephone number, Employment history (10 years), and Education: Qualifying work experience (commensurate with position)

Criminal Records Check: Never have been shown by credible evidence e.g. a court or jury, a department's investigation or other reliable evidence to have abused, neglected, neglected or deprived a child, or adult or to have subjected any person to a serious injury as a result of intentional or grossly negligent misconduct as evidenced by an oral or written statement to this effect obtained at the time of application. Not have criminal record. Verification of a satisfactory criminal records check determination.

First Aid and CPR Training: Have current evidence of successful completion of a biennial training program in cardiopulmonary resuscitation (CPR) and triennial training program in first aid which has been offered by certified or licensed health care professionals and which dealt with the provision of emergency care to infants and children. At least fifty percent (50%) of the caregiver staff shall have current evidence of first aid training and cardiopulmonary resuscitation. There must always be an employee with current evidence of first aid training and CPR on the center premises whenever children are present and on any center-sponsored field trip.

Essential Duties: Not to be suffering from any physical handicap or mental health disorder, which would interfere with the applicant's ability to perform adequately the job duties of providing for the care and supervision of children enrolled in the center in accordance with these rules.

Certification of statements on application: Not have made any material false statements concerning qualifications requirements.

Professional Development: Bright from the Start requires staff members to complete orientation prior to being assigned to a group of children and a minimum of ten clock hours of approved training annually. You may visit the website to review a schedule (www.training.decal.state.ga.us). Training topics include, but are not limited to, instruction in child development, individual assessment, special needs, cultural diversity, public safety, emergency medical procedures, communicable diseases, curriculum planning and developing, behavior modification, nutrition and food preparation, and financial budgeting. In-service training will be made available through various seminars, staff meetings, visits from community officials and professionals, and hired consultants.

Safety Rules and Regulations including Sexual Harassment

To achieve [YOUR SCHOOL'S NAME]'s goal of providing a completely safe workplace, everyone must be safety conscious. Employees are required to know and comply with Bright From The Start general safety rules and to follow safe and health work practices at all times. Employees must report any unsafe or hazardous conditions directly to their Supervisor immediately. Every effort will be made to remedy problems as quickly as possible.

[YOUR SCHOOL'S NAME] strictly prohibits all *harassment* of one employee by another employee, or of an employee by a student, on any basis including, but not limited to sex, race, color, religion, national origin, ancestry, citizenship, pregnancy, age, marital status, medical condition, physical disability, mental disability, gender, sexual orientation or any other characteristic protected by federal, state and/or local laws. Any harassment will be reported immediately to the Director, Bright From The Start, The Board of Health and DFCS. When students are involved, the parents of the students will be contacted and an incident report will be completed which will include any disciplinary action taken. Any employee found responsible for harassment in violation of this policy will be subject to disciplinary action, up to and including termination of employment.

[YOUR SCHOOL'S NAME] forbids any *retaliation* against employees and/or students for reporting unlawful harassment, or for initiating or assisting in any action or proceedings regarding unlawful harassment.

Corporal Punishment should never be used in the child care setting, even with the parent's permission.

Electronic Communication Policy - [YOUR SCHOOL'S NAME] prohibits the use of cell phones or the use of any other device such as iPods or CD players, etc in the work place. The use of cell phones and electronic devices during work time is distracting to both employees and students and interferes with the responsibility to provide supervision in a learning environment. The center provides telephones and computers for business and educational use. Those should never be used for personal use. It is recognized that occasional telephone calls are necessary; however, these should be kept to a minimum both in frequency and duration. Except in the case of an emergency, telephone calls should be made only at break time. Teachers should not call parents from the classroom and teachers should also ask family and friends not to contact you by telephone at work unless absolutely necessary.

Child Care Abuse Detection and Reporting
All staff members of the center are mandatory reporters of child abuse and child neglect. As such, all employees and volunteers of the Center who come into contact with the children at the Center must be trained in all of the following:
• Child abuse and neglect law.
• How to identify children who have been abused or neglected.
• The process for reporting known or suspected cases of child abuse or neglect.

Our staff members are required by law to report all *suspicions* of child abuse or neglect to the Director and the county Department of Family and Children's Services Child Protective Services office. Our staff will follow the guidelines for clues to recognizing and reporting child abuse and neglect provided in *Caring for Our Children*, The National health and Safety Standards for educational settings. The Director will complete an incident report indicating observations or the child's report and submit it to Child Protective Services. If we believe the child's life is at risk or there is a risk of permanent injury we are required to call Emergency Medical Services (EMS)/911 immediately. All reports of child abuse are strictly confidential. These reports will not be made available to staff members, parents, or others who do not have a need to know.

Grievance Procedure

[YOUR SCHOOL'S NAME] will make all efforts to mediate problems, but if such efforts are unsuccessful, arbitration will be required. Arbitration shall be conducted by three arbitrators. Each party shall have the right to select one arbitrator. The two arbitrators selected will jointly select the third neutral arbitrator. Each party to the dispute will be responsible for the fees and expenses of his/her arbitrator and one half of the fees and expenses of the neutral third arbitrator. If the parties agree to use one arbitrator, the fee and expense will be shared equally.

Upon hiring every employee will have to sign a grievance form to be included in new hire packet.

Orientation

All employees prior to assignment to children or task will receive initial orientation on the following subjects:
a.   The center's policies and procedures
b.   The portion of rules dealing with the care, nutrition, health and safety of children including SIDS, blood borne pathogens, handwashing and medication administration
c.   The employee's assigned duties and responsibilities
d.   Reporting requirements for suspected cases of child abuse, neglect or deprivation; communicable diseases and serious injuries
e.   Emergency procedures concerning fire and water safety, severe weather plans, structural damage, and other evacuation plans
f.   Childhood injury control procedures
g.   Child care training requirements

A Documentation Form of Orientation must be signed and dated by new employee and staff performing the orientation.

Compensation

[YOUR SCHOOL'S NAME] salary ranges and schedules are based upon such factors as: (a) Program Budget (b) Federal or Georgia pay scales (c) Job description (d) Prior experience (e) Job performance.

All teachers and support staff will be paid a base hourly wage on a bi-weekly time period and are eligible for raises at the following service dates:
1. 90 day Probationary Period Ending
2. Annual Evaluation (3%)

A salary schedule outlining base wages and benefits will be given to new employees upon hire.

Attendance

To maintain a safe and productive work environment, regular and punctual attendance is an essential function of your job, and [YOUR SCHOOL'S NAME] expects you to be reliable and punctual in reporting to work.

In the event you are unable to work due to illness you should notify the Director as soon as possible, preferably two hours prior to the beginning of the workday. In case of emergency in route to the center, you should report to the Director as soon as possible.

All employees are required to be at his/her assigned area with sufficient time to store personal belongings and wash his/her hands. Several unscheduled absences and/or tardiness will be communicated as grounds for termination of employment.

In the event we are closed due to inclement weather, the closing will be aired on 104.7 FM, 97.5 FM and local television stations.

Benefits

Upon hire employees will be provided with secure storage areas for personal possessions. However [YOUR SCHOOL'S NAME] will not be responsible for the loss or theft of personal property. Each employee will be allotted one hour of unpaid lunch time and two paid fifteen minute breaks per day.

The following Federal Holidays will be observed:
Monday, September 3 Labor Day Closed
Monday, October 8 Columbus Day Early Release Staff Development
Monday, November 12 Veterans Day Early Release Staff Development
Wednesday –Friday, November 21-23 Thanksgiving Closed
Monday-Wednesday, December 24-26 Christmas Closed
Tuesday, January 1 New Year's Day Closed
Monday, January 21 Birthday of Martin Luther King, Jr. Closed Staff Development
Monday, February 18 Washington's Birthday Closed Staff Development
Monday-Friday, April Spring Break
Monday, May 27 Memorial Day Closed
Thursday, July 4 Independence Day Closed

Sick leave – full time regular employees are entitled to five days of paid sick leave per calendar year after successful completion of one year. Unused sick leave will not be carried over from year to year and unused sick leave will not be paid at termination. However, if an employee does not use the five days allotted by the end of the year, he/she will be paid for those days.

Maternity Leave will be granted in accordance with the Federal Laws.

Time Off Request – Employees will be granted paid or unpaid leave and their position guaranteed for a specific period of time for reasons such as: death of an immediate family member (Father, Mother, Sibling, Children). Proof of relation will be required within one week of leave. Some positions may not be guaranteed after the required time periods have elapsed.

Vacation Leave – Paid time off for vacation accrues for full time employees on an anniversary date basis. Vacation time may be taken on an accrual basis following the successful completion of one year. No vacation time is earned during any unpaid leave of absence or during any time periods during which an employee is not working full-time. After your first year of employment, you will accrue a total of 40 hours of vacation time. After the second through the fifth calendar years of employment, you will accrue 80 hours of vacation time. Employees working six or more years will accrue 120 hours of vacation time per calendar year. Family and Medical Leave Act does not apply to [Your school's name] Child Development Center due to the number of staff members, however, leave will be considered on an individual basis. Daily attendance records for employees must be kept by the center for a six month period.

Leave of Absence - The director may approve a leave of absence without pay to any employee because of sickness, disability, or other personal reasons. The application for such leave must be submitted in writing by the employee stating the reason for the request.

If the leave of absence request is for personal reasons including extended illness, injury, or pregnancy, it shall be accompanied by a statement from the employee's physician stating the nature of the illness or incapacity that causes the employee to be medically disabled for performance of his or her normal work.

A leave of absence may be granted for a period not exceeding ninety consecutive days.

Time spent on such leave of absence without pay shall not be considered time in service for purposes of determining sick leave or vacation leave.

Should the employee decide to return before the expiration of the leave without pay, he or she may do so after giving the executive director a minimum of three day's notice, and providing proper certification indicating that he or she is capable of performing the regular job duties without restrictions.

Upon return from leave of absence, reasonable attempts will be made to reinstate the employee in his or her former position, or one of equal status and salary.

Employees who do not report back to work or contact the office on the date due back to work will be considered to have resigned.

When an employee requests permission to return to work after being granted leave without pay as a result of illness or disability, he or she must provide a statement from his or her physician that certifies that he or she is capable of resuming normal and regular work duties without restrictions.

If an employee requests time off without pay for personal reasons, and approval of the request would burden the Center or unreasonably disrupt the Center functioning, the request may be denied. If the employee takes off in spite of the denial, the time off will be considered an unauthorized absence.

Jury Duty - Time away from the job with pay will be permitted when a full-time, salaried employee is summoned for jury duty. The employee will receive the difference in what he or she receives in pay for jury duty and his or her regular pay. The jury summons must be submitted to the immediate supervisor and documentation of the payment from the court. No employee shall receive pay for any court appearance in which he or she is a defendant, witness, or plaintiff, as this would be considered personal business.

Military Leave - Employees who provide documentation that they must report for a military physical examination may use sick leave, in an amount not to exceed eight hours, for that purpose.

Short-term military leave may be granted to employees for a period not to exceed fifteen calendar days per year. To qualify for the benefits provided, employees must provide a copy of military orders to the supervisor prior to complying with the military requirements. Military leave will be without pay.

Supervision and Evaluation

[YOUR SCHOOL'S NAME] will regularly evaluate the center's effectiveness including measuring staff competencies. Job performance and goals will be discussed on an informal day to day basis between employee and supervisor. A formal performance evaluation will be conducted after your first 90 days of employment.

Employees will be supervised for the primary purposes of:
1. To evaluate the fulfillment of the program's objectives
2. To maintain the standards of excellence set forth in national standards for child care
3. To ensure the health and safety of the children
4. To prevent favoritism, child abuse and/or neglect
5. To anticipate future needs
6. To provide vision and direction for the future
7. To encourage and recognize staff member strengths and to identify areas for improvements
8. To provide a plan for program and staff quality improvement

Staff needs will be assessed annually by a written survey and parent/child satisfaction will be assessed as well. Input from all key players is valuable to the effectiveness of the Center.

1.Staff members will meet annually to set goals and strategies monthly on how best to achieve those goals
2.Staff members will be observed in the classroom on a timely basis and provided feedback by the Supervisor or peer mentor
3.Staff members will be evaluated quarterly one on one with the Director to review quarterly goals and expectations, receiving feedback which will enhance job performance. Staff members will be evaluated annually in the following areas:
Attitude, initiative and job knowledge
Oral and written expression with children, parents and co-workers
Attendance/dependability
Appearance
Record Keeping

Adherence to the Employment agreement
Professional development and training needs

Employment Agreement

Upon offer of employment, employee will be required to sign and return an Employee Agreement form (exhibit 3 which will detail probationary periods, work schedules, calendars, uniforms etc.). With the return of the signed employee agreement an orientation will be scheduled by the Director and a Staff Handbook will be issued to the employee.

New Hires are to submit to criminal background checks and a physical examination performed by a licensed physician prior to employment. A record of the criminal background check and physical exam with the physician's certification will be placed in employee's personnel file.

Disciplinary Policies

Separation of employment, either voluntary or involuntary is an inevitable part of personnel activity within any organization. It is the policy of the Center to approach each employee termination with fairness, both to the employee and the Center. Since employment with the Center is based on mutual consent, both the employee and the Center have the right to terminate employment at will, with or without cause, any time.

In the case of voluntary separation of employment, teachers are expected to notify their supervisor two (2) weeks in advance of their last expected day of work.

These rules do not represent every conceivable type of offense, but reflect those most frequently encountered.

Misconduct not specifically described in these polices will be handled as warranted by the circumstances of the case involved. The Center may modify penalties imposed as a result of infractions of the rules when extenuating circumstances are found. Likewise, flagrant infractions of the rules of conduct may result in whatever action is deemed appropriate by the director.

All employees are expected to conduct themselves according to the highest standards of integrity and ethics. Standards of employee conduct normally expected in any place of employment will be the standards of employee conduct at the Center, whether or not such are in writing. As a basic standard of justice, employees are informed of the behavior expected of them through such avenues as job descriptions, personnel policies, and instructions of supervisors. Employees and administrators are expected to conduct themselves in a professional manner at all times. Complaints by employees should be conducted in the supervisor's office. Administrators should counsel employees in private.

Failure to conform one's conduct to reasonable requirements will result in disciplinary action. Written reports of all disciplinary action will be prepared and placed in the employee's personnel file. Disciplinary action will be taken as soon as the facts are known and a fair judgment can be made. The following disciplinary actions may be taken, depending on the nature of the offense and circumstances surrounding the particular case. Discipline may or may not be progressive.

Progressive Disciplinary Procedure
1ˢᵗ Session
1. Director will outline in writing the specific area of concern
2. Areas of concern will be discussed with the employee and attempt to address the root attitudes or

problems
3. Counsel the employee accordingly
4. Encourage employee to respond from his perspective
5. Director will document the meeting
6. Conference summary to be signed by Director and employee. A signed copy is to be given to the employee and another copy placed in the employee's file.
2nd Session
The same procedure is to be followed as with the first session and the following:
1. The teacher and director should report on the progress they each felt has been made in following the corrective action outlined in session one.
2. Any new steps of action will also be documented at this time and the teacher will be informed that failure to implement by a certain date may result in dismissal depending upon severity of the problem.
3. Any items not mentioned in the first session will be discussed and a plan of action formulated.
4. The director will invite the Center Owner to be present
5. A copy of the meeting summary will be sent to the Board

3rd Session
The director will summarize the contents of prior conferences and the steps of action not followed and problem areas not corrected. This final session will include the director and a Board Member/or Owner
1. A letter of separation notice will be given to employee which details the reasons for termination
2. Employee will be given an explanation as to how the letter will be used in future inquiries.
3. Terminated employee will be provided with an opportunity to appeal the decision directly to the Board within five business days by giving notice to the director. The Board's decision will be final. Failure to request a hearing with the center board within that time frame shall waive the person's right to such a hearing.

A Compulsory Exit Interview will be conducted for employees leaving voluntary or involuntary to determine to what extent the policies, environment and working conditions contributed to their departure.

Return of Center's Property – you are responsible for all Center property, material or written information issued to you or in your possession or control. You must return all Center property in satisfactory condition immediately upon request or upon voluntary or involuntary termination of employment. The Center will withhold from your current or final paycheck the cost of any items that are not returned when required. The Center may also take all actions deemed appropriate to recover or protect its property

HEALTH AND SAFETY

Contagious Diseases: Staff or any other persons being supervised by the staff, shall not be allowed in the center that knowingly have, or present symptoms of a fever or diarrhea.
Staff members are subject to generally the same wellness guidelines as are its students. Teachers may not participate in Center activities if they display any of the following symptoms:
- fever over 101°
- diarrhea
- flu
- unusual rash
- severe cough and/or cold
- rapid or labored breathing
- vomiting

156

- yellowish skin or eyes
- head lice
- any contagious illness

The Center maintains a roster of qualified substitute teachers and teacher's assistants, who are available for temporary classroom duty. These teachers may be candidates for teaching positions, and their substituting may be considered part of the evaluation process. Bright from the Start: Georgia Department of Early Care and Learning staff-to-child ratios will be respected. All substitute employees shall be at least eighteen (18) years of age and complete orientation before assignment to a post of duty.

Job Related Injury: An employee must always advise the director of the time, place, and cause of an on-the-job injury so that the necessary accident report can be completed. The accident must be reported immediately and a written report completed on the day on which it occurs. If the employee is unable to complete the written report, the director must do so.

An employee absent from work because of any occupational illness or service-related injury shall be entitled to reinstatement at the same rate of pay received immediately prior to the date of such illness or injury; and upon approval of a doctor to return to work. Authorization to return to work when a contract period has ended shall not be binding upon the Center for subsequent hiring consideration.

Guidance/Discipline Procedures: Children need adult guidance as they discover boundaries and learn rules for daily living. Our staff is trained to understand appropriate behavior expectations for all ages of children cared for at the center. While discipline is usually thought of as punishment, we prefer to use techniques that help the child learn appropriate ways to resolve problems and conflicts. Our goal is to create an environment where children can gain self-respect, self-control, sensitivity toward others, and learn appropriate ways to resolve problems and conflicts.

Discipline and guidance techniques include giving children choices whenever possible; making directions or suggestions through positive statements; modeling appropriate behavior; reinforcing what children do appropriately; finding logical consequences for inappropriate behavior; redirecting the activity to one that is more acceptable; ignoring misbehavior of a less serious nature; active problem-solving with the child involved; helping the child find acceptable ways of expressing strong feelings; and helping children find the words or actions to solve problems themselves. On a limited basis and as a last resort, a brief timeout may be used for children four years of age and older.

Staff will never use physical abuse or punishment; shame, frighten, or humiliate children; use consequences that are too long, punitive, or postponed; or threaten children with a loss of affection. If repeated disruptive or destructive behaviors or gross misconduct (frequently and deliberately causing harm to others and/or is frequently and deliberately destructive) becomes a concern, a conference will immediately be requested to keep you informed and to discuss possible solutions.

(Your school's name) Early Learning Center
[Street Address]
[City, state and zip]
[Telephone]
[Web address]
[Email address]

EMPLOYEE'S DOCUMENTATION CHECKLIST

Employee Name _____ Hire Date _____
(Last, First, Middle)

Yes	No	N/A	Document
			Employment Application
			Copy of Valid Driver's License or state issued i.d.
			Social Security Card
			I-9 Employment Eligibility Verification
			W-4 Federal Withholding Form
			G-4 State Withholding Form
			Physical Examination/Health Assessment Form
			Education-Training Record Verification
			Qualifying Work Experience
			Orientation Training
			Criminal Records Check Application (date submitted_____)
			Fingerprints (date submitted_____)
			CPR Training, if any
			First Aid Training, if any
			Official College Transcripts
			Certification Credential Agency _____
			Direct Deposit Payroll Form
			Other Documentation (list):

_____   _____   _____
Date Employed   Signature of Administrator/Person-in-Charge   Date

(Your school's name) Early Learning Center
[Street Address]
[City, state and zip]
[Telephone]
[Web address]
[Email address]

STAFF TRAINING RECORD

Employee Name _____ Hire Date _____
(Last, First, Middle)

Position _____

First Year of Employment

	Date	Approved Hrs	Source of Training	Required by position ✓	Documentation on file ✓
CPR					
First Aid					
Identifying, reporting, meeting the needs of abused or neglected children (2 hrs)					
Disease control, basic hygiene, cleanliness, illness detection and disposition (2 hrs)					
Childhood injury control (2 hrs)					
Food nutrition planning (preparation, serving, proper dishwashing, and food storage (administrated and cook 4 hrs)					
Fire Safety (5 hours)					
Transportation (2 hours)					
Nutrition (4 hours)					

Annual Training

Date	Competency	Approved Hours	Workshop/Session Title

(Your school's name) Early Learning Center
[Street Address]
[City, state and zip]
[Telephone]
[Web address]
[Email address]

Employee Name _____
(Last, First, Middle)

DOCUMENTATION OF ORIENTATION TRAINING

✓	Subjects
	Program Philosophy of Education
	The school or center's policies and procedures
	Federal and State Rules and Regulations regarding child care, health and safety of children (Diapering, hand washing, playground, etc.)
	Assigned duties and responsibilities
	Reporting requirements for suspected cases of child abuse, neglect or deprivation; communicable diseases and serious injuries
	Emergency procedures (Bomb Threat, Fire Drill, Severe Weather, Death or Loss of Child, Serious Illness or Injury)
	Childhood injury control
	First Year Training Requirement
	Continuing education requirement (10 hrs)
	Annual calendar, work hours and schedule options, lunch schedules, leave policies, annual leave, sick leave, overtime and compensatory time and holidays. Time off request procedure.
	Tour location of telephones, mailboxes, time clock, copy machines, fax machines, restrooms, mop closet, laundry, playground, etc.
	Building/property security procedures esp. opening/closing duties
	Introductions to co-workers, supervisors, and managers, and explanation of the relationship of their work to the employee's.
	Telephone system/voice mail, computer and e-mail access, if applicable.
	Issue uniform, name tag, etc.

_____   _____
Employee Signature   Signature of Person conducting orientation

_____
Date Orientation Completed

Child Care Staff Health Assessment

Employer completes this section.
Adapted from *Model child care health policies*. 4th ed. Pennsylvania Chapter, American Academy of Pediatrics. 2002.
Washington, DC: National Association for the Education of Young Children. And Centers for Disease Control and Prevention.
2006. Preventing Tetanus, Diphtheria, and Pertussis Among Adults: Use of Tetanus Toxoid, Reduced Diphtheria Toxoid and
Acellular Pertussis Vaccine. *MMWR* 55(RR17): 1-33.

Name of person to be examined: _____
[Your school's name, address, and phone number]

 Purpose of examination:
_pre-employment (with conditional offer of employment) _annual re-examination

Type of activity on the job: _lifting, carrying children _close contact with children _food preparation
_extended computer screen time _outdoor activities with children _cleaning and sanitizing
_driver of vehicles _facility maintenance

Part I and Part II below must be completed and signed by a licensed physician or CRNP.

To the Physician:
**This examination is needed to determine the physical ability of this person to care for children as a
worker in a educational organization or child care center, i.e. work may entail bending, lifting,
standing for long periods of time, cleaning with bleach, outdoor activity for extended periods, etc.**

Based on a review of the medical record, health history, and examination, does this person have any of
the following conditions or problems that might affect job performance or require accommodation?
____yes ____ no

Date of exam: _____
Part I: Health Problems (circle yes or no)
Visual acuity less than 20/40 (combined, obtained with lenses if needed)?   yes no
Decreased hearing or difficulty functioning in a noisy environment (less than 20 db at 500, 1000, 2000,
4000 Hz)? yes no
Respiratory problems (asthma, emphysema, airway allergies, current smoker, other)? yes no
Heart, blood pressure, or other cardiovascular problems? yes no
Gastrointestinal problems (ulcer, colitis, special dietary requirements, obesity, other)? yes no
Endocrine problems (diabetes, thyroid, other)? yes no
Emotional disorders or addiction (depression, substance dependency, difficulty handling stress, other)?
yes no
Neurologic problems (epilepsy, Parkinsonism, other)? yes no
Musculoskeletal problems (low back pain or susceptibility to back injury, neck problems, arthritis,
limitations on activity)? yes no
Skin problems (eczema, rashes, conditions incompatible with frequent handwashing, other)? yes no
Immune system problems (from medication, inherent susceptibility to infection, illness, allergies)? yes no
Need for more frequent health visits or sick days than the average person? yes no
Other special medical problem or chronic disease that requires work restrictions or accommodation?
yes no

Part II: Infectious Disease Status

Female of childbearing age susceptible to CMV or parvovirus? yes no

Immunizations now due/overdue for:

Tdap* yes no

MMR (2 doses for persons born after 1989; 1 dose for those born in or after 1957) yes no

Polio (OPV or IPV in childhood) yes no

Hepatitis B (3 dose series) yes no

Varicella (2 doses or had the disease) yes no

Influenza yes no

Pneumococcal vaccine yes no

Comments: _____

Evaluation of tuberculosis status shows a risk for communicable TB? Yes no

(Circle Test Used) Tuberculin Skin Test (TST)   Interferon-Gamma Release Assay (IGRA)

Test Date: _____ Result: _____

Transmission of tuberculosis infection should be controlled by requiring all adolescents and adults who are present while children are in care to have their tuberculosis status assessed with a tuberculin skin test (TST) or interferon-gamma release assay (IGRA) blood test before caregiving activities are initiated. In people with a reactive TST or positive IGRA, chest radiography without evidence of active pulmonary disease and/or documentation of completion of therapy for latent tuberculosis infection (LTBI) or completion of therapy for active disease should be required.

Health professions should consult the current edition of *Red Book: Report of the Committee on Infectious Diseases* (www.aapredbook.org) for guidance on TB screening. For current adult immunization requirements see: www.cispimmunize.org www.aapredbook.org; and www.cdc.ogv/vaccines/recs/schedules/default.htm.

I have read and understand the above information.

Please attach additional sheets to explain all "yes" answers above. Include the plan for follow up.

Signature: _____ MD DO CRNP

Printed last name:_____ Title: _____

Phone number of physician or CRNP: _____

162

(Your school's name) Early Learning Center
[Street Address]
[City, state and zip]
[Telephone]
[Web address]

INSTRUCTIONAL STAFF DUTIES AND RESPONSIBILITIES

NATURE OF THE WORK

Teachers play an important role in fostering the intellectual and social development of children during their formative years. The education that teachers impart plays a key role in determining the future prospects of their students. Whether in preschools or high schools or in private or public schools, teachers provide the tools and the environment for their students to develop into responsible adults.

Teachers act as facilitators or coaches, using classroom presentations or individual instruction to help students learn and apply concepts in subjects such as science, mathematics, or English. They plan, evaluate, and assign lessons; prepare, administer, and grade tests; listen to oral presentations; and maintain classroom discipline. Teachers observe and evaluate a student's performance and potential and increasingly are asked to use new assessment methods. For example, teachers may examine a portfolio of a student's artwork or writing in order to judge the student's overall progress. They then can provide additional assistance in areas in which a student needs help. Teachers also grade papers, prepare report cards, and meet with parents and school staff to discuss a student's academic progress or personal problems.

Many teachers use a "hands-on" approach that uses "props" or "manipulatives" to help children understand abstract concepts, solve problems, and develop critical thought processes. For example, they teach the concepts of numbers or of addition and subtraction by playing board games. As the children get older, teachers use more sophisticated materials, such as science apparatus, cameras, or computers. They also encourage collaboration in solving problems by having students work in groups to discuss and solve problems together. To be prepared for success later in life, students must be able to interact with others, adapt to new technology, and think through problems logically.

Preschool, kindergarten, and elementary school teachers play a vital role in the development of children. What children learn and experience during their early years can shape their views of themselves and the world and can affect their later success or failure in school, work, and their personal lives. Preschool, kindergarten, and elementary school teachers introduce children to mathematics, language, science, and social studies. They use games, music, artwork, films, books, computers, and other tools to teach basic skills.

Preschool children learn mainly through play and interactive activities. *Preschool teachers* capitalize on children's play to further language and vocabulary development (using storytelling, rhyming games, and acting games), improve social skills (having the children work together to build a neighborhood in a sandbox), and introduce scientific and mathematical concepts (showing the children how to balance and count blocks when building a bridge or how to mix colors when painting). Thus, a less structured approach, including small-group lessons, one-on-one instruction, and learning through creative activities such as art, dance, and music, is adopted to teach preschool children. Play and hands-on teaching also are used by *kindergarten teachers*, but academics begin to take priority in kindergarten classrooms. Letter recognition, phonics, numbers, and awareness of nature and science, introduced at the preschool level, are taught primarily in kindergarten.

Adapted from the United Stated Department of Labor

Qualifications

1. High school diploma or GED
2. Child Development Associate or equivalent early childhood certificate
3. Technical College Diploma in Early childhood Education
4. Bachelor's Degree in Early Childhood Education
5. Satisfactory Criminal Record Check
6. First aid and CPR

7. One year of experience in working with preschool children
8. Above average communication skills

Staff members must be knowledgeable about the subjects they teach, and possess the ability to communicate, inspire trust and confidence, and motivate students, as well as understand the students' educational and emotional needs. Teachers must be able to recognize and respond to individual and cultural differences in students and employ different teaching methods that will result in higher student achievement. They should be organized, dependable, patient, and creative. Teachers also must be able to work cooperatively and communicate effectively with other teachers, support staff, parents, and members of the community.

Classroom Organization

1. Greet children and parents with a smile and a friendly hello, then encourage the children to get involved with class activities, minimizing the departure of the parent.
2. Bulletin boards should reflect a theme and also display children's artwork. Bulletin boards should be changed monthly.
3. All Learning Centers must be left in a clean, orderly condition at the conclusion of each activity. Children should be taught to assist in returning materials to the proper storage areas.
4. Storage areas must be kept neat and clean.
5. Each child must have a cubby labeled with his/her name.
6. Each child must have a sheet and blanket on his/her mat at naptime. Mats must be assigned to an individual child. Mat covers must be removed after naptime and placed in that child's cubby.
7. Allow three feet of space between each mat. Children must be placed in an alternating head-feet arrangement. Leave a walk space for exiting to the outside, in case of fire.
8. Teachers must eat with the children, modeling appropriate table conversation and manners.
9. Cleaning supplies must always be kept out of reach of children. Supply room doors must be kept closed and locked at all times.
10. Clean room according to daily checklist.

Education

1. Weekly lesson plans must be prepared and posted by 9:00am each Monday. A copy of the lesson plan must be available for substitute teachers.
2. A Monthly Activity Calendar must be prepared and posted at the beginning of each month to include a theme and any scheduled events such as field trips.
3. Materials should be prepared before the scheduled day.
4. Television time is limited to thirty minutes per week. Programs should be G rated and primarily educational. The Director must approve special movies or entertainment videos. Computer time is no more than 15 minutes at a time except for school-aged children completing school homework assignments and for children with special health needs who require and consistently use assistive and adaptive computer technology. Any screen media must be free of violent, sexually explicit, stereotyped content (including cartoons), advertising, and brand placement.
5. Each classroom must have a Parent Awareness Board. The following should be posted: daily schedule, weekly lesson plan, special events, and allergy list.
6. Children should take home art projects at least twice a week.
7. One half of playground time must be organized group activities.

Supervision

1. Constant supervision is required at all times. Children are never to be left unattended in classroom or on the playground. The proper teacher/child ratio must always be maintained.
2. Toddler Times and Infant Reports must be completed daily on each child.
3. The early morning and late afternoon teachers must include enrichment activities for the combined group of children. REMEMBER, this is the only time that some parents observe our center.
4. Children should always leave the center with clean faces and hands, shoes tied, and clothes straightened.
5. All accidents must be reported to the Director. If injuries occur, an Incident Report must be completed by the teacher, signed by the director, and given to the parent the day of the injury.
6. Do not burden parents with petty incidences. Discuss serious concerns with the Director.
7. Children are not permitted in the kitchen. In addition, staff with diaper changing responsibilities shall not be simultaneously assigned to kitchen food preparation duties.

Other Job Requirements

1. Lifting, lowering, and carrying up to 50 pounds.
2. Evacuation and/or driving in emergency situations.
3. Being outside in summer and winter temperatures.
4. Using large and small muscle groups - walking, running, jumping, lacing, cutting with scissors, sorting.
5. Apply first aid/CPR
6. Bending, crawling, kneeling
7. Eye hand coordination
8. Lead field trips
9. Visual acuity
10. Speak and hear clearly
11. On time arrival
12. Regular attendance
13. Use of chemicals and/or solvents for cleaning and disinfecting

Teacher Candidate Interview Questions

Questions about personal qualifications and background

- Tell me a little about yourself.
- Why did you decide to teach?
- What do you think of yourself?
- What is your best quality?
- What is your concept of a good life? Do you believe you have been living one?
- What are your strengths? What are your weaknesses?
- How would a friend or acquaintance describe you?
- Do you see yourself as a competitive person?
- Do you feel your grades should be considered a statement of your abilities? Why or why not?
- Are you, or do you consider yourself a perfectionist?
- What do you enjoy doing with your leisure time?

Questions about interpersonal relationships

- List and explain on a scale of 1 to 9 how you would rate yourself on the following items:
  o communicating with people older than yourself
  o getting along with students
- In past jobs, what was your relationship with your employers?
- How do you respond to criticism? How do you tell the difference between constructive criticism and just plain old criticism?
- What kind of student really "gets to you"? Why?
- To what personality types are you attracted?
- What personality types rub you the wrong way? Did you have any of that type in your students? How did you get along?
- What difficulties, if any, have you had in getting along with fellow students and teachers?
- What kind of relationship would you like to have with students, your fellow teachers, and program administrators?
- What techniques do you use in developing rapport with students?
- What quality in other people is most important to you?

Questions about the teaching-learning process

- What did you find to be the hardest thing about or during your directed teaching?
- What would you do if a student started swearing at you? And if that did not work, then what would you do?
- What would you do or how would you treat a student who refused to do the work you assigned? And then what?
- How do students react to your teaching?
- Did you have any disciplinary problems during your student teaching? If yes, what and how did you handle it?
- What is the most important thing in the school building? Why?

Questions about professional qualifications and experiences

- Briefly, what is your philosophy of education?
- How would you describe yourself as a teacher?
- Which age group would you prefer and why?
- What level (high, middle, low) of students do you want to teach? Why?
- How do you run your classroom in terms of discipline?
- What do you see your relationship to be with the parents of the students in the classroom?
- How would you work with aides and parent volunteers?
- What procedures work best for you in maintaining discipline?
- What do you believe your role and obligations to be toward other faculty members?
- Do you criticize constructively?
- Are you interested in team teaching?
- Why will you make a good teacher?
- What do you think is the job of the Director?

- What is the most effective teaching technique you have used in your directed teaching?

Miscellaneous questions

- What was the most traumatic ethnic experience you have had in the classroom?
- What do you think is the most interesting part about being a teacher?
- What are the qualities of some of the best teachers you studied with? Do you share any of their qualities?
- Why should I hire you instead of other applicants?
- What was your most important learning experience during your student teaching?
- What was your most important learning experience outside of school?

(Your school's name) Early Learning Center
[Street Address]
[City, state and zip]
[Telephone]
[Web address]
[Email address]

Interview Rating Scale

Applicant _____ Interview Date _____

Position Title _____ Time _____

	Excellent 10 pts. each	Average 5 pts. each	Poor 0 pts. each
Personal qualifications and backgrounds			
Knowledge of the teaching and learning process			
Interpersonal relationships (Public contact, tact and diplomacy)			
Professional qualifications Certification(s) or degree(s)			
Professional Experience (0-1 year, 1-3 years, 4+ years)			
Portfolio			
Computer Skills (Basic typing, Microsoft Word, Excel, Educational Software and Equipment)			
Oral & Written Skills (Communication)			

____ Recommend for position without reservation

____ Recommend for position with some reservation (please attach reasons)

____ Cannot recommend for position (please attach reasons)

Other comments:

_____   _____

Interviewer   Date Notice Provided to Applicant

Notified of decision by: Telephone Email Postcard Letter Other:

_____

[Your school's address]

Instructional Performance Evaluation

Employee Name _____ Date of Hire _____

Date of Evaluation _____

Position _____ Classroom _____

Please check the column that most closely applies:
1-Outstanding
2-Above Average
3-Satisfactory
4-Improvement needed
5-No Opportunity to Observe

	1	2	3	4	5
1.Understands and demonstrates the principles of child growth and development.					
2. Establishes and maintains a safe, healthy learning environment.					
3. Advances physical and intellectual competence.					
4. Supports social and emotional development and provides positive guidance.					
5. Establishes positive and productive relationships with families.					
6. Ensures a well-run, purposeful program responsive to each individual child's needs.					
7. Maintains a commitment to profession development.					
8. Accepts and acts upon instructional feedback from administration.					
9. Relates well with colleagues.					
10. Attendance and dependability					
11. Adheres to dress code.					
12. Oral and written expression with children, parents, and co-workers.					
13. Attitude, initiative and job knowledge					
14. Adherence to the employment agreement.					

Based upon Georgia Early Care and Education Early Care and Education ((ECE) For those who work with children from birth through the age of five) Professional Development Competencies.

Performance Planning

Areas needing improvement	Expected Outcomes and Goal Dates
Improvement Strategies	Evidence of achieving expected outcomes

Evaluator's comments:

<table>
<tr><td></td></tr>
<tr><td>Employee's comments:</td></tr>
</table>

The employee's signature indicates the above evaluation has been discussed.
Initial Conference:

Evaluator's signature _____ Date _____
Employee's signature _____ Date _____

<table>
<tr><td>Evaluator's comments:</td></tr>
<tr><td>Employee's comments:</td></tr>
</table>

Review Conference(s)
Evaluator's signature _____ Date _____

Employee's signature _____ Date _____

<table>
<tr><td>Evaluator's comments:</td></tr>
<tr><td>Employee's comments:</td></tr>
</table>

Review Conference(s)
Evaluator's signature _____ Date _____

Employee's signature _____ Date _____

[Your school's name address]

Classroom Observation

Employee Name _____ Date of Hire _____

Position _____ Classroom _____

Date of Observation _____ Time _____ Activity _____

Please check the column that most closely applies:

1-Outstanding
2-Above Average
3-Satisfactory
4-Improvement needed
5-No Opportunity to Observe

	1	2	3	4	5
1. Management of Instructional Time Comments:					
2. Management of Student Behavior Comments:					
3. Instructional Presentation (Utilizes a variety of teaching techniques and resources) Comments:					
4. Instructional Monitoring of Student Performance Comments:					
5. Rapport with students (Ability to engage all students) Comments:					
6. Facilitating Instruction (lesson planning, materials, centers, etc) Comments:					
7. Interacting within the educational environment Comments:					

8. Classroom Appearance, Safety, Orderliness and Cleanliness Comments:					
9. Family Communications (bulletin boards, newsletters, etc.) Comments:					
10. Appearance Comments:					

The employee's signature below indicates the above observation has been or will be discussed as needed.

Evaluator's comments:
Employee's comments:

Evaluator's signature _____ Date _____

Employee's signature _____ Date _____

[Your school's name and address]

Instructional Performance Evaluation

Domain 1: Planning and Preparation	**Check one**
1. Demonstrates knowledge of content and pedagogy – *teacher displays extensive content knowledge and works to increase this knowledge; builds on prior knowledge and relationships in content to diagnose student learning problems; continues to search for best practices to teach the content.*	☐*Strength* ☐*Area for Growth* ☐*No basis for evaluation*
2. Demonstrates knowledge of students – *teacher varies instruction according to knowledge of: age-group and developmental characteristics; knowledge of group and individual student skills (ability levels and learning styles); knowledge of the interests or cultural heritage of each student; knowledge of group and individual exceptionalities (special needs, gifted, and learning disabilities)*	☐*Strength* ☐*Area for Growth* ☐*No basis for evaluation*
3. Designs coherent instruction – *teaching is based on unit plans, using lesson plans as incremental steps, which establish goals with high expectations, are clear, and written in the form of observable student learning ("students will be able to..."); goals target significant concepts and Bloom's levels of thinking.*	☐*Strength* ☐*Area for Growth* ☐*No basis for evaluation*
4. Selects instructional objectives – *lesson objectives are phrased in observable verbs, clearly stated, and are implemented through instructional tasks and assessments.*	☐*Strength* ☐*Area for Growth* ☐*No basis for evaluation*
5. Selects instructional outcomes/goals – *unit and course outcomes/goals are phrased in observable verbs, clearly stated, and are implemented through instructional tasks.*	☐*Strength* ☐*Area for Growth* ☐*No basis for evaluation*
6. Assesses student learning – *assessments are completely congruent with instructional objectives and goals, have clear criteria, and the results are used to adjust curriculum planning for individuals and classes.*	☐*Strength* ☐*Area for Growth* ☐*No basis for evaluation*
7. Demonstrates knowledge of resources – *in addition to program resources, teacher seeks other materials/resources to enhance instruction and promotes independent student interest, growth, and learning.*	☐*Strength* ☐*Area for Growth* ☐*No basis for evaluation*

For the entire domain of *planning and preparation...*
the single area of greatest strength is:
the single area in most need of growth is:

Domain 2: The Classroom Environment	**Check one**
1. Establishes a culture for learning – *students actively participate, demonstrate curiosity, and pay attention to detail; students take pride in work and initiate improvements in it; both students and teacher maintain high expectations for the learning of all students.*	☐*Strength* ☐*Area for Growth* ☐*No basis for evaluation*
2. Manages classroom procedures – *regular routines and transitions are seamless and engage students; non-instructional/administrative routines are efficient and engage students; students working independently or in groups are productive and responsible at all times.*	☐*Strength* ☐*Area for Growth* ☐*No basis for evaluation*
3. Manages student behavior – *teacher clearly states appropriate and relevant expectations for student conduct, uses discrete and preventive monitoring of behavior, responds effectively and appropriately to misbehavior.*	☐*Strength* ☐*Area for Growth* ☐*No basis for evaluation*
4. Organizes physical space – *classroom is safe and uncluttered; students/teacher adjust furniture to enhance learning; students/teacher use available physical resources (board, overhead, technology, learning centers,*	☐*Strength* ☐*Area for Growth* ☐*No basis for*

	evaluation
resource areas, etc.) optimally; learning and resources equally accessible to all students.	

For the entire domain of *classroom environment...*
the single area of greatest strength is:
the single area in most need of growth is:

Domain 3: Instruction	Check one
1. Communicates clearly and accurately – *teacher articulates clear directions and procedures, anticipates possible student misunderstanding, uses spoken and written language correctly, expressively and to enrich lessons.*	☐ *Strength* ☐ *Area for Growth* ☐ *No basis for evaluation*
2. Uses questioning and discussion techniques – *teacher asks questions of uniformly high quality with adequate response time; teacher encourages student formulation of questions, initiation of discussion topics, and a self-monitoring format to ensure all students are heard.*	☐ *Strength* ☐ *Area for Growth* ☐ *No basis for evaluation*
3. Engages students in learning – *all students are cognitively engaged in content exploration and creativity; grouping is productive for all students and provides for student initiative in learning; appropriate materials and resources are provided in student work; structure of lesson/activity provides adequate/appropriate pacing for all students and for coherent reflection and closure*	☐ *Strength* ☐ *Area for Growth* ☐ *No basis for evaluation*
4. Provides feedback to students – *teacher uses various forms of verbal and written feedback (ex. graded work, conferences, revision) to provide structured and consistent response to and review of student work and progress; feedback is provided in a timely manner, consistently of high quality, and is provided in a form that is useful for and promotes continued student learning.*	☐ *Strength* ☐ *Area for Growth* ☐ *No basis for evaluation*
5. Modifies instruction according to developmental level and learning styles of students – *teacher makes adjustments to lessons and materials and varies instruction to address the developmental level and different learning styles of students; creates assessments which challenge appropriately all students.*	☐ *Strength* ☐ *Area for Growth* ☐ *No basis for evaluation*
6. Modifies instruction for children with learning exceptionalities – *teacher makes adjustments to lessons and materials to address learning disabilities and gifted abilities; seeks appropriate help from colleagues, administration, parents and community professionals to improve these students' learning; creates assessments which challenge appropriately all students.*	☐ *Strength* ☐ *Area for Growth* ☐ *No basis for evaluation*

For the domain of *instruction...*
the single area of greatest strength is:
the single area in most need of growth is:

Domain 4: Professional Responsibilities	Check one
1. Maintains accurate records – *teacher maintains effectively a record of grades, documentation of notable incidents, non-instructional activities, the latter providing for student participation in its maintenance; the records track student progress in a way that is effective for teacher, student, and parent participation in learning.*	☐ *Strength* ☐ *Area for Growth* ☐ *No basis for evaluation*
2. Communicates with parents and guardians – *teacher provides frequent information to families about: the instructional program, student progress, behaviors, response(s) to parents concern(s); teacher is consistently sensitive and discrete in and about this communication; communication establishes the basis for the partnership between parents and teachers in the interest of the student.*	☐ *Strength* ☐ *Area for Growth* ☐ *No basis for evaluation*
3. Grows and develops professionally – *teacher seeks resources and opportunities for improvement, actively reflects on classroom experiences for improvement of teaching, and cooperates and contributes to improve self, colleagues, and the profession.*	☐ *Strength* ☐ *Area for Growth* ☐ *No basis for evaluation*

For the domain of *professional responsibilities...*

the single area of greatest strength is:

the single area in most need of growth is:

COMMUNITY	Check one
1. Contributes to the school community – *teacher supports and cooperates with colleagues and administration, takes initiative to participate and volunteer in program events and projects, contributes and offers leadership in some aspect of the center.*	☐ *Strength* ☐ *Area for Growth* ☐ *No basis for evaluation*
2. Contributes to the larger community – *teacher personally engages in service activities with the civic community and takes initiative to better these communities.*	☐ *Strength* ☐ *Area for Growth* ☐ *No basis for evaluation*
3. Promotes student engagement with community resources – *teacher connects students to the community beyond the program through overt participation, speakers, field trips, service, technology and/or other means.*	☐ *Strength* ☐ *Area for Growth* ☐ *No basis for evaluation*

For the pillar of *community...*

the single area of greatest strength is:

the single area in most need of growth is:

PROFESSIONALISM	Check one
1. Creates environment of respect and rapport – *teacher demonstrates genuine caring and respect for individual students; teacher and many/most students exhibit mutual respect and caring for each other within the roles of student and teacher and as persons beyond these roles.*	☐ *Strength* ☐ *Area for Growth* ☐ *No basis for evaluation*
2. Fosters character and ethical development – *teacher integrates peace and justice into the classroom demonstrated through behaviors and/or academics.*	☐ *Strength* ☐ *Area for Growth* ☐ *No basis for evaluation*
3. Serves as an ethical role model – *teacher recognizes the impact of her/his public life and behaviors in influencing the students.*	☐ *Strength* ☐ *Area for Growth* ☐ *No basis for evaluation*

For the pillar of *professionalism...*

the single area of greatest strength is:

Signature on this form signifies knowledge of its content, not necessarily agreement.

Initial Conference:

Evaluator's signature _____ Date _____

Employee's signature _____ Date _____

Notification of Unsatisfactory Performance

Teacher _____

Evaluator _____

Evaluation Period _____

Your supervisor is charged with the responsibility of making the initial recommendation concerning your future employment status with [FAITH BASED PRESCHOOL]. This form constitutes official notice from your immediate supervisor your performance in the area(s) indicated has been judged to be less than satisfactory.

Areas Requiring Improvement

I.

II.

III.

This notification has been discussed with this employee. The employee acknowledges the receipt of this form.

_____

Teacher's Signature   **Date**

_____

Evaluator's Signature   **Date**

[Your school's name]
[Your school's address]

PASTORAL/CHURCH LEADER REFERENCE FORM

As part of the application process at FAITH BASED PRESCHOOL, this reference letter must be completed by a church leader who personally knows, but is not related to, the candidate. The person completing this form must be a pastor, elder, deacon, or other leader within the church where the candidate attends and must be personally acquainted with the candidate's relationship with Christ. Please provide this form and a stamped envelope addressed to the school to the church leader.

To be completed by the candidate:

Candidate's Name _____

Address _____

City _____ State _____ Zip _____ Phone_____

Church Name _____

Church Phone _____ Church Leader's Name _____

Church Leader's Title _____

Church Address _____

Have you attended this church for more than one year?_____ If less than one year, please explain.

_____

_____

To be completed by the Church Leader:

Dear Pastoral Staff,

Our school requires that candidates for employment be professing Christians. The candidate above has applied for a position at FAITH BASED PRESCHOOL and has listed your church as their church home. We would appreciate your candid assessment of this candidate and mail the form back to our school.

1. Do you personally know the candidate? _____
2. Having read the school's statement of faith (on reverse side), to your knowledge does this candidate agree with these statements?   ___Yes ___No

If no, please explain._____

_____

3. Level of involvement of the applicant. Please circle the appropriate responses.
    a. Member: ___ Yes ___ No
    b. Attendance: Regular Occasional Infrequent Never
    4. Please list the auxiliaries in which the candidate serves and frequency:

_____

Pastor's Name (please print) _____

Signature _____ Date _____

FAITH BASED PRESCHOOL
[Your school's address]
STATEMENT OF FAITH

I. We believe the Bible to be the inspired, the only infallible, authoritative, inerrant Word of God (2 Tim. 3:16-17; 2 Peter 1:20-21).

II. We believe there is one God, eternally existent in three persons -- Father, Son and Holy Spirit (Deut. 6:4; Matt. 28:19; 2 Cor. 13:14).

a. We believe in God the Father whose love was exemplified in that He gave His only begotten Son for the salvation of men (John 3:16; Eph. 1:3).

b. We believe in the Deity of the Son, the Lord Jesus Christ. When coming to earth He never ceased to be God and that His humiliation did not consist of laying aside His Deity. As a man, He was miraculously begotten of the Holy Spirit and born of the Virgin Mary. By his atonement and resurrection He accomplished the redemption and justification before God of all who truly believe in Him and accept Him as Lord (Isa. 7:14; 9:6; Luke 1:35; Gal. 4:4-5; Phil. 2:5-8).

c. We believe that the ministry of the Holy Spirit is to glorify the Lord Jesus Christ and during this age to convict men, regenerate the believing sinner, indwell, guide, instruct, comfort, sanctify, seal, reprove and empower the believer for Godly living and service (John 16:7-8; Rom. 8:9; Eph. 1:13-14).

III. We believe Satan is an angelic being who rebelled with other angels against the authority of God. Satan was given temporary rule over the earth for an age to deceive as many of mankind as he is able (Job 1:6-7; Isa. 14:12; Matt. 4:2-11; Matt. 25:41; Rev. 20:10).

IV. We believe that God created the heaven and earth, including all life, by direct act, and not by a process of evolution, in six literal, 24-hour periods (Gen. 1:1-2:3; Ex. 20:11).

V. We believe God's grace provides salvation and eternal life through Christ's death, burial and resurrection to all people who repent and receive Him as Savior and Lord. Salvation is based solely upon faith in God's promise (John 1: 12-13; 2 Cor. 5:17; Eph. 1:7, 2:8-9; Gal. 2:16).

VI. We believe that Christ arose from the dead, ascended into heaven, and is seated at the right hand of the Father, where He intercedes for the believers as our High Priest. We believe in His personal return for His Church. We believe in the resurrection of both the saved and the lost; they that are saved unto the resurrection of life, and they that are lost
unto the resurrection of damnation (Acts 2:22-36; Rom. 3:24-26; 1 Peter 2:24; Eph. 1:7; 1 Peter 1:3-5; Acts 1:9-11; Heb. 9:24, 7:25; Rom 8:34; 1 John 2:1-2; Matt. 25:46; John 5:28-29, 11:25-26; Rev. 20:12-15).

VII. We believe that the family is ordained by God as the basic unit of His plan for His people. The institution of marriage between one man and one woman as created by God provides the foundation and definition for the family. We believe in the preservation and edification of the family to be an act of obedience to God (Gen. 2:24, 19:5,13; Lev. 18:1-30; Rom. 1:26-32; 1 Cor. 6:9-10; 1 Thes. 4:3; Heb. 13:4; Mal. 2:14-16; Rom. 7:1-3; Matt. 19:3-6; 1 Cor. 7:10-16).

VIII. We believe in the sanctity of all human life. This life should be protected, nurtured and helped from the moment of conception, when life begins, until death occurs normally (Ps. 139:13-16; Isa. 44:24, 49:1,5; Jer. 1:5; Luke 1:44).

FAITH BASED PRESCHOOL
[Your school's address]

Payroll Schedule 2013-14

PAY PERIOD BEGINNING DATE	PAY PERIOD ENDING DATE	TIME SHEET DUE DATE	CHECK DATE	CHECK NO.
April 22, 2013	May 5, 2013	May 6, 2013	May 30, 2013	1.
May 6, 2013	May 19, 2013	May 20, 2013	June 14, 2013	2.
May 20, 2013	June 9, 2013	June 10, 2013	June 28, 2013	3.
June 10, 2013	June 23, 2013	June 24, 2013	July 15, 2013	4.
June 24, 2013	July 7, 2013	July 8, 2013	July 30, 2013	5.
July 8, 2013	July 21, 2013	July 22, 2013	August 15, 2013	6.
July 22, 2013	August 4, 2013	August 5, 2013	August 30, 2013	7.
August 5, 2013	August 18, 2013	August 19, 2013	September 13, 2013	8.
August 19, 2013	September 1, 2013	September 2, 2013	September 30, 2013	9.
September 2, 2013	September 15, 2013	September 16, 2013	October 15, 2013	10.
September 16, 2013	September 29, 2013	September 30, 2013	October 30, 2013	11.
September 30, 2013	October 13, 2013	October 14, 2013	November 15, 2013	12.
October 14, 2013	October 27, 2013	October 28, 2013	November 29, 2013	13.
October 28, 2013	November 10, 2013	November 11, 2013	December 13, 2013	14.
November 11, 2013	November 24, 2013	November 25, 2013	December 30, 2013	15.
November 25, 2013	December 8, 2013	December 9, 2013	January 15, 2014	16.
December 9, 2013	December 22, 2013	December 23, 2013	January 30, 2014	17.
December 23, 2013	January 5, 2014	January 6, 2013	February 14, 2014	18.

The Payroll Department will periodically request timesheets/absentee sheets earlier than deadline.

[Your school's name and address]
Time Off – Overtime Request Form

Employee Name: _____

All foreseeable requests for time off must be submitted and approved in advance. An employee who is absent from duty for more than one (1) working day without an approved leave is considered to have automatically resigned.

Pay Code	From		Through		Total Hours
	Date	Hour	Date	Hour	
		a.m.		p.m.	
		a.m.		p.m.	

Purpose of leave: check one and fill in requested information.

☐ **Vacation:** _____

☐ **Sick Time:** (explain in detail) _____

(NOTE: Sick Time taken for medical, dental, professional appointments, or similar reasons which you have advance notice of, must be scheduled and approved at least thirty days in advance for you to qualify for payment.)

Time off recorded, as "Sick Leave" or "FMLA Sick Leave" can be used for the illness of the employee OR in a calendar year, you can use what you accrue in a six-month period of time to care for a family member.

All compensatory time must be used before Leave of Absence without Pay can be granted. If leave is for employee illness, all Sick Leave must be exhausted before LOA without Pay is granted.

☐ **Jury Duty/Court Appearance**: (NOTE: Attach a copy of summons from court and submit a certification form to Human Resources verifying your court attendance when you return to work.)

☐ **Bereavement:** List relationship to you: _____

State deceased lived in _____

☐ **Medical leave of absence** (attach physician's statement)

☐ **Uncompensated Time Off:** (explain in detail) _____

Note: If requesting leave for family care reasons or one's own serious health condition, make sure you have obtained and read the notice on Employee Obligations under the Family and Medical Leave Act (FMLA).

Pay Codes		Pay Codes- Family Leave/Medical Care	
011	Vacation	F11	FMLA Vacation*
022	Sick Leave	F22	FMLA Sick Leave*
033	Administrative Leave	F33	FMLA Administrative Leave*
044	Compensatory Time Off	F44	FMLA Compensatory Time Off *
E	Leave of Absence without pay	FE	FMLA Without Pay
11J	Jury Duty/Court Appearance	*ALL FMLA LEAVES REQUIRE MEDICAL CERTIFICATION, OR PROOF OF BIRTH, ADOPTION OR FOSTER PLACEMENT.	
11B	Bereavement Leave		

It is the employee's responsibility to request leave and provide the required documentation (including a physician's statement on a timely basis to the administration. The provision of similar documentation to another party (e.g., Long Term Disability carrier, Worker's Compensation Administrator) does not relieve the employee of his/her responsibility to provide this documentation.

_____ _____

Employee's Signature (Required)   Date

_____ _____

Administrative Approval (Required)   Date

[Insert your address and phone number]

Weekly Time Card/Attendance Record

Week Ending

Name		Department	Shift		File #	
Employee #		Social Security #			Payroll Class	

	Morning Hours		**Afternoon Hours**		**Overtime Hours**		**Office Use Only**	
	Time In	Time Out	Time In	Time Out	Time In	Time Out	Regular	Overtime
Monday								
Tuesday								
Wednesday								
Thursday								
Friday								
Saturday								
Sunday								
Totals								

Signatures

Employee	Date	Supervisor	Date
Principal	Date	Payroll Department	Date

Use of Background Investigation Results

Listed below are examples of factors that may disqualify an applicant for employment (this is not an all inclusive list, merely examples):

- Inconsistency of information provided by the candidate versus that obtained by the background investigation. (Examples might include, but not be limited to, significant differences in prior employment dates, education obtained, or licenses held.)
- Omissions of significant information by the candidate. (Examples might include, but not be limited to, failure to disclose being dismissed for cause or loss of certifications qualifying the applicant for the position.)
- Unsatisfactory information uncovered by the background investigation. (Examples might include, but not be limited to the following: Recent felony or misdemeanor convictions related to the position applied for; unsatisfactory job performance on a prior job; poor attendance or disciplinary problems on a prior job; record of moving violations (for a job requiring driving a University or state vehicle); credit history that would indicate an inability to manage finances or which would create undue personal financial pressure (for jobs handling management of significant financial resources).

4. Fair Credit Reporting Act ("FCRA") Compliance:

The FCRA and the regulations promulgated there under are intended to give a candidate for employment the opportunity to correct any factual errors in his or her consumer report, as defined in the FCRA, before an adverse employment action is taken. The candidate must be provided notice of any disqualifying information revealed by the consumer report, including, but not limited to, credit history information, and a reasonable period of time to correct discrepancies.

When the university or CSU System Office receives information in a consumer report that will disqualify a candidate from consideration, the university or CSU System Office will comply with the following FCRA protocol:

- The candidate shall be sent a letter notifying him/her that the University or CSU System Office has received disqualifying information from the consumer report.
- To the letter shall be attached a copy of the report and a summary of the candidate's rights under FCRA.
- The notification shall be sent to the candidate before any adverse employment action may be taken based on the consumer report.
- After five (5) business days, barring the receipt of any new information that changes or clarifies the consumer report and eliminates any discrepancies, the university or CSU System Office shall send the candidate a second letter rejecting his/her candidacy based on the disqualifying information generated by the consumer report.

5. Record Retention:

All information obtained, as part of a background investigation, shall be held in strictest confidence. Documentation shall be retained for the appropriate retention period for employment records promulgated by the State of Connecticut and by university and CSU System Office personnel search policies and procedures. Such records shall not be included in an employee's personnel file. Unauthorized disclosure of information gathered through the background investigation will not be tolerated and may subject the discloser to disciplinary action.

6.   **Use/Review Criteria:**

   a.   Criminal Convictions: The universities and the CSU System Office will not knowingly hire applicants who have been convicted of job-related crime within the allowable reportable time period for reporting such offenses. This time period is normally seven (7) years. This also applies to those situations when the date of disposition, release, probation, or parole (whichever is most recent) relating to the crime occurred within the past seven (7) years.

   Pursuant to Connecticut General Statutes Sections 46a-79 and 46a-80, in determining whether conviction of a criminal offense will disqualify an applicant for a particular position, the following factors will be considered:
   - o   The nature of the offense and its relationship to the position;
   - o   The degree to which the applicant has been rehabilitated; and
   - o   The length of time elapsed since conviction.

   Notification of rejection of employment will be sent via registered mail and will specifically describe the evidence presented and state the reason(s) for disqualification.

   b.   Pending Criminal Charges: If the university or CSU System Office becomes aware that the applicant has criminal charges that are currently pending, but no court disposition has yet been made, the university or CSU System Office shall assess the criminal charges on a case-by-case basis to determine if the charges are job-related.

   Pursuant to Connecticut General Statutes Section 46-80(d), no record of arrest that was not followed by conviction, or record of conviction that has been erased, shall be considered in connection with an application for employment.

   c.   Accelerated Rehabilitation: The university or CSU System Office is not prohibited from considering accelerated rehabilitation or other alternative dispositions when evaluating an applicant. The university or CSU System Office shall consider the accelerated rehabilitation as it would a pending charge.

   d.   Motor Vehicle Records Check: Motor vehicle records which evidence a revoked or restricted driver's license, invalid driver's license, or traffic violations (including, but not limited to, alcohol-related violations) shall be reviewed as they relate to positions requiring driving duties and in conjunction with all other factors disclosed by the background investigation.

e. Credit History: An applicant's credit history shall be reviewed as it relates to jobs requiring financial responsibilities. An applicant's credit history shall be considered in conjunction with all other factors disclosed by the background investigation and alone shall not be a determining factor in denying employment.

Statutory/Administrative Regulation:

Fair Credit Reporting Act - Connecticut General Statutes, Sections 31-51i, 46a-79, 46a-80, 46a-80(d), 46b-146, 54-760, 54-142a

HIRING PRACTICE CHECKLIST

The school's recruitment procedures are established to assure equal opportunity and impartial review of all applications for instructional and support positions. These procedures are not intended to interfere with the selection of qualified candidates; however, no offer of employment and no actual work should be performed until all steps of the recruitment process are completed. In order to adequately implement these procedures, it is recommended that the organization create a committee to establish the criteria for review of the applications and face-to-face interviews, as well as interview questions, tests or skill evaluation tools, if not already available. Applicant search activities meeting Affirmative Action requirements are required for all full and part-time positions. The extent of the search will differ according to the nature of the position.

STEP # 1 – To Begin Recruitment
Before a position can be posted and/or announced, the following must be completed and approved by the owner or board:
- Job description (including qualifications, duties, and responsibilities)
- Job classification and suggested salary range for the current recruitment
- Interview questions
- Test/Skill evaluation tools (suggested if used)
- Criteria for evaluating candidates (objective interview rating scale)

Applicant receives the following forms:
Job Description and Announcement
Application for Employment
Criminal Record Check Form
Reference Check Forms

STEP # 2 – Announcement of Positions
The administrator will announce the open position and process any requested advertisements. Job announcement advertisements should be sent to employment agencies, institutions and organizations (State University System, State Employment Offices, community groups etc.,). The initial announcement should remain open for a minimum of ten (10) - thirty (30) days for all positions.

STEP # 3 – Application/Resume Review Process
Applicants are to be screened using job related criteria based on the actual job description and input from the hiring committee. the criteria for evaluation should be determined before the screening process begins. After reviewing all applications, using job-related criteria, and checking references the hiring committee will interview at least three (3) applicants. Candidates selected for further review should have at least three references checked. The Hiring Manager should personally speak to each reference and complete the "Candidate Reference Check" form before any offer will be approved. The hiring committee may not indicate or announce an applicant's employment status until all recruitment procedures are completed.

References: What can you say when asked to give a reference on a former employee? "When asked for a reference for a former employee, our policy is to state: a) job title, b) eligibility for rehire, and c) the dates of her/his employment." When requesting a reference however, you can ask anything. I typically advise faxing a list of questions and getting it emailed or faxed back. See the interview questions list.

1. **Consent for employer to give a reference**-If you feel that you must give a reference, have an employee sign this statement. "I, _____, an employee of _____ childcare, agree to hold _____childcare harmless for the recommendation that organization may give me."
2. **Job descriptions**: "Functional requirements of the job" focus on the task to be accomplished, not the attribute needed, e.g. evacuating six infants in a crib or diapering a baby weighing 20 lbs. or more, rather than lifting 20 #. The Americans with Disabilities Act of 1990 (ADA) makes it unlawful to discriminate in employment against a qualified individual with a disability. Essential job functions are the fundamental duties of the job. A job function may be considered essential for any of several reasons, such as: 1. the job exists to perform that function 2. The function requires specialized skills or expertise and the person is hired for that expertise 3. There are only a limited number of employees to perform the function. An individual with a disability must also be qualified to perform the essential functions of the job with or without reasonable accommodation, in order to be protected by the ADA. It is wise to list both job functions and physical demands in the job announcement and description.
3. **Interview questions**: a) allow the applicant to demonstrate the ability to perform the functional requirement of the job, b) ask same questions of each applicant.
ADAAA (Americans w/ Disabilities Act Amended 2009): requires that persons with a **handicap** (restriction of a major life activity like breathing, walking) **who otherwise qualify** for the job, be given **reasonable accommodations** to apply for or perform the job, unless doing so will cause the employer an **undue hardship.** Employers may not ask the applicant/employee if s/he he is handicapped. Below are some helpful comments from a recent Human Resources Leadership Association conference in Mystic, Connecticut. Farrell, legal editor at BLR® and Attorney Patricia Trainor, SPHR, senior managing editor at BLR shared three basic Americans With Disabilities Act factors to consider in an analysis:
• Does the person have a disability?
• Is the person qualified? (Can he or she perform the essential functions of the job with or without reasonable accommodation?)
• Is there a reasonable accommodation? (Is there a possible accommodation? If so, is it reasonable or would it cause undue hardship?)
Furthermore, conditions are to be evaluated without considering mitigating measures. You look at the potential disability (e.g., diabetes, HIV, cancer) in its untreated state, says Farrell.   Since the American Medical Association (AMA) has determined that obesity is a disease, Farrell adds, obesity may be a disability, especially if it substantially limits walking or standing.
Also, in the new DSM-5 (American Psychiatric Association's *Diagnostic and Statistical Manual of Mental Disorders*) there are diseases such as "social communication disorder" that could rise to the level of a disability if they substantially limit a major life activity, Farrell notes. DSM-5 could also have a broader impact under state law, she adds.
4. **Equal opportunity** law forbids discriminating against **protected classes** (age, gender, race, religion, national origin (Patriot Act exceptions), and marital status.

STEP # 4 – Committee/Face to Face Interviews
Interviews shall be conducted in a fair and impartial manner. Only questions related to specific job tasks may be asked. Each Interviewer should complete an objective Interview Rating scale/Evaluation form for each applicant interviewed. Administration will administer typing tests, mock teaching opportunities, or
skills evaluations to determine levels of competency.

STEP # 5 – Job offer

California's Fair Housing and Employment Act (FEHA) prohibits employers from requiring job applicants to take a medical or psychological examination. (Cal. Gov't Code §§ 12900–12996) The FEHA also prohibits employers from inquiring about any mental or physical disability or medical condition. However, the employer may ask about an applicant's ability to perform any job-related functions. Also, if an applicant requests a reasonable accommodation on the job, the employer may respond by asking why it's necessary. For example an applicant with a disability that prevents using a computer keyboard may ask for voice-recognition software.

After extending an offer, the employer may ask the applicant to have a pre-employment medical exam or laboratory test, as long as it relates specifically to the requirements of the job. (Cal. Gov't Code § 12940(e-f)) While California law requires employers to keep *employee* medical records confidential (Cal. Civ. Code § 56.20), it's not clear whether they have the same responsibility concerning *job applicants'* medical records.

New employees must complete the personnel and payroll forms listed below and bring them when reporting for work on the first day of employment.

Upon Job Offer
Offer Letter
Employment Agreement
Medical and Physical Examination Form
Employee Information Sheet
Salary Schedule
Medical Benefits list
G-4 - State Withholding Allowance Certificate
W-4 Federal Withholding Form
I-9 - Employment Eligibility Verification

Upon Hire-Orientation Day
Staff Handbook
Documentation of Orientation
Training Record
Health Insurance Premium Rates (if applicable)
Health Benefit Plan Declination (if applicable)
Direct Payroll Deposit /Debit Master Card Form (if applicable)

TERMINATING AN EMPLOYEE CHECKLIST

1. Employees "**at will**" can resign or be fired without notice. Employer says: "It's just not working out." Provide a separation notice with one of the following reasons indicated:
Voluntary reasons:
- ☐ Without notice or reason
- ☐ Another job, relocation or illness
- ☐ Working conditions
- ☐ Work schedule
- ☐ Problem with supervisor or co-worker
- ☐ Personal problem
- ☐ Return to school
- ☐ Retirement
- ☐ Refused suitable work
- ☐ LOA-Did not return

Involuntary reasons:
- ☐ Absenteeism
- ☐ Insubordination
- ☐ Violation of work rules
- ☐ Lack of work
- ☐ Tardiness
- ☐ Unsatisfactory performance
- ☐ Refusal to follow instruction
- ☐ Job eliminated or changed
- ☐ Disability

2. **Probation period** is the easiest and best time to let an employee go. (90 days, 120 days, etc.)
3. **Progressive discipline's procedures three strikes:**
- ☐ Verbal warning
- ☐ Probation
- ☐ Termination.

All three require written notice. Employer's "**Conscientious rescue effort**' includes: a) notice of what is expected, c) plan with timeline for correcting behavior, d) enhanced supervision, d) consequences of failure to improve.

4. Sample "good cause" **Grounds for termination**: poor performance, inability to deal w/ subordinates, insubordination, violations of employee regulations, refusal to participate in legal investigation. **Immediate grounds:** theft, violence, drug use.

5. **Checklist for termination:** a) followed written policies & procedures, b) could firing be viewed as retaliatory, c) consistent w/ treatment of other employees, d) if employee has been at organization for years, why terminate now, e) any question about employee's responsibility for poor performance/misconduct?

6. **Beginning trend:** Replace Progressive Discipline with "at will" process. The employee can be terminated "at will" without cause. Document…document…document the process.

AMERICANS WITH DISABILITIES ACT (ADA and ADAAA) Notes

What is a handicap? What makes an accommodation reasonable? Should I give preference to an applicant or an employee with a handicap?

Recent legislation, ADA Amendments Act (ADAAA), effective 1/1/09, overrules Supreme Court decisions interpreting the ADA narrowly, and will result in far more conditions qualifying as disabilities.

1.   **ADA protects** a person with **physical** or **mental impairment** that **substantially limits** one or more **major life activities (NEW: functioning of immune system, normal cell growth, digestive, bowel, bladder, neurological, brain, respiratory, circulatory, endocrine and reproductive functions** along with eating, sleeping, thinking, communicating, concentrating, lifting and bending)
2.   **Impairments** can be: **Physical** (deaf, blind, wheel-chaired), **conditions** (epilepsy, diabetes, AIDS), or **Mental** (bipolar, major depression, ADHD), also **Record of impairment** (cancer in remission), and/or **Regarded as impaired.**
3.   **"Who is otherwise qualified for the job"** means person meets job requirements, and is able to **perform the functional requirements of the job** with or without accommodation.
4.   **Reasonable accommodations** are adjustments or modifications to enable people with disabilities to enjoy equal employment opportunities (in applying for and performing on the job). Accommodations are individualized, tailored to fit the employee's needs. Ask for the doctor's recommendations.
5.   If an **undue hardship** would result from making a reasonable accommodation, the accommodation does not have to be made. Undue hardship includes excessive cost, putting the organization in financial jeopardy.
6.   **Direct threat exception** comes about if an employee poses a **significant risk of harm** to him/herself or others on the job. The direct threat must be **likely to occur,** not just speculative.

BABYSITTING & RELEASE TIME POLICIES & PROCEDURES.

Release time crisis procedure: If a crisis arises at the end of the day, we will take the following steps to ensure everyone's safety and well being. We will:

• Not immediately release the child. While discussing our concerns with the person picking up the child, we will engage the child with another staff member;
• The Director or other administrative staff member will contact the other parent or persons on the authorized list to enlist them in ensuring that the child leaves our care safely.
• Offer alternatives. Brainstorm with the family member alternative ways to ensure the child goes home safely.
• Release the child with reservation, notifying the appropriated authorities of our concern.
• Call in the police and/or other authorities if anyone's well being and/or safety is threatened (e.g. child not placed n the back seat or a safety seat, intoxicated or irate driver/passenger).

3 MANAGEMENT

Writing a Business Plan

A business plan clearly sets out the objectives of your educational institution. It communicates to lenders, grant makers, and other stakeholders exactly how the business intends to operate and how it will become profitable and sustainable. The plan must be credible, clear, and authoritative. You should cite specific "sources" of information that are within in the plan. Be sure to include tables and graphs that clarify numerical data. The plan should be 10-15 pages in length (excluding the introduction and any supporting documents) and it should be typed (single or double spaced) without grammatical or typographical errors. Readers of your business plan may view mistakes or sloppy presentations as examples of poor business or administrative skills.

Be sure to write in the third person. Don't say "I', "me", "we" or "our", instead, say "Castle Child Development Center", "the owner" or "Jane Doe". Be positive and write in the present tense. Don't say, "I hope to care for..." instead, say "The licensed capacity of the school is 75-90 children between the ages of ...."

Directions:
Simply answer the following questions in <u>complete sentences</u> and then separate them into paragraphs according to the topic.
New program directors may be unable to answer some questions.
Cash flow projections should be calculated for year one to five.

The Sections of the Child Care Center Business Plan

* The Business Introduction
* The Business Organization Section
* The Management/Operations Section
* The Marketing Section
* The Financial Section
* Supporting Documents

EXECUTIVE SUMMARY
Provide a brief overview (highlight and summarize primary elements) of the business plan's contents.

BUSINESS INTRODUCTION
⬝ Provide a history and description of the business
* How and why did you enter the child care field?
⬝ Mission statement
* Who are you and what do you do?
* What services do you offer?
* Who do you serve?
* Why is your program necessary?
* How will you impact the lives of your target audience?
⬝ Research market feasibility
* Is there a need for child care in the area where your business will be located?
* How many children are there in your zip code, county, city? (U.S. Census Quick Facts)
* How many licensed programs are there and what is their licensed capacity?
⬝ How much of a need is there and how much of it will you serve?
⬝ Competition
* Who are your competition?

- What services do they offer; what are their strengths and weaknesses?
- Are they a threat to your business?
- ⟩ Industry trends
- What does the child care industry itself look like at this time: is it stable or declining? (SBA, USDOL Occupational Outlook)
- ⟩ Potential market
- Given what's known about the above issues, what is the potential demand/need for your facility?

BUSINESS ORGANIZATION
- ⟩ Legal
- Will the center be a sole proprietorship, a partnership, or a corporation?
- Will it be profit making or a non-profit organization?
- Will it have a board of directors?
- Will it be employer sponsored or supported, or funded by state or local agencies?
- Who will determine the policies and budget?
- Who will provide legal representation?
- ⟩ Insurance
- What types of insurance will you carry (liability, fire, theft, health, accident) and through whom?
- What are the coverage limits?
- ⟩ Tax and bookkeeping system
- What records do you need to maintain?
- What system will you use?
- ⟩ Regulation, licensing, and/or government issues
- What licensing regulations are there for your industry?
- What are the zoning regulations for your location?
- What local building code requirements must you adhere to?

MANAGEMENT/OPERATIONS
- ⟩ Personnel/management team
- Who are they?
- What are their qualifications?
- What education have they had?
- Are they competent, capable, and experienced?
- ⟩ Benefits
- What benefits are being offered to employees, if any?
- ⟩ Employee requirements and job descriptions
- What are your hiring practices?
- What is your wage scale?
- How is your payscale determined?
- What are your staffing patterns?
- What will specific employees be expected to do?
- ⟩ Business operations
- How will you actually run your business?
- What are your major business policies?
- What is your schedule of daily program activities and how will they provide you with a competitive edge?
- ⟩ Suppliers
- What equipment and materials do you need?
- Where will they be obtained?
- Provide breakdown of costs by supplier.
- ⟩ External partners

- Will a lawyer, accountant, or early childhood specialist's served be used?
] Technology needs
- Do you need or will you need any technology to help you, such as computers, telephone add-ons, etc.?

MARKETING
] Describe your services
- What do you offer and to whom?
- Do you offer any special services that may not be offered elsewhere?
] Describe the target market for you facility
- Who will be served?
- What is the average or median household income level?
- What is the average number of children per household within the targeted age range?
- What is your relative market share projection: the size and fraction of that market that you hope to cover?
Relative market share (RMS): # of licensed slots available + # of slots in your center/# of slots needed
] Identify your location
- Where is your facility located?
- Has is met local and state inspections and zoning requirements?
- Does it accommodate special needs?
- What features about your site are desirable for child care and families?
] Pricing strategies
- How will fees be determined?
- Will there be late fees, paid holidays and vacations, sick days, etc.?
- Will you charge for special services, i.e., transportation?
- How do your rates compare to your competitor's? Explain differences.
] Promotional strategies
- How will you reach your customers?
- What advertising methods will you use?

FINANCIAL
] Start-up costs
- If applicable, what will you need to purchase to begin?
- What operating funds will be needed?
- Where will this money be obtained?
- How much, totally, is needed to successfully cover all start-up costs?
] Cash-flow projection
- Where will your income come from and where will it go?
- Why will a loan or someone's investment in shares (if relevant) make the business more profitable?
- Anticipate your income and expenses for a two-year period, month by month and by year.
] Income statement
] Balance sheet: assets, liabilities, net worth
Break even analysis: "Break-even" occurs when business revenues equal business expenses, i.e., zero profit. The break-even analysis determines the minimum enrollment necessary to make a profit.
Step one-Identify fixed and variable costs. Fixed costs (ones you must pay no matter how many children are enrolled, e.g. salary, utilities, rent/mortgage, insurance, and overhead): For example, they are $4,000 per month. Variable costs are costs that change with the number of children served, such as food, supplies, and extra teachers. Our estimate will be $8,000 per month.
Step two-Estimate income. For example sake we are charging $400 per child per month.

Step three-Divide expenses/costs by the tuition to determine the break-even point. In order to break even we need to make $12,000 per month or enroll 30 children. The break-even analysis is not an exact science. Instead of adding more children, your program could increase tuition or hire fewer teachers (a change in one variable affects the others).

- Revenue versus expenses: how much money do you need to break even?
- Can you make a profit?
- Financing plan
- Will you need to borrow money? How much?
- How will you use it and how will it be repaid?
- Identify sources of funds
- Determine how the program will be funded.
- Will you seek a bank loan?
- How much money can you provide?

SAMPLE BUDGET FORM

INCOME	
Registration fees	
Books and materials fees	
Tuition	
Gifts and contributions	
Fund-raising	
Investment income	
Government Subsidies	
Grants	
Rent	
Total Income	
EXPENSES—Personnel	
Staff salaries	
Total	
Fringe benefits*(10–15% of total):* Workers' compensation, FICA, FUTA, health insurance	
Discounted staff tuitions	
Total Salaries & Fringe Benefits	
EXPENSES—Controllable	
Advertising	
Banking fees	
Bookkeeping/Audit	
Cleaning service	
Consultant services	
Custodial Supplies	
Discounted sibling tuitions and vacancies	
Educational	
Educational	
Equipment	
Food	
Housekeeping	
Internet service	
Office	
Office	
Paper products (kitchen, bathroom, office, etc.)	
Supplies & materials	
Transportation	
Uncollected tuitions	
Website domain	

EXPENSES—Fixed	
Insurance	
Marketing	
Space costs (rent/mortgage)	
Taxes	
Telephone	
Utilities	
Other costs	
TOTAL EXPENSES	
Cost per child (total expenses _ number of children)	
NET (income minus expenses)	

SUPPORTING DOCUMENTS

☐ Personal resume(s)
☐ Letters of reference
☐ Accreditations or distinctions earned by the program or its leaders
☐ Job descriptions
☐ Contracts, leases, licenses to operate business
☐ Client lists

(Your school's name) Early Learning Center
[Street Address]
[City, state and zip]
[Telephone]
[Web address]
[Email address]

DIRECT DEPOSIT AUTHORIZATION FORM

How Direct Deposit works –

The [Insert your school's name] notifies your financial institution electronically of the funds to be deposited on your behalf. Your financial institution records this transaction into an account of your choice, creating immediate access on the day of deposit. You receive an earnings statement documenting this payment. If you desire to make a direct deposit to more than one institution, you must complete a form for each institution. Only one deposit can be made to one account at each institution.

✓   *It's convenient* -saves you a trip to the bank.
✓   *It's faster* - most banks post the funds to your account at the beginning of the day's business on payday allowing immediate access
✓   *It's safer* – Direct Deposit eliminates the worry of a lost or stolen paycheck
✓   *It's confidential* – funds are automatically processed and you can instruct the bank to apply them to your savings or checking account

Name _____ Social Security Number _____

I hereby authorize the [insert your school's name] to **(circle one)   Start / Change / Stop** total bi-weekly payroll deduction to the Financial Institution shown below. You may designate any bank, savings and loan association, or credit union in the U.S. that (1) is a member of the Federal Reserve System and (2) accepts electronic funds transfer. Payroll will notify you if the institution you choose does not qualify.

Financial Institution's Name _____

Transit Routing Number _____

Account Number _____

Type of Account (Checking or Savings)

Deduction Amount (Dollar Amount) $_____

Effective with pay date of _____

I have an established account at the Financial Institution indicated above, and authorize [insert your name] to initiate credit entries and to initiate debit entries and adjustments for any credit entries in error to my (our) account(s) indicated above.

I have provided a copy of a voided check (see attached) solely for the purpose of verifying my account number and the Financial Institution's routing number. My authorization will remain in effect until revoked by me in writing or I terminate my employment with [insert your name].

Signature _____ Date _____

Co-Signature (If Joint Account) _____

(Your school's name) Early Learning Center
[Street Address]
[City, state and zip]
[Telephone]
[Web address]
[Email address]

DELINQUENT TUITION LETTER

Date

Name
Address

Dear _____:

    We are delighted that you have chosen to enroll your child here. According to our financial agreement, tuition should be paid each Monday in advance. It has come to my attention that your payment for the week of __/___/14 - __/___/2014 has not been paid. The tuition payments are the primary source of revenue for our program and must be paid in order for us to meet our obligations to our personnel and vendors. Please remit the past due payment of $_____.___ including the $5/day late payment fee on or before ___/___/2014, in order for _____ to continue in class. We understand this may be an oversight on our part, if so, please let provide a copy of your cancelled check and receipt for the aforementioned payment. Please contact me if I can be of any assistance to you.

    Your prompt attention to this matter is greatly appreciated.

Sincerely,

Grant Readiness Checklist/Assessment

Organization Name: _____

Person (name, title) performing readiness assessment: _____

Date of assessment: _____

Assessment Directions: *Enter a "1" under each column for each assessment sub-criteria. Total tally on last line should total scores for "strong," "needs improvement," "incomplete," & "N/A"*	**Strong**	**Needs Improvement**	**Incomplete**	**N/A (Not applicable)**
ORGANIZATION				
1. DUNS number (see: http://www.dnb.com/US/duns_update/)				
2. EIN/TIN number (see: http://www.irs.gov/businesses/small/article/0,,id=102767,00.html)				
3. Business/Organizational Charter				
4. 501c3 determination letter				
5. Governance structure				
• List of Board members (biographical summaries)				
• Organizational bylaws (current, updated)				
• Board financial commitment (documentation thereof)				
6. Key Staff structure (list by name, title &/or functionality)				
• List of key program staff (& biographical summaries)				
• List of key administrative staff (& biographical summaries)				
• List of key consulting and/or contract staff (& biographical summaries)				
ONLINE REGISTRATIONS *(Note: most government grant registrations take 2-4 business weeks to complete. Many must be in place in **advance** of e-submission of grants. All accounts should be current/updated.)*				
1. CCR (Central Contractor Registration) (see registration link: http://www.bpn.gov/ccr/)				
2. Grants.gov (accounts: eBiz point of contact, SO, AOR) (see registration link: http://grants.gov/applicants/get_registered.jsp)				
3. eRA Commons (accounts: eBiz point of contact, SO, AOR, PI) (see link: http://era.nih.gov/commons/index.cfm)				
4. Others (please specify: _____)				
MISSION AND VISION				
1. Mission &/or Vision statements				
2. Programming Agenda (for 1 yr, 2 yrs, 3 yrs)				
3. Strategic Goals & Objectives (project/program; organizational/operational)				

	Strong	**Needs Improvement**	**Incomplete**	**N/A (Not applicable)**
FINANCIAL OVERVIEW				
1. Identification of funding/budget period(s): *(organizational fiscal year; proposed project budget period)*				
2. Financial management/controls *(including staff policies & procedures if available, staff name & title/functionality, Board oversight policies)*				
3. Financial statements *(including audited statements if available)*				
4. Project/program Budget				
5. Overall organizational budget				
6. Identification of other funding sources *(existing/current and/or*				

planned/projected by source name, amount & funding period) (for Project/Program and for organization)				
GRANTS MANAGEMENT READINESS				
1. Procedures & Personnel for acctg. *(receipt & uses of grant funding)*				
2. Procedures & Personnel for compliance *(grantors/funders reporting requirements)*				
PAST PERFORMANCE/TRACK RECORD				
Community Relations/Strategic Partnerships *(identify by agency/org. name, role, tenure—timeframe of relationship)*				
Past Program, Project &/or Organizational Performance Results *(quantitative & qualitative reports)*				
Grant funding performance: existing &/or previous grants *(by program/project title & description, funding source, funding amount, funding period, outcomes/results)*				
Documentation				
TOTAL SCORE				

If you scored the most points in *"strong,"* congratulations! You are ready to apply for grants. If you scored most points in *"needs improvement"* & *"incomplete,"* then it's time to execute a "readiness" plan so that you will be prepared to submit competitive grants.

Penn Consulting offers basic education grant writing workshops and services. Contact us for price quotes and training schedules.

INVOICE

(Your school's name) **Early Learning Center**
[Your Company Slogan]

INVOICE # [100]
DATE: JULY 20, 2014

[Street Address], [City, ST ZIP Code]
Phone [000.000.0000] Fax [000.000.0000]
[e-mail]

Bill to: [Family Name or Responsible Party]
       [Street Address]
       [City, State, Zip]
       [Phone]
Student Name: [name]

DATE	DESCRIPTION OF FEE	AMOUNT	CREDIT	BALANCE
1/1/2008	Registration	$ 175.00		$ 175.00
1/1/2008	Field Trip Fee	$ 35.00		$ 210.00
1/1/2008	Curriculum/Consumables	$ 65.00		$ 275.00
1/1/2008	Field Trip Shirt Fee	$ 8.00		$ 283.00
1/1/2008	Tuition 01/01/08-01/04/08	$ 150.00		$ 433.00
1/1/2008	Payment-Thank You-Check No. 2001		$ 433.00	$ -
				$ -
				$ -
				$ -
	Total Due			$ -

Payment terms: (check one)
- ☐ PIA - Payment in advance
- ☐ Net 7 - Payment seven days after invoice date
- ☐ Net 10 - Payment ten days after invoice date
- ☐ Net 30 - Payment 30 days after invoice date
- ☐ Net 60 - Payment 60 days after invoice date
- ☐ Net 90 - Payment 90 days after invoice date
- ☐ EOM - End of month
- ☐ 21 MFI - 21st of the month following invoice date
- ☐ 1% 10 Net 30 - 1% discount if payment received within ten days otherwise payment
- ☐ 30 days after invoice date
- ☐ CIA - Cash in advance

Make all checks payable to [Your Company Name]

THANK YOU FOR THE OPPORTUNITY TO SERVE YOUR FAMILY!

Person Completing Form and Title:	Date:		# Students:	# Staff:

Attach to this form a list of all staff and visitors who participated in the drill.

FAITH BASED PRESCHOOL

Emergency Drill Reporting Form

Time Alarm Sounded:	Time Drill Concluded:	Time to Evacuate: (fire evacuation drills only)
Type of Drill:	**Classes:**	**Weather Conditions:**
☐ Fire / Evacuation ☐ Lockdown ☐ Modified Lockdown ☐ Shelter-in-Place ☐ Earthquake ☐ Tsunami ☐ Medical Emergency ☐ Weather Emergency ☐ Other:	☐ Infant ☐ Toddler ☐ Preschool ☐ School Age ☐ Other	☐ Clear ☐ Cloudy ☐ Raining ☐ Rain and wind ☐ Windy ☐ Snow / Sleet ☐ Hail
Participants:	**Notification Method:**	**Situation:**
☐ School Administrators ☐ Teachers / Assistants ☐ Custodial Staff ☐ Students ☐ School Security Officers ☐ Law Enforcement ☐ Fire Department ☐ Emergency Medical Services ☐ County Emergency Mgmt. ☐ Other	☐ Bell or Buzzer ☐ Enhanced Alert System ☐ Intercom ☐ Phone ☐ Voice Notification ☐ Siren ☐ Other:	☐ Before School ☐ During Class Time ☐ Passing Time ☐ Recess ☐ Lunch Time ☐ Assembly ☐ After School ☐ Other:
# of administrative or supplemental staff available to assist teachers:	**Staff previously trained on emergency procedures this year?**	**Students previously trained on emergency procedures this year?**
	☐ Yes ☐ No	☐ Yes ☐ No

FAITH BASED PRESCHOOL Emergency Drill Reporting Form (Cont'd)	
Problems Encountered:	
☐ Congestion in hallways ☐ Alarm not heard ☐ Students unsure of what to do / proper ☐ Staff unsure of responsibilities / response ☐ Weather-related problems ☐ Unable to lock doors ☐ Windows left open ☐ Doors left open ☐ Lights left on ☐ Students not accounted for / attendance ☐ Difficulties with evacuation of disabled students or staff ☐ Students unaccounted for (note # below)	☐ Radio communication problems ☐ Network / computer problems ☐ Noise impedes communications ☐ Students not out of sight (lockdown drill) ☐ Long time to evacuate building ☐ Students not serious about drill ☐ Frightened students (lockdown drill) ☐ Improper or unavailable supplies ☐ Confusion ☐ Doors or Exits blocked ☐ Transportation ☐ Interagency miscommunications ☐ Other:
Extenuating Circumstances - Factors / Special Conditions Simulated:	
Mitigation / Plans for Improvement: (check all that apply and explain below)	
☐ Additional staff training ☐ Additional student training ☐ Address need for additional equipment ☐ Improved emergency supplies	☐ Cooperative planning with responders ☐ Revised emergency procedures ☐ Other

[Your school's name]
[School's address and phone number)

Incident Report Form

Fill in all blanks and boxes that apply.

Name of Child_____

Sex M F Birth Date: _____ Incident Date: _____ Incident Time: _____am/pm

Name of Parent/Guardian of Child _____

___Not notified ___Notified Time Notified: _____am/pm By whom: _____

Method of Notification_____

Address _____

Work Number _____ Home Number _____

Cell Number_____

List any failed attempts to notify a parent (of the incident) below, including the name of the attempted parent, as well as the date and time of each attempt.

1.) _____

2.) _____

3.) _____

Circle officials notified: EMS, law enforcement, child protective services, pediatrician or other medical professional _____

___Not notified ___Notified Time Notified: _____am/pm By whom: _____

Describe the activity the child was engaged in at the time of the incident: _____

_____

Location of incident (circle): playground classroom bathroom hall kitchen doorway gym stairway

Other: _____

Equipment/Product involved (circle): climber slide swing playground surface bike/trike   hand toy sandbox Other: _____

Cause of injury (circle): N/A

Fall to surface (Estimated height of fall ____ ft) Type of surface _____

Fall from running/tripping   Bitten by child Motor vehicle Hit or pushed by child Eating or Choking

Injured by object _____ Insect sting/bite Animal bite Exposure to heat/cold

Other: _____

Parts of body injured (circle): head neck arm hand wrist finger throat back leg feet ankle knee eye ear nose face mouth Other: _____

Name(s) of staff present at the activity: _____

Total # staff/children present: _____

Name(s) and telephone number of other witnesses: _____

_____

When did child receive professional medical attention? NA or _____

Name and address of facility/physician which provided medical care: NA or _____

_____

Describe medical attention/care/steps to locate child by school: _____

_____

_____

Describe care provided by medical facility/physician: NA or _____

_____

Describe the child's injury: NA or

_____

_____

Number of days of limited activity from this incident: _____ Follow-up plan of care: _____

_____

Does the child remain enrolled in the facility? Yes No

Describe action(s) taken to prevent reoccurrence:

_____

_____

Additional Comments: _____

Signature of Director/Provider _____ Date _____

Signature of Parent/Guardian_____ Date _____

Signature of Staff Person_____ Date _____

Name of official notified _____

Telephone number _____ Date and time _____
(Distribution: copy #1 to child's record; copy #2 to licensing consultant; copy #3 to parents)
** Please notify your consultant that the incident report is being faxed to ensure that it is received.**
Form may be submitted without parent's signature to ensure it is submitted within 24 hours or the next business day.

4 Instructional Resources

Your Child at 3 Years of Age (CDC Milestone Checklist)

Child's Name _____ **Age** __ **Date** _____

How your child plays, learns, speaks, and acts offers important clues about your child's development. Developmental milestones are things most children can do by a certain age. Check the milestones your child has reached by his or her 3rd birthday. Take this with you and talk with your child's doctor at every visit about the milestones your child has reached and what to expect next.

What Most Children Do at this Age:

Social/Emotional
☐ Copies adults and friends
☐ Shows affection for friends without prompting
☐ Takes turns in games q Shows concern for a crying friend
☐ Understands the idea of "mine" and "his" or "hers"
☐ Shows a wide range of emotions
☐ Separates easily from mom and dad
☐ May get upset with major changes in routine
☐ Dresses and undresses self

Language/Communication
☐ Follows instructions with 2 or 3 steps
☐ Can name most familiar things q Understands words like "in," "on," and "under"
☐ Says first name, age, and sex
☐ Names a friend
☐ Says words like "I," "me," "we," and "you" and some plurals
☐ (cars, dogs, cats)
☐ Talks well enough for strangers to understand most of the time
☐ Carries on a conversation using 2 to 3 sentences

Cognitive (learning, thinking, problem-solving)
☐ Can work toys with buttons, levers, and moving parts
☐ Plays make-believe with dolls, animals, and people
☐ Does puzzles with 3 or 4 pieces
☐ Understands what "two" means
☐ Copies a circle with pencil or crayon
☐ Turns book pages one at a time
☐ Builds towers of more than 6 blocks
☐ Screws and unscrews jar lids or turns door handle

Movement/Physical Development
☐ Climbs well
☐ Runs easily
☐ Pedals a tricycle (3-wheel bike)
☐ Walks up and down stairs, one foot on each step

Act Early by Talking to Your Child's Doctor if Your Child:
☐ Falls down a lot or has trouble with stairs
☐ Drools or has very unclear speech
☐ Can't work simple toys (such as peg boards, simple puzzles, turning handle)
☐ Doesn't speak in sentences
☐ Doesn't understand simple instructions

- ☐ Doesn't play pretend or make-believe
- ☐ Doesn't want to play with other children or with toys
- ☐ Doesn't make eye contact
- ☐ Loses skills he once had

Tell your child's doctor or nurse if you notice any of these signs of possible developmental delay for this age, and talk with someone in your community who is familiar with services for young children in your area, such as your local public school. For more information, go to **www.cdc.gov/concerned** or call **1-800-CDC-INFO**.

Adapted from CARING FOR YOUR BABY AND YOUNG CHILD: BIRTH TO AGE 5, Fifth Edition, edited by Steven Shelov and Tanya Remer Altmann © 1991, 1993, 1998, 2004, 2009 Forms are downloadable at http://www.cdc.gov/ncbddd/actearly/downloads.html

Excerpt from Disorder Fact Sheet Resource Booklet:
For parents and teachers of exceptional learners

ATTENTION DEFICIT DISORDER
SIGNS /SYMPTOMS
- Problems with paying attention
- Being very active (called hyperactivity)
- Acting before thinking (called impulsivity)

Three types of AD/HD
- Inattentive type (student can't seem to focus or stay focused on task/activity)
- Hyperactive-impulsive type (person is very active and often acts without thinking)
- Combined type (when the person is in-attentive, impulsive, and too active)

SIGNS TO LOOK FOR IN THE CLASSROOM
- Denies events or misattributes blame or responsibility
- Temper tantrums due to overstimulation (sensory or affective)
- May break things due to carelessness, accidental
- On first meeting someone generally pleasant toward others
- May have difficulty settling down and may get up early
- Even with interest and motivation have significant difficulty staying fully involved in academic tasks
- Symptoms often improve as the child gets older
- Stimulant medication may cause an improvement in symptoms

STRATEGIES FOR INSTRUCTION
- Determine which specific tasks are difficult for the student. Example: Student may have trouble starting a task-Another may have trouble ending one task and starting the next- each student needs different help.
- Review rules, schedules, and assignments. Clear rules and routines will help a student with AD/HD
- Teach study skills and learning strategies and reinforce regularly
- Help student channel his/her physical activity (let student do some work standing up)
- Provide regularly scheduled breaks
- Make sure directions are given step by step, and that student is following the directions
- Give directions both verbally and in writing. ADHD students benefit from doing the steps as separate tasks.
- Work with student's parents to create and implement an educational plan tailored to meet the student's needs
- Regularly share information about how the student is doing at home and at school
- Be willing to try new ways of doing things.
- Be patient and maximize the student's chances for success.

The *Disorder Fact Sheet Booklet: For parents and teachers of exceptional learners* is available at www.amazon.com or www.barnesandnoble.com

The Shepherd's Christian School

___ Grade Teaching and Learning Goals

Semester 1, Week(s) 7-12, October 17-November 25, 2011

Bible: (8:15-9:00) The student will develop an understanding of God's Word; understand how to use the Bible as a practical and spiritual resource; and understand the different stories in the Bible as being a part of history. Answer 5 W's and a H. *Test each Monday*

Wk. 7 Memory Verse: Eph. 4:32 Lessons Jacob blesses his children, Genesis 48-49, Moses and the Exodus

Wk. 8 MV: Proverbs 20:11 Lessons: Exodus 2-15 Moses and the burning bush, the plagues, the Passover, crossing the Red Sea

Wk. 9 MV: Psalm 106:1 Lessons: Exodus 15-16 Israel in the Wilderness, God provides quail and manna, the Ten Commandments

Wk. 10 MV: Ephesians 5:20 Lessons: The Ways of God, The twelve Spies, The Bronze Serpent Numbers 1-2

Wk. 11 MV: Psalm 100 Good bye Moses, Promised Land, Rahab Believes Joshua, The Fall of Jericho

Wk. 12 MV: Psalm 100 Christian Heritage Thanksgiving week

Language Arts: (9:00-10:00) Developing Christian character through the reading of God's Word. Eccl. 12:12-14, Phil. 4:8 The student writes clear and coherent sentences and paragraphs that develop a central idea. His writing shows he considers the audience and purpose. He will progress through the stages of the writing process (e.g., prewriting, drafting, revising, editing successive versions). Create readable documents with legible handwriting. Understand the purposes of various reference materials (e.g., dictionary, thesaurus, atlas). Student writes compositions that describe and explain familiar objects, events, and experiences. Student writing demonstrates a command of standard American English and the drafting, research, and organizational strategies. Student will distinguish between complete and incomplete sentences and identify and correctly use various parts of speech, including nouns and verbs, in writing and speaking. Use commas in the greeting and closure of a letter and with dates and items in a series. Use quotation marks correctly. Capitalize all proper nouns, words at the beginning of sentences and greetings, months and days of the week, and titles and initials of people. Spell frequently used and irregular words correctly (e.g., was, were, says, said, who, what, why). Spelling word list (vocabulary): **Test Mondays. Speech Club 1st and 3rd Fridays** at Crossroads Presbyterian Church: Student delivers brief recitations and oral presentations about familiar experiences or interests that are organized around a coherent thesis statement. Describe story elements (e.g., characters, plot, setting). Journal 3 times each week.

Reading: The Children's Treasury of Virtues (HONESTY/LOYALTY/FRIENDSHIP)

The Pasture, George Washington and the Cherry Tree, God Make My Life a Little Light, The Indian, Cinderella, Little Boy Blue, The Boy Who Cried "Wolf", The Honest Woodman, Why Frog and Snake Never Play Together, Heroes, Opportunity About Angels, A Prayer at Valley Forge, Only a Dad, The Sphinx, Jackie Robinson, Sail On! Sail On!

Arithmetic: (10:15-11:05) In second grade mathematics the student is taught to see that the addition and multiplication tables are part of the truth and order that God has built into reality. Student counts, reads, and writes whole numbers to 1,000 and identifies the place value for each digit. The student uses words, models, and expanded forms (e.g., 45 = 4 tens + 5) to represent numbers (to 1,000); Orders and compares whole numbers to 1,000 by using the symbols <, =, >. Student estimates, calculates, and solves problems involving addition and subtraction of two-and three-digit numbers (inverse relationships between addition and subtraction (e.g., an opposite number sentence for 8 + 6 = 14 is 14 - 6 = 8) to solve problems and check solutions); Finds the sum or difference of two whole numbers up to three digits long; Uses mental arithmetic to find the sum or difference of two two-digit numbers; Recognizes, names, and compares unit fractions from 1 /12 to 1 /2; Solves problems using combinations of coins and bills; Know and use the decimal notation and the dollar and cent symbols for money; Uses the commutative and associative rules to simplify mental calculations and to check results; Relates problem situations to number sentences involving addition and subtraction; Solves addition and subtraction problems by using data from simple charts, picture graphs, and number sentences; Measures the length of an object to the nearest inch and/or centimeter; Tells time to the nearest quarter hour and know relationships of time (e.g., minutes in an hour, days in a month, weeks in a year); and Records numerical data in systematic ways, keeping track of what has been counted. Calendar skills in Spanish.

Science: (12:00-1:50 Wednesday and Thursday) The student will be aware of the importance of curiosity, honesty, openness, and skepticism in science and will exhibit these traits in their own efforts to understand how God's creation (the world) works. Earth is made of materials that have distinct properties and provide resources for human activities. As a basis for understanding this concept: we will compare the physical properties of different kinds of rocks and know that rock is composed of different combinations of minerals; smaller rocks come from the breakage and weathering of larger rocks; soil is made partly from weathered rock and partly from organic materials and that soils differ in their color, texture, capacity to retain water, and ability to support the growth of many kinds of plants; fossils provide evidence about the plants and animals that lived long ago and that scientists learn about the past history of Earth by studying fossils; and rock, water, plants, and soil provide many resources, including food, fuel, and building materials, that humans use. The student will: Make predictions based on observed patterns and not random guessing; Measure length, weight, temperature, and liquid volume with appropriate tools and express those measurements in standard metric system units; Compare and sort common objects according to two or more physical attributes (e.g., color, shape, texture, size, weight); Write or draw descriptions of a sequence of steps, events, and observations; Construct bar graphs to record data, using appropriately labeled axes; Use magnifiers or microscopes to observe and draw descriptions of small objects or small features of objects; and Follow oral instructions for a scientific investigation.

Social Studies: (12:00-1:50 Monday and Tuesday) To inspire each student that he has a divine place and purpose in Christ. His Story. Student understands the importance of providence, individual action and character and explains how heroes from long ago and the recent past have made a difference in others' lives (e.g., from biographies of Abraham Lincoln, Louis Pasteur, Sitting Bull, George Washington Carver, Marie Curie, Albert Einstein, Jackie Robinson, Sally Ride). You Can Change the World: Learning to Pray for People Around the World (Volume II) Working with Maps, Globes, and Other Geographic Tools: Name specific continent, country, state, and community; Understand that maps have keys or legends with symbols and their uses; Find directions on a map: east, west, north, south; Identify major oceans: Pacific, Atlantic, Indian, Arctic; The seven continents: Asia, Europe, Africa, North America, South America, Antarctica, Australia (Oceania); Locate: Canada, United States, Mexico, Central America; Locate: the Equator, Northern Hemisphere and Southern Hemisphere, North and South Poles. Reading: *The Story of the World* history from ancient times until the present. Africa, China, Europe, the Americas—world's civilizations (nomads to the last Roman emperor).

Integrated Art: To develop the disciplined use of God-given talents to produce visual are for the glory of God and to encourage creative expressions thereby building self-esteem.
Integrated Music: To recognize music as a gift from God to mankind. To participate in music making, praise and worship as technical abilities and understanding increase. Singing, moving, playing and understanding instruments, appreciation, hearing, and music theory.
Computer: Students use technology tools to enhance learning, increase productivity and promote creativity all to God's glory. Accelerated Reader software will be used to assess students' reading with four types of quizzes: reading practice, vocabulary practice, literacy skills, and textbook quizzes. This will build a lifelong love of reading and learning
Physical Education (Daily): To develop and strengthen the child in both body and spirit through conditioning (skill, coordination, endurance, and health). Wednesday Hiking with Hiking Exploring Group

Homework:
Practice memory verse 10-15 minutes and Spelling Words
Complete worksheets (if applicable) and get communication folder signed
Monthly Christian Home school Group Meeting
1st Thursday 7 p.m. at Word from Above Ministry and Church

DIFFERENTIATED LEARNING PLAN

Subject   **Date**

Standards: What should students know, understand, and be able to do? (Grade Level Expectations, Depth of Knowledge, Show Me Standards, Common Core State Standards)	

Assessment/Criteria for Success: How will you know students have gained an understanding of the concepts? (Identify tools for data collection, logs, checklists, journals, agendas, observations, portfolios, rubrics, contracts, etc.)

Essential Questions:

Content: (Bible Truths, Concepts, Vocabulary, Facts)

Developmental Domains Addressed:	✓	(Check all that apply to the lesson(s)) Notes:
Spiritual		
Ethical		
Cognitive		
Psychological		
Language		
Physical		
Social		
Cultural		

Skills Development:

Monday	
Tuesday	
Wednesday	
Thursday	
Friday	

Procedures:	Materials:
Engagement (Activate or Motivate): How will you pre-assess, gain, and maintain students' attention?	
Process/Acquire: (How will the lesson be taught?)	
Lesson Segment 1 (Explain-Model):	
Activities (Explanation):	
Lesson Segment 2 (Explore-Guided Practice):	
Activities (Explanation):	
Lesson Segment 3 (Elaboration and Extension-Independent Practice):	
Activities (Explanation):	
Evaluate (Feedback or Closure)	

Instructional Strategies Employed:	Tool	✓
1. Identifying similarities and differences		
2. Summarizing and note taking		

3. Reinforcing effort and providing recognition		
4. Homework and practice		
5. Nonlinguistic representations		
6. Cooperative learning		
7. Setting objectives and providing feedback		
8. Generating and testing hypotheses		
9. Cues, questions, and advance organizers		

Grouping Decisions: Check selection or identify activity in space provided. *Apply and adjust as needed.*
✓

TAPS: Total-whole, Alone, Partner	
Small Groups	
Random	
Heterogeneous	
Homogeneous	
Interest	
Task	
Constructed	
Brain Compatible Strategies: Which will you use to deliver the content?	✓
Brainstorming/Discussion	
Drawing/Artwork	
Fieldtrips	
Games	
Mnemonic Devices	
Music/Rhythm/Rhyme/Rap	
Reciprocal Teaching/Cooperative Learning	
Storytelling	
Technology	
Graphic Organizers/Semantic Maps/Word Webs/Thinking Maps	
Humor	
Work study/Apprenticeships	
Manipulative/Experiments/Labs/Models	
Role play/Drama/Charades/Metaphor/Analogy/Simile	
Movement	
Writing/Journals	
Visuals	
Project/Problem-based Instruction	
Visualization/Guided Practice	

Evaluation: (report, quiz, test, performance, products, presentations, demonstrations, logs, journals, checklists, portfolios, rubric, meta-cognition)

Teacher's Lesson Reflection:
Describe

Analyze

Reflect

Instructional supervisor or peer observer suggestions:	**Initials**

Childcare Health and Safety Checklist

☐ Health and Safety checks are completed at the BEGINNING OF EACH DAY

☐ (✓check if in compliance)

☐ Program is smoke free.

☐ All entrances/exits are kept clear of clutter, snow, ice, etc.

☐ Staff purses and personal items are locked out of reach of children.

☐ Hands are washed by staff and children upon arrival to classroom.

☐ Each child has brief health check by classroom teacher (includes parent/caregiver communication).

☐ Bleach solution is made daily, labeled and inaccessible to children.

☐ All hygiene supplies are available (soap, paper towels, toilet paper, lined garbage can, warm water).

☐ Area is generally clean and clutter-free (garbage emptied, floors swept, toys and work space, bathroom clean).

☐ All chemicals are locked/out of reach of children.

☐ Air fresheners are not used.

☐ All electrical outlets are covered.

☐ Furniture and equipment is in good repair (check for broken toys, accessories, wrinkled/disrepair rugs/carpet).

☐ Heavy toys/items are stored on lowest shelf.

☐ Window cords are adjusted to prevent strangulation.

☐ Children's personal/nap items are kept separated (use of cubbies, bags, or storage containers).

☐ Tables and chairs are not stacked while children are present.

☐ Playground and equipment is checked for garbage, standing water and other hazards before use.

☐ Diapering supplies are gathered and within reach before beginning (including a lined and covered foot operated garbage can).

☐ Cots/mats/cribs are placed 3 ft apart or have barrier and assigned to a specific child or cleaned and sanitized after each use.

☐ Approved safety gates are used on stairways, if necessary.

☐ Screens, in good repair/secure and used in open windows and doors.

☐ First aid kit is available in each room/appropriately stocked.

☐ All bottles have full name/date and refrigerated immediately.

☐ Infants always placed on their back to sleep in cribs/pack-n-plays.

☐ Cribs are free of soft bedding, bumper pads, pillows and stuffed toys.

☐ Cribs have tight fitting mattress and a secure fitted sheet.

☐ High chairs are in good repair and cleaned and sanitized before/after use.

☐ Safety restraints are used on infant seats, swings, strollers and high chairs.

☐ Staff and children's hands are washed after arriving/before leaving, before and after preparing/serving food, eating, toileting, water/sand/play dough play, after outside play, wiping noses, when visibly dirty and as frequently as possible.

☐ Eating areas are cleaned with soap/water/rinsed and sanitized (let stand for 2 min) before and after use.

☐ Spills are cleaned up immediately.

☐ Infants are ALWAYS put on their back to sleep. No blanket or objects in the crib.

☐ Always hold infants when feeding a bottle.

☐ Plastic bags are stored out of reach of children and tied in a knot before discarding.

☐ All medication is always stored in original container and labeled with the child's first and last name, date and instructions. Medicines should be in a locked box if refrigerated and out of reach of children if not refrigerated. Authorization is renewed every ten days.

☐ Medication administration to a child is always recorded. (Right child, Right Medication, Right

Time, Right Amount, Right Method, Right Child (double check)
- [ ] Vehicles are checked by two different people to ensure they are empty.
- [ ] Gates and exits are locked. (alarms indicate a child leaving the room or facility)

Weekly Lesson Plan

Teacher Name _____ Date _____

Age Group (Circle One):

Infant (   )   Toddler (18-35 months) Preschool (3-5 years)

	Monday	Tuesday	Wednesday	Thursday	Friday
Circle Time Developmental Goal or Learning Standard	Identity of self, Recognition of own skills and accomplishments, Comprehends meaning				
Activity	Book: I Learn with My Senses Song: 'This is a Song about Colors'				
Materials	Book CD and player				
Domain(s)					
Small Group Time Developmental Goal or Learning Standard					
Activity					
Materials					
Domain(s)					

ABOUT THE AUTHOR

Althea Penn, M.Ed.Adm., NAC, PDS is a national conference speaker and professional development specialist with over thirty years of experience in education as a teacher, principal, and Children's ministry leader. She has a passion for children and those who serve them. She is an inspirational communicator and has served as a conference speaker and seminar leader for The Georgia Preschool Association, the National Black Child Development Institute, Kid's Advocacy Coalition, Quality Care for Children, the Association of Christian Schools International, and other organizations which share her passion for intentionally cultivating potential. As an educational consultant, she has trained thousands of educational organization program administrators and educators. Althea is married to her best friend and high school sweetheart. They are the parents of two adult children.

Penn Consulting is an education consulting firm specializing in professional development for early childhood educators. We provide motivating staff development and business consulting for administrators and teachers of programs for young children. Our objectives are to ensure optimal development of children by developing programs that engage every learner and to improve processes and performance in order to promote student achievement and program sustainability. We provide organization development services (including strategic planning, licensing, and accreditation consultation) for those seeking to start private schools, preschools, afterschool programs, and other educational institutions.

Connect with me online at:
Twitter: http://twitter.com/pennconsulting
Facebook: http://www.facebook.com/althea.penn
Website: http://altheapenn.tripod.com or www.penntraining.com
Email: penntraining@yahoo.com

Book Order Form
Equipping early educators

Title	Regular	Discounted Price	Quantity	Amount
Christian Education Mandate	$19.99	$10.00		
Disorder Fact Sheet Booklet	$9.99	$5.00		
Subtotal				
Shipping $4 first book, $1 each additional				
Subtotal				
Tax (Georgia residents only 6%) $5.00=$.30 $10.00=$.60 $15.00=$.90 $20.00=$1.20 $25.00=$1.50 $30.00=$1.80 $35.00=$2.10 $40.00=$2.40 $45.00-$2.70 $50.00=$3.00				
Total Due				

Please make checks payable to: Penn Consulting

Check enclosed: Amount _____ No. _____
Credit Card Authorization (Please print)

Cardholder name
_____

Card number _____
Exp. Date _____

CSC/CVV # _____ Circle one: American Express   MasterCard   Visa
☐ Shipping address same as billing (otherwise write both below)

Billing/Shipping Address
_____

City/State _____ Zip _____

Phone _____ Email _____

Penn Consulting
Child Development: Cultivating a love of learning and fostering competence in young children.

Professional Development: Training teachers whose lives and scholarship become a living textbook to their students.

Organization Development: Enhancing educational program sustainability and success through best practices in administration and program planning.

Organization Development Services
✝ Articles of Incorporation/Bylaws Drafting
✝ 501© 3 Tax Exemption Applications
✝ BFTS Licensing Application
✝ CAC Food Program Application
✝ Grant writing
✝ Student and Exchange Visitor Program (SEVP) I-17 Student Visa Application
✝ Marketing (Website, Brochures)
✝ Employee Orientation-Personality Styles in the Workplace, Policy and Procedure Review
✝ Mock Inspections
✝ Teacher Observations
✝ Parenting Seminars-see topics below!

Professional Development Services
Child Development Associate Courses and CDA Council Verification Visit

Workshops
Healthy and Happy Children – (6 hours or 3 2-hour sessions)
Injury Control, Infectious Diseases, and Child Abuse and Neglect
The Way Kids Learn – Learning Styles (2 hours)
Reading is "Fun"-damental - Early literacy birth-nine years (4 hours)
Effective Discipline Principles and Techniques – (4 hours)
Professionalism (21ˢᵗ Century Parents and Teachers) - (4 hours)
Administering and Planning Educational Programs for Young Children - (40 Hours) * **4 PLUs**
Classroom Management Strategy Toolbox - (4 hours)
Every Child Learns Differently - **Differentiated Instruction PreK-3rd grade (6 hours)**
*Shining Stars (Differentiated Instruction-6 hours and Classroom Management-2 hours) *1 PLU*
Artistic Encounters - Integrating art across the subjects-S.T.E.A.M. (2 hours)
Purposeful actions - Building trusting relationships (parents and teachers) (2 hours)
Money, Money, Money [Basic Grant Writing for Educators] - (4 hours)
Kids Count on You - Strengthening Families and Protective Factors Initiative - (2 hours).
Moral Development (2 hours)
Planning Healthy Meals (3 hours)
Infant and Toddler Development (30 hours)
Child Development - the Preschool Years (30 hours)
The workshops listed above are approved for early childhood educators pursuant to the University of Georgia's contract with Bright from the Start: Georgia Department of Early Care and Learning. All workshops are available onsite, many are available online.
* Also approved for Professional Learning Units by the Georgia Department of Education Office of Professional Learning.

Parenting Seminars

Positive Discipline is Teaching - 90 minutes
Bringing up Healthy Children – USDA Nutrition Guidelines – 90 minutes
Literacy Begins at Home – Phonics Instruction Primer 90 minutes
Raising Spiritual Champions – Biblical Discipline 90 minutes

Penn Consulting Standardized Testing Services

Spring Achievement Testing

The *Stanford 10 Achievement Test*® is a multiple-choice assessment that helps educators and parents find out what students know and are able to do. This testing instrument is a reliable tool which provides objective measurement of achievement and guidance for instruction. The Stanford Achievement Tests are also available in combination with OLSAT (*Otis-Lennon School Ability Test*®). The OLSAT measures the cognitive abilities that relate to a student's ability to learn in school. By assessing a student's abstract thinking and reasoning abilities, OLSAT supplies educators with information they can use to enhance the insight that traditional achievement tests provide. Combining the Stanford achievement tests and the OLSAT learning ability test will help you develop reasonable expectations for your student's progress, based on his or her abilities. Once you are able to discern whether your student is reaching his or her academic potential, you can understand how to tailor your teaching to your child's learning style.

Testing Price

• Stanford 10 Achievement Test and OLSAT combination (Spring-April)—$60/$80 per student (includes testing preview materials, test taking materials, postage, computerized scoring report, diagnostic consultation)*
• Wide Range Achievement Test (Year round)—$25 per student (includes scoring report, diagnostic consultation)

The Stanford 10 Achievement Test Evaluates:

1. Word study skills
2. Reading skills/ comprehension
3. Vocabulary
4. Mathematics
5. Language
6. Spelling
7. Social studies/science
8. Listening

Parents receive confidential results:

1. Norm-referenced scores: scaled, grade equivalent, stanine, and percentile rank
2. Graphed achievement percentiles
3. Content cluster skills evaluations
4. Skills performance ratings
5. Score interpretation brochure

Year Round Standardized Testing

The widely respected *Wide Range Achievement Test*® (WRAT) accurately measures the basic academic skills of word reading, sentence comprehension, spelling, and math computation. This quick, simple, psychometrically sound assessment of a student's important fundamental academic skills serves as an excellent initial evaluation, re-evaluation, or progress measure for any student—especially those referred for learning, behavioral, or vocational difficulties. Assessments can be obtained in as little as 45 minutes for younger children (K-3rd) and as little as one hour for older students (4-12th grade). The test can be administered and scored at a local library individually.

Student Eligibility—*Homeschool students*—For a student to be defined as "homeschooled," the majority of his education must be privately funded and provided at home rather than in a traditional classroom setting. Students whose education is home-based but provided by a publicly funded school would not be considered "homeschooled" for these testing purposes.

ADA Accessible—Special accommodations can be made upon request for students requiring a wheelchair accessible desk or other special arrangement.

Private Testing Session—Private testing sessions are available upon request, for an additional charge. (*This may be necessary if your child has an IEP and diagnosed learning difficulty.-additional $15*)

Test Results Consultation—Up to one half-hour consultation sessions on score interpretation and curriculum recommendations are available at no extra charge. (Scoring SAT10/OLSAT-10 business days and WRAT-immediately)

Testing Dates—SAT10/OLSAT April of each year-Computerized results and diagnostic feedback are available ten days after test administration.

Registration—To sign up, simply register your student(s) at www.pennconsulting.org. Register early as space is limited. Early bird discount available for students registered by March 1 of each year.

PLEASE NOTE: All test materials are secure and confidential and may not be viewed by anyone other than the student(s) and approved administrator(s) *during testing*. The test questions or answers may not be discussed with any parent, student, or other individual before, during, or after testing.

Test Administrators—Penn Consulting representatives adhere to all guidelines for implementing test security, while ensuring that its highly qualified staff maintains a thorough knowledge of testing procedures and professional conduct. Mrs. Penn, the test administrator and all proctors meet the qualifications for administering the paper and online assessments. They are credentialed, experienced, have attended test administration training, and completed assessment college coursework. They understand the concepts of standardized testing, security importance, and the implications of testing irregularities.

Benefits of Standardized Testing
1. It provides students with reliable feedback about their own level of knowledge and skills.
2. It helps students to associate personal effort with rewards and motivates them to work harder.
3. The testing and its feedback identify teaching and learning objectives.
4. It motivates educators to work harder and more effectively.
5. It helps educators to identify areas of strength and weakness in their teaching plans and methodology.
6. The tests yield quantifiable information (scores, proficiency levels, and so forth).

7.   The tests can be used to assess students' progress over time
8.   The tests can be used to register your child for TIP - Duke's gifted program or the Davidson Institute.
9.   The test can be used to meet the Department of Education's assessment requirement (Students should be evaluated at least every three years beginning at the end of the third grade).
10. They help educators to identify learning styles, unknown talents or abilities
"Test scores do not indicate whether children are learning to think from God's point of view or whether they enjoy what they are doing and are starting on the path of lifelong learning. And tests cannot tell the overall story of how a child's experience in school is preparing him for life. Such results—the results that matter most—must be evaluated by parents and teachers along the way, using a multitude of tools of which a standardized test score is only one." James Deuink, *The Proper Use of Standardized Tests*

Made in the USA
Coppell, TX
28 December 2021

70229583R00129